How to
Overcome
Trauma
and Find
Yourself
Again

How to
Overcome
Trauma
and Find
Yourself
Again

How to Overcome Trauma and Find Yourself Again

Seven Steps to Grow from Pain

DR JESSAMY HIBBERD

ASTER*

ASTER*

First published in Great Britain in 2023 by Aster, an imprint of
Octopus Publishing Group Ltd
Carmelite House
50 Victoria Embankment
London EC4Y 0DZ
www.octopusbooks.co.uk

An Hachette UK Company
www.hachette.co.uk

First published in paperback in 2024

Distributed in the US by
Hachette Book Group
1290 Avenue of the Americas
4th and 5th Floors
New York, NY 10104

Distributed in Canada by
Canadian Manda Group
664 Annette St.
Toronto, Ontario, Canada M6S 2C8

ISBN 978-1-78325-553-5

A CIP catalogue record for this book is available from the British Library.

Typeset in 11/15pt Sabon LT Pro by Jouve (UK), Milton Keynes.

Printed and bound in Great Britain.

13 5 7 9 10 8 6 4 2

Commissioning Editors: Natalie Bradley and Nicola Crane
Editor: Sarah Allen
Design Director: Mel Four
Production Controller: Serena Savini

This FSC® label means that materials used
for the product have been responsibly sourced.

MIX
Paper | Supporting
responsible forestry
FSC® C104740

For my mum and dad – for everything
and Jack – for building your dreams around me

CONTENTS

CONTENTS

INTRODUCTION

Most of us will suffer a trauma at some point in our lives. Trauma does not discriminate. It occurs across different cultures and socio-economic groups. Suffering a trauma is simply part of life. Yet our brain finds a way to trick us into believing that these things happen to other people. We put trauma away, out of sight, so that we can imagine the world is safe and we are fully in control of our lives. We do our best to avoid discomfort or pain and try to live our lives perfectly. We want to believe that good things happen to good people and that we can find a path through life where we can eliminate negative emotions and never get hurt – that if we just work hard enough and do the right things, we can avoid struggle.

But when we believe we can be in control of life, we're setting ourselves up to fail. In truth, trying to avoid hardship is exhausting and pointless. People we love die, relationships break down, our trust is broken, we can be hurt by others, we can work ourselves into the ground, jobs are not guaranteed, we cannot trust in our health, terrible things happen.

Once we openly discuss trauma, we have a chance to see how common it is. This allows us to share our experiences with others, but also allows us to remove the idea that the person suffering the trauma is somehow to blame.

In Japan, broken pottery is often repaired with seams of gold. The flaws are seen as a unique piece of the object's history, adding to its beauty. To me, this is how it should be for trauma. The person we have become is the result of what we have been through. It's the tougher times that have fundamentally changed us and restructured the way we think about our lives and live them. Any significant change alters us, but that change does not have to define us.

The question is not how we avoid these difficult experiences, but how we learn to live with them. Rather than deny their existence, we need to look at how best to cope when they happen – because they will. We can use these incredibly tough times to look within ourselves and to re-evaluate. They can remind us how precious life is and what is important, and give us the potential for a more meaningful life.

In his seminal book *Man's Search for Meaning*, Viktor E Frankl describes how he survived the Nazi labour camps, an unthinkably harrowing experience. He believed that as humans we cannot avoid suffering, but we can choose how to cope with it, find meaning within it and move forward with renewed purpose. He suggests that those who survived in concentration camps, himself included, were not necessarily the strongest or fittest, but those who saw their lives as meaningful: 'When we are no longer able to change a situation – we are challenged to change ourselves.'

Frankl's work on meaning laid the foundation for research in this area and these ideas are echoed throughout psychology literature - when we have meaning we thrive, but without it we suffer. Carl Rogers' Self-actualization Theory and Irvin Yalom's

Existential Psychotherapy (two of my favourite psychologists) highlight meaning as central to human life.

Trauma forms the core of my work as a psychologist. It's at the heart of every problem I see. But I've also found there is another side to trauma. I see the people I work with go through unimaginable pain but emerge stronger from the darkest of times. When they manage to open up and share their stories, they can use their experiences to look again at their lives. I have seen that experiencing loss can also open the door to living a more fulfilling and happier life. When we face our limits, it can make us more resilient.

When we are going through a trauma, it might feel like our problems are insurmountable. But what if a traumatic experience, rather than stopping us in our tracks or being something to get over as quickly as possible, is in fact an important part of fully becoming ourselves? What if we treat it as a chance to discover who we are and what we want from our lives?

I've seen it time and again in my clinic and in my personal life. We *can* grow from these difficult and painful times and become stronger. With this book as a guide, you can become stronger too.

THE SEVEN STEPS TO OVERCOMING TRAUMA

When our lives are broken open, it is a reminder that we are vulnerable, and cannot control everything that happens to us. It shatters our understanding of our lives into pieces and forces us to look at things we naturally avoid – the fragility of life, our mortality, how we are living, whether we are making a difference. It is only when things break that we are forced to stop and put them back together again.

When all the pieces are on the ground, picking them up

and reassembling them can feel impossible. Yet, in time, we do find a way to put the pieces back together and overcome these setbacks. Sometimes things fall apart to make space for something better.

We cannot alter what has happened, but we *do* have a choice in how we move forward.

These experiences can give us new perspectives, which we were previously blinded to, showing us how to live our lives more fully. They can provide an opportunity to re-evaluate, develop a new understanding of ourselves and think seriously about what living means. It is a chance to consider who we are, how we want to approach life and the kind of future we hope for.

In this book, I will guide you through seven steps to overcome your trauma. I will help you to become more resilient, cope better with adversity and find yourself again. The steps are best taken in order, as in each you gain knowledge and skills putting you in the best position to move forward. However, as you'll see in the stories in this book, the steps are not always linear – there is no right or wrong way through trauma. Steps 1 to 4 are the building blocks, teaching you to understand and manage the effect of the trauma on you. These steps focus on coping with the first three phases of trauma – outcry, numbness and denial, and intrusive re-experiencing. I'll introduce you to the five phases of trauma in more detail in Chapter 3.

Steps 5, 6 and 7 will lead you through the final two phases of trauma – working through, and completion. In step 5, I will help you to tell your story and process what has happened, before grieving and letting go in step 6 so you can move forward to acceptance. Finally, in step 7, I will help you to re-evaluate what you want from your life, see how you have grown from the experience and find meaning.

Step 1: Care

Step 1 forms a solid foundation to begin the work and puts you in the best position to overcome trauma. I'll be looking at this in Chapter 3. It's a bit like essential maintenance. First you need to ensure you are caring for yourself and have the basics in place: sleep, nutrition, hydration and rest. Alongside hope and support.

Hope and support are necessary components for overcoming trauma. Both are predictors of post-traumatic growth. Hope is a catalyst for change, a belief that things can get better, and this mitigates the effects of trauma, opening up space to think differently. Relationships on this journey are also key. Support from others provides a buffer to the emotional effects of trauma and protects you from experiencing more intense distress.

Step 2: Looking after your body

Step 2 helps you to feel safe in your body again. Using the mind–body link, I will teach you how to move out of the body's 'threat zone', regulate your emotions and begin to process your emotional pain. I'll be looking at this in Chapters 5 and 6.

How we feel is anchored in our connection with our body. Understanding our reactions to adversity and stress and the physical impact of trauma lets us see that before we can do anything else, we need to manage the physical effects of trauma by bringing our nervous system back into equilibrium. I will help you to tune back into your body and understand what you are feeling so you can learn to trust it again. By the end of this step you will have developed a toolkit of strategies to look after your body, including techniques to calm and ground yourself, and exercises to build resilience and look after your emotional health.

Step 3: Looking back to look forwards

Step 3 is a chance to think about your history as a way to understand and get to know yourself better. Our childhood experiences affect the development of our brain and are the foundation on which the rest of our lives are built, influencing the adult we become. Yet this connection is something we are not always fully aware of.

Reviewing your experiences growing up is a chance to understand the effects of your childhood and how these might have shaped your meaning framework (see page 43) and your current thoughts, feelings and behaviours. There is something empowering about knowing where your beliefs about yourself, other people and the world come from and how this informs what you expect. It can also help you to understand your emotions and how you cope, behave and relate to others. Step 3 will be covered in Chapter 7.

Step 4: Coping with trauma

Step 4 will teach you to understand and listen to your feelings and help you to take action using emotion-focused and active coping techniques. Emotion-focused coping (or 'feeling your way through') means learning strategies to regulate your emotional response. Active coping means accepting the impact of trauma on your life and taking direct action to change things where you can.

In this step, I will help you to take ownership of your situation. By allowing yourself to feel your emotions, you can make sense of your experience, understand what they are telling you and find ways to soothe them. Getting more comfortable with your emotions will also put you in the best position to tell your story. It's important to 'feel your way through' in parallel with active coping in order to overcome trauma. These themes form part of every chapter, with a specific focus on this in Chapter 8.

Step 5: Telling your story

Step 5 will empower you to tell your story so you have a coherent understanding of what happened – each step before has been building to this point. The stories we tell about our lives shape us and give us a sense of who we are. When we experience trauma, it disrupts our life story and this challenges our belief system.

Putting your experience into words allows you to make sense of what has happened and feel the emotions connected to the trauma so they become less frightening and painful, letting you file away the memory so it no longer intrudes on your life. We'll cover this in Chapter 9. When you acknowledge and feel your distress, symptoms subside and make space for growth – letting you piece back together your meaning framework in a new way and begin to build a new understanding about life.

Step 6: Grieving, letting go and accepting

Step 6 is a chance to grieve your losses and let go of the past as a route to acceptance. This is perhaps the hardest step, but it is only when you grieve that you can make space for what you have gained. In this step, which is dealt with in Chapter 10, I will show you how to update your story and unlock yourself from negative emotional states, such as anger and resentment, so you can free yourself from the continuing hurt of these destructive emotions. What has happened will never be forgotten, but you can choose how you respond to the past.

We all have the power to shape our story to live with more meaning and purpose. Letting go is recognizing that you cannot change what has happened and making a choice to release the past so it doesn't continue to hold you back or hurt you. This means giving yourself permission to move forward and become present in your life again.

Step 7: Becoming yourself

Finding meaning in what has happened is at the core of how we overcome trauma and grow from the experience. Chapter 11 will guide you to look past the difficulty and value the positive changes. This gives you the freedom to review your life, reflect on what you have learned and take responsibility for how you want to live now.

In this final step, I will show you how to use your experiences to see clearly what life is about and channel what has happened into a determination to change things for the better. It is only by letting go of your old life that you can begin to consciously choose how you want your future to be.

OVERCOMING TRAUMA

It can be hard to recognize that awful events can lead to something good. In this book, I never forget how terrible trauma is, or dismiss its impact and the suffering and pain that come with it. No trauma is good. There is nothing inherently positive about loss, illness, disaster or violence. But while adversity is not something any of us would seek out, it is often a point from which change occurs.

This book will help you find a way to move beyond the hurt and to heal. I want to empower you to take charge of your story and build the life you choose. We know that those who strive to understand the meaning of their own lives are better able to interpret and organize their experiences and achieve a sense of their own worth. This is why building a positive life narrative is so important, and why telling your story and finding meaning should be your ultimate aim.

This book can be helpful if you have experienced childhood trauma, but due to its scope, I will not be focusing specifically on this area. If you would like to read more on the topic, I recommend *The Body Keeps the Score*, *What Happened to You?* and *How to Do the Work* (see References, Resources and Further Reading, page 293), which are all excellent books with a specific focus on childhood trauma and the ways it can continue to impact us in our adult years.

If you are reading this book to support someone going through trauma, they are very lucky to have you. When we are going through difficult times, we all need someone to talk to and to know that somebody cares. If you can, ask them how you can support them; don't just say 'I'm here' and wait for them to ask you to help. Keep checking in, offer practical support that they can accept in a way that fits with their needs and understand that even if you're not able to get it right all of the time, it will still be hugely appreciated.

ABOUT ME

This book is written based on my professional experience as a clinical psychologist as well as my personal experience of trying to make sense of life (and frequently falling short). Everything in its pages is underpinned by extensive research and evidence-based therapy. However, I am still just one person, with one approach informed by my work and research, and I am sharing what has worked for me.

Trauma and meaning in life has always been an area that has fascinated me. I first studied it for my doctorate, where I investigated the effects of working in a war zone and compared mental health outcomes in two groups of diplomats: those who had been posted to Iraq or Afghanistan and those who had worked in what were classed as 'non-hardship' overseas posts. (What really mattered was the *meaning* individuals gave to an event and how they made sense of it, not where they were posted.)

In my clinic, I have also treated a number of people who have suffered from significant personal trauma. I have witnessed first hand how working through a trauma, reframing it and building a positive life narrative can have dramatic results, helping them to find meaning, contentment and a new-found sense of who they are.

Despite all my experience with trauma, I was a firm member of the 'life is what you make it' camp. Emotionally, I was connected to the idea that if I worked hard and achieved my goals, everything would slot into place (despite an overwhelming amount of evidence to the contrary). But then a significant personal trauma happened and I had to face up to reality. It threw me into a situation I had never expected to be in, and it was this experience, and the work I did to get through it, that inspired this book.

Clinical psychology training follows a scientist/practitioner model. This means that I was trained in both research and clinical practice. I had to understand not just the theory, but how to apply it. I'll use the same approach in this book, so you can understand why you are feeling the things you do, and what you can do to feel differently.

Since completing my doctorate, I have trained in many different approaches to psychology. At the Institute of Psychiatry, Psychology and Neuroscience, I became accredited in cognitive behavioural therapy (CBT). I then completed training in compassion-focused therapy, became accredited in schema therapy, and most recently studied at the Tavistock and Portman in psychodynamic, systemic and child development theories. All these various strands of psychology have been woven into the strategies outlined in this book.

HOW TO GET THE MOST FROM THIS BOOK

Picking up this book is a brilliant start. It means you hope for things to be different. Hope is the key to change. To move forward, you now need to take action. It's all too easy to put things off and wait until you feel ready, but there's no better time than now. Working through the steps and trying the strategies outlined here means you at least have a *chance* of achieving what you're hoping for, and there are positives no matter what the outcome.

Going through this will be painful and difficult. The process of struggle and growth is rarely quick or smooth, and you may encounter obstacles as you forge a new way. But with each step you will learn more about yourself and connect to your inner strength. Resilience doesn't mean that you never experience pain or suffering; it means that you keep going in spite of these things. Together we will plant the seeds of change, but it is up to you to nurture them, take care of them and bring them into bloom.

Be gentle with yourself as you work through the steps. What you need may change from day to day. When we're overcapacity, it can be hard to even think about trying things differently, and we can become rigid and inflexible in our approach. To give yourself the best chance, it is important that you are kind to yourself and try to find compassion for what you have been through. This approach will give you a much better chance of success. Allow yourself time – you've been through a lot; things won't change overnight. Have faith in the process and hang on to hope that there is a way through this. I promise it will be worth it.

TAKE A DAY-BY-DAY APPROACH

Go through the book at a pace that feels comfortable to you, and put it down if you need to. It is meant to be used as a guide to explore your life, to learn and make mistakes. It doesn't matter if you stop along the way or go off course; there is no set path through trauma. It is all about the process and what you learn along the way – if you are only focused on the destination, you won't appreciate the full benefits of your journey.

Consistency is key. Instead of thinking, *How will I ever get over this?* try thinking, *What small thing can I do today?* Doing something each day, no matter how modest, means you are thinking about yourself and what you need (this is one of the most important changes you will make). How we feel is a natural product of all our choices, but especially the small choices that each of us makes every day.

Small steps might not sound so dramatic, but they add up. You don't set off up a mountain and suddenly you're at the top; it's many steps that take you to the summit. When you're at the bottom of the mountain, looking up, it might seem like an impossible journey, but when you think about just taking the next step and putting one foot in front of the other, it seems much more doable. Remind yourself that if you do what you need to do today, that will get you to tomorrow, and in the longer term to where you want to go. Keep this idea with you as you work through the book.

SHARED STORIES

Stories of personal growth and other people's experiences can be a way to find strength and hope in your own situation. Sharing your vulnerability is not a weakness, but a strength. It is our idiosyncrasies and flaws that make us alive and human. That's why stories form the heart of this book. You'll find them interspaced between the theory and strategies, and they will illuminate the seven steps. Each one is someone I know who has experienced trauma (though some names have been changed for confidentiality). They are the real stars of this book and have been incredibly generous in letting me write about their experiences in the hope that they might help others.

You'll read about:

- Akemi, whose husband told her when she was six weeks pregnant with their second child that he had been having multiple affairs and was leaving her and wanted her to abort their baby.
- Jess and Finn, who tragically lost their mother only ten months after her cancer diagnosis, a woman who was a pillar of the community and respected and loved by all who knew her.
- Sophie, who experienced insomnia from the age of 15, and at 29 experienced her first breakdown. She was then hit by another trauma when her marriage broke down.
- David, a commanding officer of an infantry battalion in Afghanistan, who was shot in the right leg. Rather than amputation, he opted for reconstruction, and over the course of some three and a half years (for most of which he was in a wheelchair), he rebuilt his leg and his future outside the army.
- Peter, who overcame his alcoholism aged 47, after a lifetime of mental health problems and suicide attempts.
- Naomi, who at the age of 40 discovered a lump in her breast. Less than a year later, at the end of her successful

breast cancer treatment, a routine check showed she had
stomach cancer, something she is still in active treatment
for now.

I hope that reading these stories will help you feel a little less
alone and remind you that growth after trauma is not an unusual
story or something reserved for the lucky few.

WHAT DO YOU WANT TO BE DIFFERENT?

Before you continue, take a minute to think about your reasons
for change. What do you want to gain from this book? What do
you want to be different? Think about the impact this could have.

Although you may not realize it yet, you are the hero of your
own story. Everything you need is already within you. You have
the strength to make changes so you can heal and overcome what
has happened to you. It is only by taking responsibility for yourself
that you can regain control of your life and emerge stronger.

Part One

UNDERSTANDING TRAUMA

1

TRAUMA

We think of traumatic events happening in far-off places, where there is war, poverty and natural disasters. Or that people are more likely to be affected if they work in jobs that put them at higher risk. When we hear stories of trauma, we might even believe, deep down, that the person affected must have done something wrong – that the world is rational and bad things only happen to bad people.

We usually visualize trauma as the result of a major event – the pandemic, 9/11, the Manchester arena bombing, a forest fire. Sadly, the reality is that most traumas are the result of the actions of those close to us. It is the ones we love who cut us most deeply.

It is estimated that 75 per cent of people in the developed world will experience some form of trauma in life, and 1 in 5 will experience a potentially traumatic event in any year. This estimate is conservative, as the study did not include medical illness or the loss of a loved one. The first UK-based study of its kind, published in *The Lancet Psychiatry*, found 31 per cent of young people had a traumatic experience during childhood.

As I write this book, we are still not over the Coronavirus pandemic. There is a war in Ukraine. Flooding in Pakistan from June to August 2022 killed more than 1,391 people and caused a huge amount of damage to the country. The highest ever number of rapes in England and Wales was recorded by police in the year ending 2022, at over 70,000. On average someone is diagnosed with cancer every 90 seconds in the UK. Divorce rates are also currently at around 40 per cent. Trauma is a common experience.

WHAT DO I MEAN BY TRAUMA?

The Diagnostic Statistical Manual of Mental Disorders (DSM-5) used in the USA, defines trauma as 'actual or threatened death, serious injury, or sexual violence' experienced by you or someone close to you.

Post-traumatic stress disorder (PTSD)

The DSM-5 is used as a route to diagnosing PTSD, a mental health condition that can be triggered in response to trauma. Symptoms include:

- Re-experiencing the traumatic event: these internal reminders typically present as nightmares, flashbacks and intrusive memories in which you feel like you are in the situation again.
- Avoidance of external reminders: either trying not to think about the traumatic event, suppressing the feelings associated with it, or avoiding reminders of the event, e.g., driving after a road traffic accident.
- Altered anxiety state: feeling more physically anxious and on edge (hyperarousal); exaggerated startle response and constantly on the lookout for danger (hypervigilance).

- Changes in mood or thinking. Seeing the world as a very dangerous place. Feeling isolated, angry, irritable, anxious, hopeless or depressed. Persistent negative beliefs or expectations about yourself. Giving up activities you previously enjoyed. Increased risk-taking.
- Emotional numbing: feeling detached from emotions and others, dissociation; amnesia associated with significant parts of the event.

Most people who go through a traumatic event have temporary difficulty adjusting and coping, but in time they usually get better. Research suggests you will be at higher risk of PTSD if you have experienced childhood trauma or previous trauma. Poor outcomes are also more likely in those who feel guilt, shame and helplessness; who blame themselves or are less emotionally expressive; who lack social support or who have to deal with other life events after the trauma.

These symptoms can be really distressing. If you think you might be suffering from PTSD, or if your symptoms are having an impact on your daily functioning, it is important to see your GP. Getting effective treatment is critical, though this book might be helpful alongside any treatment. There are many evidence-based treatments that are proven to help you overcome PTSD, including CBT and EMDR (eye movement desensitization and reprocessing).

However, there is now thankfully a general acknowledgement that the DSM-5 definition does not encompass the full scope of trauma. In this book, I am thinking about trauma not just as the psychiatric textbooks define it, but more broadly to include any deeply distressing or disturbing experience that causes emotional and physical pain, and at a deeper level, challenges our beliefs and how we understand and live our lives. Relationship breakdown, bereavement, miscarriage, burnout, addiction, infertility, illness, redundancy, abuse, bullying, racism, homophobia, poverty, living with an alcoholic, a significant stressor or a life crisis. We need to be aware of the situations that can be traumatic, but there should not be a hierarchy of what counts or does not – each situation must be given the validity it deserves.

It is important to remember that trauma is personal – that it is specific to the individual. It is not what happens but how we *interpret* it that is the key. As useful as the statistics are, they do not describe the individual and their unique experience or story. What is most important is how *you* feel in response to whatever happened. It is what *you* find distressing or disturbing and *your* interpretation of events that shapes the way you will be affected by the trauma, as my work with the diplomats showed (see page 10). Our appraisal of an event depends on multiple factors such as our personality and previous experiences.

To take one recent example: the coronavirus pandemic has impacted everyone, but its effect has differed from person to person. Some people have lost loved ones; others their jobs. For some it has negatively impacted their health, while others are concerned about wider society. While most of us were negatively affected, a minority were fortunate and did not find the experience distressing; perhaps it brought them closer to their family, or they were able to change how they lived or worked in a positive way. Within this, the specifics of what has happened will also be different. For one person, losing their job might mean having to sell their home, while for someone else it could be a chance to retrain or set up their own company. The same experience, but a different response. This is something you'll also see in Jess and Finn's story.

We are all different, which is why we all react differently to the same events. It is our interpretation of what has happened and the meaning we take from it that shapes the way we are affected by the trauma.

MY DEFINITION OF TRAUMA

When we experience adversity or face difficult life events, I think of it as opening up a gap between the life we thought we knew (and all the expectations that ran alongside this) and our new reality – how life is now as a result of what has happened. This gap represents the loss of what we thought our life was. We experience grief as we let go of the life we knew and our imagined future. Or if you've never known this safety or were born into a life of abuse, it represents the loss of what you didn't have. These are experiences of loss that I see commonly in my clinic:

- Loss of the life you knew
- Loss of a loved one
- Loss of your health
- Loss of a relationship
- Loss of a job
- Loss of your identity
- Loss of who you thought you were
- Loss of your naivety
- Loss of an imagined future and the life you thought you'd have
- Loss of your mobility

- Loss of places and things you loved
- Loss of a safe childhood
- Loss of trust
- Loss of connection or support networks
- Loss of normality
- Loss of a child
- Loss of the things you have worked for
- Loss of structure and stability
- Loss of a clear view of the future
- Loss of freedom
- Loss of control

Trauma brings into sharp focus the reality of life. It shows us that our situation is uncertain and unpredictable. It reminds us that we are vulnerable, fragile and not ultimately in control of our lives.

These types of experiences often feel unreal, as they place us in situations we never imagined being in, outside what we thought we knew or expected from life. They challenge our view of the world, forcing us to rethink what we believe and making us struggle at a deeper level, rocking the foundations of how we understand and live our lives.

We often think of trauma happening in a moment – one significant event, an overwhelming experience, like David being shot, or Naomi's double cancer diagnosis. But it can also be many different moments, the drip, drip of a bad situation that grows and becomes more potent over time, like Sophie's insomnia or Peter's drift into addiction. This type of trauma is often more subtle, yet it can affect us deeply, leaving us feeling shame or guilt and corroding our self-esteem. Childhood trauma; an emotionally abusive relationship; facing one difficulty after another, grinding us down so we no longer trust in life. Feeling lost, stuck, disconnected or disillusioned; wider social factors such as poverty, discrimination and inequality; or a slow giving up on life. Trauma can be something that challenges our identity or sense of self.

Even with clearly defined moments of trauma, it is too simplistic to say that the next step is straight to recovery. Trauma is complex and messy. It has an ongoing ripple effect on our lives, creating a constantly changing picture of what's happening so that we have to adjust and readjust our hopes and expectations. Distress happens from the outside inwards, but also from the inside out. It is what happens to us, but also our reaction to it.

Trauma affects our lives now, but also the future we imagined – how we expected our lives to be. I worked with a woman who was struggling with infertility. She had always imagined her life with children in it; it was what mattered most to her. Every dream and future thought had included these imagined children. It was a huge loss to let this go. Akemi believed she was in a trusting relationship, looking forward to the birth of a longed-for second child with someone she would spend the rest of her life with. She was then faced with a reality in which the person she loved told her that he did not want to be in the relationship, did not want a second child and had never been invested in their life together.

With any loss, we have to grieve for what has happened and for the change to the life we thought we knew. These experiences cause anguish, confusion and struggle, making us feel powerless or helpless. They can make us question *everything*, irreversibly altering how we see our lives. They can threaten our sense of who we are, and often we struggle to find a sense of self-worth, meaning and identity. Sadly, they often come with a sense of stigma, and messages from wider society can increase our feelings

23

of shame, guilt, self-blame and fear. This makes the experiences difficult to talk about, and can make us feel isolated and like we're going through them on our own.

PUSHED OVERCAPACITY

Trauma can shake us to our core. It's like suddenly being thrown into darkness, unable to see where we are or what is ahead. Our ideas about life are broken, and this understandably takes an emotional toll on us. It affects our ability to regulate and express our feelings and to ultimately find life meaningful.

Our reaction is therefore not strange when we think of it like this, but an understandable response to our life being turned upside down. Stephen Joseph was a pioneer in recognizing this. In his brilliant book *What Doesn't Kill Us*, he describes this idea in the context of post-traumatic stress: 'Post-traumatic stress can be understood as a search for meaning in which the drive to revisit, remember and think about the trauma is a normal urge to make sense of a shocking experience, to grasp new realities and incorporate them into one's own life story.'

Of course, when we experience something that affects us so deeply, we will have a response to what has happened. It is normal to experience anxiety, nightmares, sadness or anger, and the physical symptoms that go with these. To question everything or be confronted by sudden reminders and flashbacks to what has happened. These are not signs that we are not coping – we have to go through these feelings to process what has happened.

It would be more unusual if we had no emotional response. All emotions are normal; we have the full spectrum because they are all necessary and useful to us, whether in response to a larger event or smaller day-to-day incidents. This reaction is our brain and body working through what has happened, and research shows that experiencing and accepting these emotions is vital for our mental health. As much as we may want to feel happy all the time, life isn't straightforward. Negative emotions are just as crucial as positive ones in acknowledging what's happened and making sense of it.

We need to see this resulting emotional distress or troubled behaviour as a reaction to our circumstances and life experiences rather than an issue in itself. When I work with people at my clinic, I think about their presentation – anxiety, depression, intrusive thoughts, low self-esteem – not as the problem, but as symptoms of the problem. While it's important to treat the symptoms and improve how the person is feeling so they can function more fully in their life again, it is also important to think about the underlying concerns that are causing these symptoms. Treating the symptoms will only be a temporary fix. When your house suffers from damp, you can replaster and repaint so it all looks good again, but unless you treat the source of the damp, it will come back.

This allows us to see our reaction to adversity as a natural process and to see that experiencing distress post-trauma is also the beginning of change. The struggle to find all the pieces of our lives and put them back together again in a new pattern is a normal response to trauma, with the potential to lead to post-traumatic growth. The events that happen to us are all part of our life story and define who we are.

I find it helpful to think about this in terms of capacity. When we experience trauma, it pushes us over our limit. Capacity varies from person to person, but is always finite. A simple way to think about this is to imagine capacity as a pan sitting on the hob. When life is straightforward, there is a small amount of water in the pan and it can bubble away without a problem. As things are added in, whether it's work, chores, commitments or relationships, the water level rises. Alongside this are the emotions we're experiencing and how we're feeling physically; so for example, when we're tired, stressed or feeling overwhelmed, there is even more water in the pan.

As we work through life events and deal with them, the water level goes down, but sometimes the pan gets so full that it starts to bubble over, and even small things can make it overflow. This is what trauma does. One of the major signs that we are over-capacity is that it becomes difficult to regulate our emotions. We frequently feel irritable or have angry outbursts. We're more likely to overreact, and even small things that go wrong can have a big impact. If your reactions seem out of proportion to what's going on, it's a signal you're struggling to cope.

SYMPTOMS

When you're overcapacity, life feels much harder. You might be more forgetful as your brain struggles to keep up with everything you're meant to do. Leaving your key in the lock, mixing up your words. It can make you clumsy, breaking or dropping things. Other signs include feeling tired or demotivated. Or feeling like life is out of control and you can't manage. And if you've been pushing yourself for too long, you can become rundown and physically unwell. Being overcapacity shrinks your life and steals your confidence. It can make you take tight control of everything to try and ensure you know what to expect and eliminate uncertainty. It can even leave you feeling like you are going crazy.

Bessel van der Kolk describes the imprint left by trauma on the mind, brain and body in his seminal book, *The Body Keeps the Score*: 'Trauma produces actual physiological changes, including a recalibration of the brain's alarm system, an increase in stress hormone activity, and alterations in the system that filters relevant information from irrelevant. We now know that trauma compromises the brain area that communicates the physical, embodied feeling of being alive.' He goes on to explain that this has important consequences for how the 'human organism' lives in the present, changing not only what we think about, 'but our very capacity to think'. These changes explain why after trauma it's common to become hypervigilant to threat, something that impacts our ability to engage with our day-to-day lives.

Trauma is a disrupter and affects us on multiple levels, with a range of interlinked symptoms both physical and emotional. These can be sudden or gradual, and are all bi-directional, so have an effect on each other. For example, our nervous system might become stuck in the fight-or-flight reaction, on hyperarousal. This makes us hypervigilant, both internally to what's going on in our bodies and externally to what's going on around us.

The physical discomfort can make it much harder to do things. When we do manage to do something, it can be difficult to engage, with so much going on. Feeling like this changes how we think about and see our lives. It can distort and intensify our thoughts, making us more likely to recall troubling memories and less able to see the good things. We might get stuck questioning or ruminating on what's happened or obsessing about the future.

It can also make us sensitive to reminders of the event. Think of how, after food poisoning, you can't look at that food again or think of eating it; it takes time to remember that you are safe and that things are OK. We might have sensory triggers – sounds, smells or situations that we try to avoid. This link between our feelings, behaviours and thoughts is cyclical – they all feed into each other, as you can see in the diagram overleaf. And all these symptoms have their origin in the body's response to the original trauma. We'll be looking at the physiology of this in more detail in Chapter 5.

On page 30, I will run you through some of the symptoms of trauma – though this is not an exhaustive list. From an evolutionary standpoint, many of these symptoms are stress responses, and these are typically categorized into fight, flight, freeze and fawn. Most of us are familiar with the fight, flight and freeze responses – fight and flight are the hyperalert reactions like

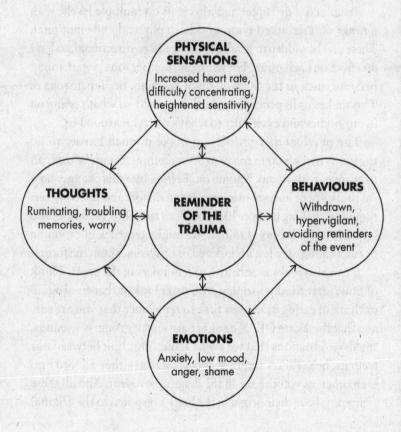

PHYSICAL SENSATIONS
Increased heart rate, difficulty concentrating, heightened sensitivity

THOUGHTS
Ruminating, troubling memories, worry

REMINDER OF THE TRAUMA

BEHAVIOURS
Withdrawn, hypervigilant, avoiding reminders of the event

EMOTIONS
Anxiety, low mood, anger, shame

increased heart rate or hypervigilance, and freeze describes the shutdown responses like dissociation or numbness.

The term 'fawn' was defined by Peter Walker, a C-PTSD (complex post-traumatic stress disorder) survivor, and such responses are more common when someone is exposed to prolonged trauma or abuse. Rather than trying to fight, run away or shut down, the person seeks safety by merging with the needs, wishes and demands of others, trying to please them to avoid conflict and ignoring their own needs and feelings as a result. This response typically develops in childhood and is carried into adult relationships, but it can occur at any time of life.

As you read through this list, it is important to remember that trauma is personal and specific to you, and so the symptoms will be too. Recognizing the symptoms you are experiencing is the first step to finding a way to manage them.

I hope that seeing the symptoms in black and white also shows you that they are all a normal response. The reason I can write this list is not because I know you and your story, but because the research shows that these are common symptoms in reaction to traumatic events.

THE PARADOX OF TRAUMA

There is no avoiding the emotional turmoil that comes with trauma. Trauma involves suffering and pain and it leaves us with scars, both physical and emotional. For many it changes their lives for the worse and they are left emotionally overwhelmed by the experience, unable to move forward. It is important that we hear these stories and never forget how truly devastating trauma can be.

But it is also important to listen to the quieter story of what can happen in response to trauma, a story that does not always

Emotions	Physical sensations	Thoughts	Change to behaviour
Grief	Anxiety symptoms: increased heart rate, faster breathing, tense muscles, heaviness in your body, tight chest	Difficulty remembering what happened	Hypervigilance
Shame	Clenched jaw	Distressing or intrusive memories	Avoiding anything that reminds you of what has happened
Guilt	Feeling sick	Ruminating – being plagued by what's happened	Hostility
Sadness	Dizziness	Self-blame – if only I'd done . . .	Social withdrawal
Anxiety	Headaches/migraines	Confusion – nothing makes sense any more	Self-sabotage/problematic coping e.g. drinking too much or using drugs, emotional eating
Fear	Fainting	Negative outlook	Loss of trust in others
Confusion	Increased startle response	Flashbacks	Going through the motions
Anguish	Sleep disturbance, vivid dreams or nightmares	Mental avoidance	Putting your guard up to protect you from life

Emotions	Physical sensations	Thoughts	Change to behaviour
Anger	Physical health problems: eczema, psoriasis, strep throat, digestive issues, being rundown	Rigid and inflexible thinking	Difficult to do the things you normally enjoy
Irritability	Poor memory/ brain fog	Obsessing/ catastrophizing/ pessimism	Stopping caring as a way to protect yourself
Rage	Shutdown or dissociated	Wishing you could turn back the clock – I wish I'd said . . . why didn't I . . .	Becoming unreliable
Hopelessness	Exhaustion	Difficulty thinking about the future	Life shrinks – sticking to known routines
Resentment	Feeling trapped	Fear of what others think	Being less tolerant of others
Dread	Disorientated	Disappointment – why hasn't it worked out, what's wrong with me?	Harder to communicate with other people
Embarrassment	Feeling out of control	Unfairness – questioning why	Difficulty functioning in relationships
Low self-esteem or insecurity	Distracted	Feeling hard done by	People-pleasing

Emotions	Physical sensations	Thoughts	Change to behaviour
Disgust	Disconnected	Feeling like life is against you	Codependence
Panic	Difficulty concentrating	Not feeling satisfied	Difficulty speaking up for yourself
Humiliation	Feeling deadened or numb	Life no longer feels meaningful	No boundaries
Surprise	Spaced out	Feeling like something bad is going to happen	Perfectionism

get heard. Trauma undoubtedly brings immense challenges, but while it is tempting to believe that it is something we cannot withstand or recover from, PTSD and mental health problems like anxiety and depression are not the only outcome. We are not simply reduced by these events. The story is not only one of despair. Humans have an amazing ability to adapt, and it is possible, through trauma, to become more resilient to what life throws at us.

Together we will look at what has happened and observe what it has brought us: the good, the bad and the ugly. Trauma can be a turning point. It can bring everything into sharper focus. A chance to re-evaluate our priorities, strip away the unimportant and focus on what really matters to us. To refocus our energy on a new path or goal. To learn more about ourselves and to see our strengths. Rather than being the end of our life, it may simply be the end of our life as we know it, as these experiences can be a catalyst for change and a time of transformation.

Trauma challenges our assumptions about how the world

works and our place within it, but it's a curious paradox. Our losses can result in valuable gains. At a time when we feel lost, it can give us direction. It makes us more vulnerable, yet stronger, and gives us a sense that although it has been painful, valuable lessons have been learned.

KEY TAKEAWAYS

- Trauma is specific to the individual – it is how we interpret what happens to us that shapes the way we are affected.
- Trauma opens a gap between the life we used to know and the life we know now; it represents the loss of what we thought our life was.
- Our reaction to adversity is a natural way to make sense of a shocking experience, as we struggle to put the pieces of our life back together.
- Trauma affects us on multiple levels: how we think, how we feel physically, our emotions and how we behave.
- Paradoxically, trauma can make us stronger.

2

BURNING DOWN THE HOUSE

SHATTERED ASSUMPTIONS

In my therapy room I see how brutal life can be. But the truth is, I didn't *really* see it until it started to affect me and the people I love. It seems crazy. When trauma is so common, how can we believe that we could possibly be exempt, and why does it feel so personal when it does happen to us? I'll be exploring why in this chapter.

Imagining we can live life without struggle is bordering on delusional, and yet we all too often do exactly that. The human mind is amazing at minimizing risk. We get married expecting our relationship will last, despite the stats. We still cross the road, get in the car, ride a bike or walk in the dark.

To understand how this is possible, we first need to look at our brain and the beliefs we hold tight that help us to understand the world. When it comes to trauma, we have a whole set of beliefs that have an impact on us.

MEANING FRAMEWORKS

Our brain is essentially a meaning-making machine; it loves to find meaning or purpose in life. It is always trying to understand the significance of events, and to enable this we have a framework of beliefs that our brain uses to decode situations and make sense of the world around us. At its core are fundamental assumptions about how life is and our place within it.

I think of it like a map that helps us to navigate our lives and understand ourselves and others, so that we know what to expect and can make sense of where we have been, our current situation and where we are going. It is central to how we operate in our lives and feeds into everything we do.

These mental maps are built from childhood (something we'll look at in more detail in Chapter 7) through our experiences, and help us to interpret and organize new information quickly and automatically by filtering it through existing expectations and referencing past experiences and memories. We are always making unsaid assumptions and generating ideas due to our societal, historical and personal experience and discourse. This allows us to take shortcuts in interpreting the vast amount of information that is available in our environment. If we tried to process everything as if we were encountering it for the first time, we would not get much done. These shortcuts allow us to follow routines without thinking too much about them, and can search our environment for what is relevant. Think of your morning routine or a normal week – it saves you time and energy to run some of your life on autopilot. We will be looking in more detail at autopilot in Chapter 4.

These maps are relatively stable; the main structures and major roads do not change much. But they are constantly updated, refined and renewed as we move through life, adding our experiences to give richness and depth. This adjusts our expectations and revises our view of the world based on what we know – often without us even noticing. If we are let down by a friend, we may change our view of them as reliable; if they let us down on several occasions, we become more wary of them, but the overall map of life remains the same. We do not presume that everyone we know is unreliable, just that specific individual.

What is really interesting is that research shows we all tend to hold similar beliefs. In essence, the main roads that appear on our maps are surprisingly alike. Ronnie Janoff-Bulman, a thought leader in this area, found that in Western culture, we grow up with three fundamental assumptions. These assumptions are our representation of the world and form the framework of our lives, and they explain why trauma feels so distant from our everyday lives.

Janoff-Bulman's three fundamental assumptions

- *The world is benevolent*: we believe the world is a good place and the people in it are kind and well intentioned. We tend to overestimate the probability that good things will happen to us and underestimate the extent to which we are vulnerable to adversity. We get up in the morning and expect life to continue as normal.
- *The world is meaningful*: we believe that life makes sense and is predictable, controllable, fair and just. We think of what happens in life as a cause-and-effect relationship between events and outcomes. If we work hard and do the right things, we can have a good life. Good things happen to good people and bad things will happen to those who are bad or careless. This is why it can feel so unfair or wrong when something happens to us or someone we care about.

- *We are worthy*: we tend to view ourselves as capable, moral and decent, and think that in some way this makes us more deserving of positive outcomes. This helps to maintain the belief that we have the ability to control what happens to us in both positive and negative terms.

These beliefs protect us from the reality of life, where we are vulnerable, death is inevitable and we do not have ultimate control over our lives. In some ways they are useful, allowing us to live our lives and keep fear at bay in a world that could otherwise be pretty scary. We manage risk on a daily basis, without it causing us problems, and free up mental space so we can continue to function and enjoy life.

These beliefs are not something we consciously think about; they lie below the level of awareness and are unquestioned, informing how we think and act. We might notice that we seek these things out in our own lives and hold beliefs about what we expect. Think about the way we use external order as a way to manage and calm internal disorder – it can feel so satisfying when everything is tidy and in the right place (or maybe that's just me!). Other examples include:

- Sticking to routines
- Caring about fairness
- Craving stability
- Preferring things to be predictable
- Trying to be in control of life

We might also hold beliefs that link to these assumptions:

- If I stay healthy, wear sunscreen and don't smoke, I won't get cancer.
- If I work hard and do the right thing, I can have a good life.
- If I am a good parent to my child, they will not encounter problems or go off the rails.
- Problems affect people in other parts of the world.
- Bad things should not happen to good people.

It is not that we believe bad things do not happen; rationally we know that life is not straightforward and that no one is immune to the harder parts of it. We see on the news or amongst people we know the effects of things like bereavement, serious illness, job loss, natural disasters and war. Yet we believe these things are unlikely to happen to us – although we know this isn't quite right on a deeper level – and we are genuinely surprised when something bad does happen.

Decades of research following Neil Weinstein's seminal study on this topic in 1980 suggests that when it comes to personal risk, we have an optimistic bias and are often overly optimistic about the future. Weinstein asked more than 250 college students: 'Compared to other students, the same sex as you, what are the chances that the following events will happen to you?' He listed 24 negative events ranging from buying a bad car to developing cancer. For nearly every event, four times as many students thought they were safer than average than thought they were at greater risk than average.

This is based on the phenomenon often referred to as unrealistic optimism. Studies report that people perceive their own future as more positive than the average person's, rating negative future events as less likely to happen to them than to the average person, and positive events as more likely to happen to them than to the average person. We are also more accepting of outcomes when the results of a chance or random event is something positive. I met my husband at a music festival in Serbia – the fact we both chose to go that year, were at the same music stage and stood in the same place meant we got chatting. Yet when something negative happens, or we are in the wrong place at the wrong time, it is much harder for us to process or accept.

THE DOWNSIDES

Most information we receive fits into our framework of beliefs – people generally behave as we expect, most jobs reward those who work hard – so we can stay safely in our belief that the world is a good place and feel that we are in control of our lives. Our mental maps give us enough information to know where we are going and roughly what to expect so we can move through life without too much difficulty.

Our brain is invested in proving our beliefs right, but there are some negative consequences. These beliefs really do function as assumptions, with our brain accepting them as intrinsically true or certain to happen, even without any proof. This means that our mental maps are not our guide, but our master.

My work showed me what life was like, but I believed that these things would not happen to me or the people I loved. To continue to hold these beliefs in the face of such contradictory information shows how strongly they operate. To keep the belief in place, our brain seeks out information that fits with it and gives more weight to this information. When faced with information that does not fit, we find ways to put it away again – we might try to ignore, distort or deny facts that do not match our belief. You'll also see this later, when you read about Akemi.

This is known as confirmation bias. A good example of it is dating. When someone has not called as they said they would (we've all been there), instead of confronting the idea that they are not interested, we keep ourselves in denial. 'They've lost their phone', 'they're really busy', 'they didn't get my text', 'their phone died'. Anything but the fact that they just have not rung. It can take a lot before we change our mind, even in the face of irrefutable proof, as it is easier to deny what is in front of us than recognize that we were actually wrong the whole time. Think about a belief you hold strongly: how much would it take to change your mind?

Another common but more damaging way that we stay in denial and away from the truth is our tendency to blame and judge. In some ways this is a protective strategy. When we hear about awful things happening, it forces us to question our beliefs that the world is a good place. We might start to wonder if the same thing could happen to us. To comfort ourselves and keep our sense of safety, we have to find a way to distance us from the experience. We do this often without consciously realizing, as our brain is desperate to keep hold of our beliefs.

We all have a friend who did not see the (obvious in retrospect) signs that their partner was cheating, and we convince ourselves that we would never be so stupid. Or a friend has a motorbike accident, and we think they were not sensible to ride it in the first place. Parenting is another great example. I was a much better parent before I had kids!

When you judge someone, you are making them responsible for what has happened. Blame says it is their fault and therefore it will not happen to us. It keeps us separate from what has

41

happened, positioning ourselves as superior, and this works to distance the event from ever occurring in our life. We think we know better, or could do better.

We might even blame ourselves. If only I had not walked home that way in the dark. If only I had been a better partner. Blame lets us believe that what happened was preventable and that we *can* live our best life if we just try hard enough. This is how we keep our beliefs of safety and control in play and ourselves away from vulnerability, rather than facing up to the reality that it could also happen to us and that life is not straightforward.

Blame also brings with it a more serious problem. When we do not check these thoughts, it pulls us into seeing the worst in ourselves and others. It makes us unkind and leaves less space for compassion. This makes it much harder for people to talk about negative events for fear of judgement, keeping them shrouded in secrecy and shame just when the support of others is needed most. It is important to remember that we never know what is going on in other people's lives. In my experience, there is *always* context to what is going on; it is never black and white. Blame in any scenario is a useless and harmful waste of time. Being aware of our tendency for blame is really important, so that we can step back from it, let the thoughts go and concentrate on what is most important – being there for the person who needs our help, or being there for ourselves.

WHAT HAPPENS WHEN YOU EXPERIENCE ADVERSITY?

Imagine our meaning framework as a house designed to keep us safe and contained. Ordinarily we operate on the basis of unchallenged, unquestioned assumptions about ourselves and the world, and this means our brain can happily keep our beliefs intact. The daily difficulties or struggles we face are like wear and tear on the house. There is very little damage and it is easy to repair. The information slots easily into our meaning framework and our beliefs are unaffected.

Something more serious will cause greater damage and will need a more significant repair, but the house looks like it did before and it is not obvious to others that there has been a change. This is how adversity affects some people. If the new information is unexpected or does not easily fit, it can take longer to sink in as our brain finds a way to place it securely within the framework. Perhaps you hear about a friend having an accident. The thought takes longer to put away and is likely to come back to you and pop up on you as you adjust to this new information and find a space for it.

While this type of experience challenges us, we can fit what has happened into our original mental map relatively easily, without having to abandon our worldview. The experience may knock or even break some of our beliefs, causing us to reflect and look at our life, but it does not fundamentally change the way we think about things.

Trauma shatters our fundamental assumptions about life. It rips up our mental map and our beliefs come crashing down, bringing us face to face with a different picture. This is like burning down the house. Initially, with all the bricks on the ground and the house in tatters, it might seem impossible to repair. These experiences lie so far outside of our mental map that we cannot use our meaning framework to make sense of what has happened. We have never imagined being in this situation so we have no mental map to guide us or make sense of things, and this feels destabilizing.

In the wake of a loved one's death, it becomes increasingly difficult to ignore the reality that those close to us can be taken from us. This can also make us face our own mortality. When you have always prided yourself on being healthy and you get cancer, it is impossible to believe the world is fair and just.

This creates the gap we discussed when defining trauma in the last chapter: the gap between the life we thought we knew (and all the expectations that ran alongside this) and our new reality – how life is now as a result of what has happened. What we thought we knew about life is broken, often shattered into so many pieces that we do not know where we stand any more. We can no longer tell ourselves that the world is good and we are safe when our experience so clearly shows us something different. It is like our mental map has missed out a continent.

You could take the parts and try to quickly put them back together and build the same house again, but doing this does not take into consideration why the house fell down in the first place. While it might look the same from a distance, on closer inspection it is only just held together and is no longer sturdy. A quick repair isn't the long-term answer. The house is not going to feel very safe or secure when you are inside, and it will not take much for it to be knocked down again.

Although after suffering trauma it might feel preferable to keep hold of your original beliefs, put things back together without obvious change and carry on as before, this means you are not dealing with or looking at what has happened. Like living in a patched-up house, this leaves you vulnerable.

Letting go of your beliefs is hard. But slowly you realize that you will have to start over. Continuing to believe that the world is safe and good things happen to good people means overlooking the reality of the trauma or fooling yourself into thinking it was not so bad. If you force these new pieces of information into the framework, it will no longer be strong.

44

The best approach is to learn from what has happened and rebuild the house with this new knowledge so that it is stronger and more resilient to future problems. Rebuilding is daunting. When the bricks are all on the ground, it can be hard to imagine how the house can come together again. Yet with this approach, you can start again with more solid foundations and a new design more suited to the way you want to live now.

Taking time and effort to rebuild and cement what you have learned and this new understanding of life will mean a far stronger fix. One that will weather future storms and stand you in good stead to face any future difficulties. It will also provide a safe place for you to stay internally, with a more intimate understanding of what it took to rebuild.

When you are in the midst of the building works, it is a nightmare. You have lost what used to be your home and you cannot imagine it ever being something you would feel comfortable and safe in again. Yet when the work is finished, you are in a much better place than before and it is easier to put the struggle it took to get there out of your mind and enjoy where you are now.

This is what happens when we face tough times. As hard as it feels, if we look at all the pieces and work out a new way of putting them together, we can become stronger. Working through and growing from trauma means rebuilding the framework and creating a new set of beliefs about life. This approach is challenging, but it leads to much better results. It is only by dismantling what we thought we knew that we grow stronger. When we do this, we are taking charge of what has happened and making conscious choices about how best to manage. It is this approach that leads to growth.

In a way, rebuilding represents the death of who we once were.

We are forced to rethink our ideas about the world we live in, who we are, the kind of people that surround us and how our future will be. We question *why?* Before trauma, we believed that the world is logical, that bad things happen for a reason. Afterwards, it is impossible to reconcile this worldview. We see that we *are* vulnerable, the world is not always fair and we do not have control over our lives.

This is incredibly painful and can leave you feeling lost and struggling. It strips you of your security and can make life seem meaningless and random. When you think about it in these terms, it is no wonder it can be such a confusing and frightening experience. But those who accept that life cannot be the same again can think instead about how best to move forward. In time, you can discover that these worlds can live alongside each other; you cherish the good in life even more than before, understanding that it is not guaranteed. You see the scars, but it adds to the beauty.

You'll see this in Akemi's story on the next page. I've known Akemi since school; she's one of my favourite people. Someone everyone loves and wants to be around. Kind and thoughtful, clever, but great fun too. When she married Leo, we all knew how lucky he was to get to spend his life with her. We never imagined what would happen next.

AKEMI'S STORY:

BETRAYAL OF TRUST

I trusted Leo fully. I thought we had a strong relationship. I knew he was a character and a bit of a live wire, but I felt secure. I never suspected he was having an affair. I can now see my marriage for what it was. As well as the cheating, there were lots of little signs that I was losing myself. That I wasn't happy. We were together for over ten years, and I am resigned to the fact that my whole relationship was a complete farce.

The relationship progressed in the standard way – we met in 2002, were engaged by 2004 and then married two years later. Our first child was born in 2010. It seemed steady and all very normal until everything came out in 2014. In truth, the lying, cheating and controlling had been happening for all of our marriage.

In the final year we were together, we were going through fertility treatment. We were desperate for another baby and had been trying for six months. At the first consultation there was something nonchalant about him, as if he knew it wasn't him who had fertility issues. I now realize it's because he had made two other women pregnant during our relationship.

Around this time, Leo had been really stressed out over what I thought was work. He was getting frequent migraines, was constantly grumpy and stressed. We went to Paris in February for our ten-year anniversary and it was a weird trip. He had frequent 'work calls', but I think in truth the other woman was making ultimatums. He was also switching between two extremes when interacting with me: on one side he'd make nasty offhand comments and was constantly hurtful; yet he'd also leave me cards saying I was the best wife and mother and gave me an eternity ring.

He had lied about a few things. It sounds silly, but he'd lie about smoking. His clothes would smell of smoke, but when I questioned it, he told me I was mental and paranoid. He'd turn his phone off on work nights out, but again he made me feel like a nagging wife if I brought it up. Sometimes I wonder how I didn't see what he was up to, but I could always explain it away.

I found out I was pregnant when he was in Canada. I was so excited, but I wanted to tell him in person, so I waited until he got back. When I delivered the news, he just took a deep breath and rolled his head back – no cuddle, no excitement. I'm non-confrontational, so I didn't challenge it, and I thought to myself that he was like that when he learned about our first child too. What I now know is that when I was pregnant the first time, he'd also got someone else pregnant, and he'd done it again for the second pregnancy.

Over the next week, he was withdrawn and had headaches. One morning the following week, he was at home when I woke up – usually he would have already left for work. He said he had a conference to go to and didn't need to leave until later. He then offered to take our boy to the nursery, something he never did.

When he came back, he just walked in the door and said, 'I

need to talk to you about something.' He told me to sit down, then said: 'I've been having an affair for the last nine months. And it's not the first. There have been multiple affairs in our relationship.'

'Is this a joke?' I said.

'No, it's not a joke.'

'But I'm pregnant.'

'I know.'

He was totally stone cold with no emotion. At no point did he apologize or take any blame. I just sat there in total shock. Finally, I got up, went outside and rang my brother. Not a huge amount more was said between us at that point. I don't think I even cried. I just remember I kept repeating, 'What the fuck, I can't believe this has fucking happened, what the fuck, what am I going to fucking do?' I was just in utter shock.

My dad came and picked me up. My first child was at nursery, Leo was in my home. My family urged me take control somehow. Dad managed to get an appointment at Relate, a relationship counselling centre, so I put on a dress, did my make-up and went to see the counsellor – totally on autopilot. Leo just sat there so cold, with no emotion, and gave no apology.

The counsellor turned to look at me and said, 'This is not your fault, he's got a serious problem.' I remember feeling some sort of relief. Leo had always had a lack of empathy; he never really reacted to other people crying. But then afterwards, he got upset and I found myself consoling him. He kept repeating, 'What am I going to do?' It was only later that I reflected he was only concerned about himself and the impact this would have on him.

After this, I just went into coping mode. I had to push my feelings aside to keep going. I was pregnant, had a four-year-old and a puppy, and I wasn't working, as Leo had encouraged me to give up my teaching job to focus on having another baby. I'd just had this absolute shocker and then I had to go and collect my son from the nursery, bring him home and do all the bedtime routine as if nothing had even happened. I just did it, almost dissociating from myself.

I also had to go through a full sexual health screen while pregnant, as he hadn't practised safe sex with all the women. It was clear, thank goodness, but it was another thing to deal with at the time.

The next few days were a blur. I had to decide about the baby. Leo was desperate for me to terminate, but my father is Catholic and I really wanted this baby. He was so wished for and so, so wanted. I went to see the GP for advice, and he was very calm and said to me, 'You're either a single mother of one or a single mother of two – there's not an in-between.' That was my decision.

By then Leo had told me more about what had been going on. He had slept with someone two weeks before our wedding. He'd had an affair while I was pregnant with our first child (and got her pregnant) and had been in a serious affair for the last nine months. Those were just the ones he told me about – I'm sure there had been many more.

I told a few of my friends straight away. Leo was angry that I had started sharing. He said it was my fault that it couldn't work out now because I had told people. He immediately started shifting the blame to me. He then became obsessed with the termination. He was ringing and ringing me telling me I had to make the decision: 'It's just a tablet, go in and take it and it will be better for everyone.'

He told me that if I ended the pregnancy, we might have a chance. That if I had the baby, it was over, but if I terminated, we might be able to work it out as it would be one less thing to think about. By that point I knew exactly what he was doing. He then said that if I went ahead with the pregnancy, he wouldn't have a relationship with this child. He told me I would never cope on my own, that I would be a burden to my family. That I wasn't being fair to our child. It was relentless. He knew exactly what buttons to push to hurt me. He didn't want me to go to the eight-week scan as he knew there would be no going back for me after that. I remember lying in bed and wishing that I would miscarry overnight as then I wouldn't have to make any decisions. The decision would be made for me.

Up until then, everything was going to plan. My life had followed the pattern I was expecting and had hoped for. We were going to have two children. He had a good job, so I was going to have some time not working to bring up the children. We were looking at buying a bigger house, just up the road. Even mid-affair, weeks before he left, he was enquiring about mortgages, and we had a viewing on the house. I even thought we were happy together. But then in one moment, everything that I thought my life was just disappeared. Everything completely changed.

I felt totally at peace when I finally made the decision to continue the pregnancy. I just thought to myself that what's meant to be is meant to be. If I manage to hold this pregnancy then it's got to be a tough cookie, given the amount of stress I'm under. It was an incredibly emotional time – I was constantly in tears. But once that decision was there, then it was easier. I had something to focus on, as there was no room to be upset. You can't just leave a four-year-old to fend for themselves.

When I reflect on that time, I can't believe I was contemplating a termination. That's the emotional bit. I was put in this awful position with something I so desperately wanted. I look at my son now and that's who I think about. Not about the trauma, but about him.

Leo was furious. He tried for ages to change my mind. But he couldn't manipulate me on this one. That's when it started to change. This was the first time that I hadn't been manipulated by him. It was a big thing that I didn't give in to what he wanted.

His behaviour from then on made me see the whole marriage in a different light. I asked him not to take his new girlfriend to our house while I was away, but then I found a meal for two in the recycling. He went crazy at me when I asked him about it and told me I was paranoid. 'This is why I did what I did, because you always behave like this. You are mental. This is what you're like.' As always, I ended up apologizing. But later that week the dog walker confirmed that she had been there. I can see now that our whole marriage was like this, with me being constantly manipulated. He lied the whole way through, and I'd never stood up to him.

Our marriage was a slow process of losing trust in myself. He took my voice, my inner voice, and replaced it with his. I look back and feel thankful that it ended when it did. That helps me get through life now. I didn't question anything, I didn't have an opinion on anything. We were great around a dinner party table, good fun, both loud. But behind closed doors, it was very different. My confidence in my body was destroyed by him.

When I reflect on it, I lost myself. Anything I wanted to do that I knew he might not approve of I'd tread carefully around. Any suggestion I had would have to be worded in a particular way so that it would sound like his idea. I'd try to help him and support him on weekends because he was always so tired. But that was because he was being unfaithful all week and lying about it. When he finally confessed, I remember him saying he'd rather be anywhere else than with us and that he dreaded the weekends with me and our child. That's an awful thing to say to your wife.

What started to emerge was this huge web of lies for the past ten years that no one knew about. There were hidden credit cards with huge spending on – weekends away, hotel rooms, sex shops, restaurant meals, private sexual health clinic bills – all types of secrets that started to come out. It became very clear that 'work trips' were not work at all. I eventually recognized that there was something fundamentally wrong with him. I could have eaten myself up if I analysed what I'd done wrong, but I figured out that it had no use. His behaviours were so extreme. I took myself out of the role of victim.

I was very open about what was happening, which gave space for people to be there for me. My friends and family were amazing. I was really embarrassed my marriage had failed, but I found it therapeutic to tell the story. Getting it out there was part of the healing process. I didn't want to feel shame.

It was amazing how people pulled together around me. One of the dads I knew used to drive over with a meal. Lots of food would turn up at my house. Some days I'd wake up and my dad would be outside doing the gardening. My neighbour was kind about things I might need. A nursery mum offered to walk the dog. My brother and his partner relocated to be closer, and my mother was a constant support. I had to keep thinking about the positives, and the way people helped me was really one of them.

I had to shift my mindset to thinking about coping, managing, organizing and sorting. I was busy with a four-year-old and with a baby on the way. The single parenting was OK, I knew I could do it. The hardest thing was dealing with Leo, and that has remained a challenge. He was harassing me constantly and a nightmare to deal with. He wasn't being easy about the divorce and was trying to get me out of the house and made an application to court to do so. I didn't really have any space to look around, reflect or feel sorry for myself as there was so much going on and my focus was on my son.

I felt very angry that Leo had married me. He didn't have to propose. It's not like it turned sour and he started having affairs, as he was doing it right from the start of our relationship. I've got two gorgeous children, but who knows what my life would have been, who I might have met. Instead he decided to marry me, manipulate me and control my life. It was so, so selfish. It was so traumatic, I wouldn't wish it on anyone, ever, but I'm pleased it happened and that at no point did I try and beg him to come back.

It felt quite clear that there were a couple of directions I could go. I could either let it eat me up or just move forward – I chose to let go of the past. I had to think logically how to get through this, what to plan for. I didn't think too emotionally, which is surprising as I'm a very emotional person, but if I'd allowed myself to sit and get upset, I really could have.

I think I'm a better person because of it, a better parent, a stronger individual. I joke that it was easier parenting my second child on my own than my first with him. I had to get up in the nights on my own, it was extraordinarily tiring, but there were some beautiful things about it. I never questioned any decision I made as I was the only one who had to make them. It was never like that before. It was just me, being myself.

When the baby was born, he was a 'floppy baby' and the doctors hit the alarm. I just lay there thinking, *Is this a joke? I can't believe this. If I've gone through all of this to now lose this baby.* I was lying there in shock while they were pumping him. My mum was there and she's had the trauma of losing a baby, so it was hard. He was not breathing for a while, but, thank God, he was revived. At 8 p.m., everyone went home and I was on my own in the postnatal ward. It really hit me then – I am truly on my own with a newborn. By then I'd accepted that Leo would have nothing to do with him; even the baby's name was entirely my choice. I had taken control.

My parents had lost a baby at six months so they tried to put it in perspective – it's bad, but it could be worse. In their eyes it was a case of we've got through that, we can get through this. I've never seen them wallow, so in my head there was never really another way. The acceptance of my situation had started to come, I knew I just had to roll with it. I cried a lot during my counselling sessions. I saw that as an outlet, but the rest of the time I held it together.

I know lots of people who have experienced tricky times now, but at that time I felt like I was the only one. None of my friends had gone through a divorce yet and I was going through it with a new baby! We did well most of that time, but when one of us became sick, that's when the wheels would fall off. When I saw friends, I couldn't help sometimes feeling annoyed when they would say how tired they were. If only they knew!

There are so many cool things that have come out of me being a single parent. The three of us actually rather loved it, in lots of ways. There isn't really sibling rivalry because from the word go we were the three musketeers, we had to look after each other. It changed the dynamic and we have such a tight relationship. Eventually, I started to feel grateful for how simple my life was and how lucky we were. I looked at my friends in their relationships where they were bickering and putting each other down and I felt quite liberated.

Once I'd gone through that grieving process of what I'd lost, I could then really focus on how much I had, how much I'd gained and how my life would be. At the start I would beat myself up about not giving the kids what I'd considered a normal family life. I spent a long time feeling sensitive about that. But now I reflect on how much they have gained. They've never seen any arguing in their house. In some family homes, children watch their parents fighting day in day out. My kids don't have that. They're also part of a very safe, very secure unit, and in all honesty they're lucky Leo is not in their lives that much. He's a terrible role model.

I started working as a teacher again and went back to using my maiden name. I was proud to have my name back. To be me again. Leo left in March, and by the following June, I was working two days a week. I was open about what had happened when I got there. No one knew him, they all just thought he was a dick. The job was very important to me as it meant I was not just a single mum, I was a teacher now as well.

Work started to go well and I went up to three days, then full-time alongside studying to become a special educational needs coordinator (SENCO). I know that I'm good at my job. I'm in control and I can do it. That's my thing now. My family always support me to push further in my job, saying that they can all help out. I could have thought of a million reasons not to go back to work, but I knew I had to get back in.

If I'd stayed with Leo, I wouldn't have ended up where I am now with my job, that's for sure. I would have gone back part-time as a form teacher or teaching assistant and I never would have fulfilled my potential. At one point I was in a full-time role, plus studying at university and looking after the boys. Finding out what I am capable of was a big confidence boost. I had a great boss who saw the potential in me and encouraged me to go down the SENCO route. I've just signed up for another course starting in September.

I still have challenges with Leo. I still wish I had a thicker skin with him. He still has a way of creating a physical reaction in me when I see him. I think had it been what I consider a normal break-up – where you separate and there's an apology and some kind of understanding – it may have been different. But because of the constant lies and the lack of any type of remorse, there is still a lot of anger there. But I just need to make peace with that.

So many times I hope we're at the stage where we can co-parent, but we don't seem to ever get there. I've got better at saying no. It still doesn't come naturally to me, but I'm better at boundaries now.

Dating was a good thing for me, although I had to learn how to trust again. There are still triggers, like when my partner goes out after work, or if he is quiet at home for a bit. It's hard for me to trust loving words as well. Leo got me an eternity ring three months before he left – while he was having an affair – and wrote cards, telling me of his undying love, and it was all lies. That's the problem I have. But I am also resilient and have the security of knowing that if my partner left, I could cope.

I couldn't have got to this point emotionally and mentally without the struggle. It's given me perspective on life. I'm definitely stronger now, and I know how capable I am of doing big things. I'm a better mother and hopefully a good role model for my children. I say to my kids, 'Look at what Mummy does. You must work hard in life to do these things.' I'd like to think that they have been positively affected by it. I think I'm more laid-back – even my parenting style is much more holistic and relaxed. On the other side, maybe I've become a little bit impatient with people who sweat the small things.

If I could go back to when this first happened, there are definitely things I'd want to do and say – mostly just to appreciate what I was going through and validate what I was feeling. I used to turn up to events and gatherings on my own with a baby and a four-year-old and I probably could have told people at the time how hard it was. I wish I could go back to my younger self and say well done.

Everything can change in the space of a morning. My entire life did after just a five-minute conversation. I think about that a lot and how I need to appreciate what I have. Who knows what the next day can bring. But you may as well embrace the things you have some element of control over.

I am so pleased that I found myself again. I look at photos of me with Leo, my face and my eyes, and there's something different, something dead. I look at photos of myself now and there's something more ignited in them – sparkier and more alive. I have had this opportunity to really embrace the change, make the most out of it and better myself. My life since Leo left has only improved. It's got better and better and continues to do so. I feel comfortable going into my forties and fifties. It's like new chapters of a book. Every little thing that happens now is part of the journey.

I look back and reflect on all that has happened and I actually feel grateful. Grateful for my children, grateful not to be married to Leo, grateful for my family and friends and grateful that my journey has led me to my new partner. I feel confident that I will grow old in a fulfilling way. Whatever happens now, I will be happy.

MY THOUGHTS

Akemi's story shows how one moment can change your life dramatically and how trauma can rip up the meaning framework of our lives. I remember so clearly getting the call from Akemi when Leo first told her about his behaviour. Everything she thought her life was disappeared. A gap torn open between her expectations and the reality she now knew.

Why didn't I see it? The impact of our fundamental assumptions

In a trauma like this, it can be easy to fall into the trap of questioning 'Why didn't I see it?' But Akemi trusted Leo fully. She was going through fertility treatment (a decision they had made as a couple), and they had just been to Paris, where he had showered her with gifts and cards. It is not always there to be seen. This is especially true when we consider the three fundamental assumptions that most people hold (see pages 37–38).

When we look at the world through the lens of these beliefs, it shapes what we see. Our brain wants to keep our beliefs intact and pays attention to any information that fits. This confirmation bias means we also dismiss information that doesn't match up to what we believe. We might see a red flag, but our brain finds a way to put it away again. And it doesn't happen all at once, it happens slowly – Akemi and Leo were together for over ten years. It's not that we're ignoring the signs or consciously in denial; when we're so close to something, gradual changes are hard to see because of the assumptions we hold. It's only in hindsight that we view things differently. This is because we now have new information so can look back and make sense of things in a different way – the lies, the migraines, realizing that the phone calls might have been ultimatums or seeing a nonchalant approach to fertility treatment for what it is.

Losing yourself – the impact of the relationship

Leo had eroded Akemi's self-esteem and confidence. When you're with someone all the time and they put you down, or tell you you're the one who is the problem, and the message is constant, it's impossible not to be affected. Akemi stopped listening to her inner voice and her own needs. She put Leo first and tried to keep him happy, treading carefully around things he might not approve of and wording things in a certain way. Leo also removed her from lots of the things that gave her confidence.

When you're in this type of relationship, it's not easy to see how damaging it is. The damage happens very gradually and the manipulation and control isn't overt. Often we imagine abusive husbands as 'wife-beaters', but in my experience it's far more subtle than that. They are your partner, so they know you well and know the right buttons to press. They tell you you're mad, you're the problem, so you doubt yourself and stop listening to your instincts. Often they switch between two extremes: Leo at times told Akemi she was the best wife and mother, then would flip to being nasty and hurtful. The switch between the two makes you question what you're doing wrong and keeps you hoping it will be OK (something your brain desperately wants to believe). You may have read about this type of behaviour as 'love bombing'.

Rebuilding

Finding out about Leo shattered Akemi's fundamental assumptions about life, creating a gap between the life she thought she knew and her new reality. She could no longer tell herself it was a good marriage or explain away the bad behaviour. But how she interpreted what happened made a positive difference. Discovering the truth about Leo enabled her to see him more clearly. The response from family and friends and the reaction of the relationship counsellor showed her that his extreme behaviour was not her fault.

This shift in her meaning framework, although painful to go through, allowed her to see Leo as the problem. With the support of those around her and the motivation of a new baby arriving, she picked up the pieces and worked to put things back together in a new way, rebuilding her mental map. This put Akemi in a much stronger position to move forward and allowed her to take back control.

Looking back on this, I feel sad for Akemi that she didn't recognize just how common trauma is. She was the first in our friendship group to go through something like this, and although divorce and infidelity are incredibly common, it didn't feel like it to her at the time. Her meaning framework was influenced by the beliefs and attitudes that we hold about divorce – these can be explicit or implicit and are shaped by historical and cultural context as well as by family and friends. I think this added to the shame she initially felt, which left her feeling alone in what she was going through. It was by telling her story – to family and friends and her therapist – that she was eventually able to let go of this misplaced shame.

In time, Akemi began to see that her life was changing for the better. Slowly she rebuilt herself, restoring her identity and remembering herself again. She gained confidence through work and study, and thought about what she wanted, listening to her instincts and taking back her maiden name, meaning that she saw herself as capable, strong and a good mother to the boys. All the things she'd stopped doing in the relationship. Piecing together the meaning framework of her life in a new way allowed for growth. She became stronger, more resilient, with a new perspective on life. Her spark returned and she found herself again.

Trauma phases

I saw amazing strength in Akemi and how quickly she faced up to what was happening. In the next chapter, I'll introduce you to the five phases of trauma. Hold in mind Akemi's experience as you read this. After the initial phase of outcry and shock, she immediately took action. She shared what was happening with those closest to her and sought expert help. At times she just had to keep going, in coping mode, at maximum capacity – a mother to a four-year-old, pregnant, looking after a puppy, dealing with lawyers and a tricky ex-partner. Moving between numbness and denial, intrusive re-experiencing and working through the trauma.

Akemi grieved for the loss of the life she knew and a future that didn't happen, the grief of what could have been and letting go of society's family ideal. This process moved her into the working-through phase and towards letting go of the past. By allowing herself to grieve for what she had lost, she could begin to focus on how much she had, with a new understanding of herself and all she was capable of. In charge of her future and happiness while open to the idea of struggle and hard times ahead.

KEY TAKEAWAYS

- We build mental maps to help us navigate our lives.
- We believe bad things won't happen to us – this is known as unrealistic optimism.
- Our brain's confirmation bias means we ignore facts that contradict our beliefs, keeping us in denial.
- Trauma shatters our fundamental assumptions and rips up our mental map.
- Working through and growing from trauma means creating a new mental map of beliefs.

CARE (STEP 1)

THE FIVE PHASES

Psychiatrist Mardi Horowitz (1993) divided the process of going through trauma into five different phases. In this chapter, I'll be sharing his research so you have a sense of what to expect as you work through this book. People go through these phases at different speeds; we all have different circumstances, personalities and ways of coping. Remember, the path you take is your own route. Think about these phases as a guide, rather than a set process.

These stages are typical and can be helpful in thinking about your experience and normalizing the many different emotions you will be experiencing. However, it is not an exact science: the phases don't occur for everyone or always in this exact order, and we commonly move back and forth between stages. As you read through, think about where you are.

Phase 1: Outcry

This is the shock stage, in which you feel overwhelmed by feelings in response to what's happened. In this phase, what has happened can feel unbelievable, and there is little room for much else, like Akemi when Leo first told her he had been having an affair.

In this stage you might have a sense of things feeling surreal as your brain struggles to make sense of them. You might feel a mix of emotions, such as upset and anger. You might scream, yell or cry. Or hold in your feelings, suppressing them but feeling the rage inside. You might question *why?* or the unfairness of what has happened.

Life doesn't stop for you, however, and in these early stages it can feel like you only have enough energy to deal with what is urgent and no capacity for anything extra. This is a time of uncertainty, and everything feels out of control. You might have trouble managing your feelings, moving between experiencing strong emotions and feeling exhausted, tense, confused, empty and numb. Intrusive memories, nightmares, poor sleep and flashbacks are also common.

At times you might glimpse the enormity of what has happened; the rest of the time you are just coping. This is not the time to be looking for silver linings. This is the time to look after yourself, think about your needs, connect to others, find a sense of safety and seek medical or psychological support if needed. I'll be introducing you to coping strategies to manage these symptoms in Chapters 5 to 8.

Phase 2: Numbness and denial

When you experience something that is incredibly upsetting, a common reaction is to try and push it out of your mind and avoid it. To try and move on and act as if nothing has happened, particularly if the emotions are tough ones like shame or terror, or if you were left feeling weak or vulnerable. This takes up a lot of energy and capacity.

In this stage, it can feel like you are in a dream or detached from what's happening. You might also go on autopilot, moving through life as if nothing has changed, going through the motions as it's all you know – working, taking care of your family, doing the things that are part of your normal day. Like Akemi busy with a four-year-old and a baby on the way. You might purposely keep busy so you have no time for yourself or to feel the pain, or numb yourself with drugs, alcohol or food.

Many people describe a sense of feeling outside of themselves, watching from afar. Distant from family and friends, disconnected and disengaged from life. You might not even be aware you are doing this. Sometimes people tell me it's like they put up a wall to prevent themselves being hurt more. This is essentially avoidance. When there is so much going on and you don't have the space to deal with it, some detachment is necessary to manage the distressing feelings.

You can only stay in this phase for so long before the memories start knocking and just won't go away until they are dealt with. You may move between denial and intrusion – alternating between periods of distraction and disengagement and feeling what's happened intensely. This can be helpful to break up the intensity of the loss so it is more manageable and less overwhelming. I will focus on the impact of numbness and denial and introduce healthy coping strategies to help you through this phase in Chapter 8.

Phase 3: Intrusive re-experiencing

This is described by Horowitz as the phase of adjustment to trauma. Trauma activates threat mode in the part of the brain that is devoted to ensuring survival. It sits deep below our rational brain, so is impossible to ignore in the long term.

We know this is a normal reaction to experiencing trauma, as our mind tries to work out what has happened and make sense of it. The experience can come back to us when we choose to think about it, or as intrusive thoughts, flashbacks and nightmares. We may also experience intense physical sensations and emotions. When we're in this threat mode, we cannot access higher-level thinking and work things through. We have to calm ourselves physically before we can mentally engage with our recovery. We'll be looking at how to do this in Chapters 5 and 6.

Our memories can feel painful, and unless we deal with them, they will keep having a negative effect on us. I love the poem 'The Guest House', written by Rumi, a 13th-century Sufi poet who wrote about grief, sorrow, loss and transformation, and beautifully translated by Coleman Banks. It's a great reminder of how to manage emotions, something we'll be looking at in Chapters 8 and 9.

This being human is a guest house.
Every morning a new arrival.
A joy, a depression, a meanness,
some momentary awareness comes
as an unexpected visitor.
Welcome and entertain them all!
Even if they're a crowd of sorrows,
who violently sweep your house
empty of its furniture,
still treat each guest honourably
He may be clearing you out
for some new delight.
The dark thought, the shame, the malice,
meet them at the door laughing,
and invite them in.
Be grateful for whoever comes,

because each has been sent
as a guide from beyond.

Phase 4: Working through

As time progresses – this can be days, weeks, months or even years – the movement between denial (not thinking about or feeling the loss) and intrusion (thinking about it and feeling it intensely) tends to slow down, and we can work through what has happened and slowly fill in the gaps.

The intensity of the memory decreases. Often this happens naturally, rather than due to active effort, but it is key in allowing us to move forward. This is something you will see in all the stories in this book, which I would like to give you hope.

It is hard working through what has happened, as you'll see in the next story, but it's the only way to truly let go of it. It is a chance to think about events, but to also start to figure out new ways to manage. You can't go back to how things were – that reality doesn't exist any more. It is only when you face up to the truth that you know what you are dealing with. In this stage, acceptance and forgiveness takes place: acknowledging what has happened and the suffering it has caused, recognizing that it may have forever changed your life, expressing and owning your feelings of sorrow, loss, resentment or anger.

Grieving for what's happened is an important part of making sense of it and finding a way to put it away. This process is similar to the grief model developed by Elisabeth Kübler-Ross. The five stages of grief – denial, anger, bargaining, depression and acceptance – are a useful guide for understanding some of the reactions you might have in response to loss. The stages are similar to the five phases of trauma, as they are also non-linear and not everyone experiences every stage.

Grieving your losses as you let go of the life you knew sits alongside taking responsibility for your actions, allowing you to move forward and free up more mental space. We will be looking at this as a way to deal with trauma, but it's really important that when you get to this point of the book, you go at your own pace so it feels manageable, and take whatever time you need to make sense of things and take stock. I'll also be teaching you techniques to make this easier. We'll be concentrating on this in Chapter 9.

Phase 5: Completion

At some point, the process of grieving is completed enough that life starts to feel normal again. The feelings attached to what has happened are less painful, and any active trauma memories move into long-term memory so they do not continue to bother us in the same way. We can file them away and look at them only when we choose to. We might feel the loss more strongly on key dates, or when we see something that reminds us of what happened, but we will no longer feel it at the same intensity. Completion allows space to look past the difficulty and value the positive changes; we'll focus on this in Chapter 10.

THE PROCESS

This experience is personal to you. There is no right way to go through trauma; each person finds the best way through for them. If something has just happened, I'm sure you are feeling overwhelmed, and it might be difficult to imagine working through these stages and coming out the other side, but as you will see, humans have an amazing ability to adapt and adjust to difficult times.

The early days can feel chaotic as you are pushed and pulled between stages. Some days it might feel like you are making progress, that things are coming together and you are making sense of things. At other times you will find yourself thrown back into overwhelming grief, like Jess and Finn, whose story comes next, and in these moments you can't even remember how you coped the week before. There's no quick route through this type of pain. Some people take time to move forwards; others might go straight to coping, like David, who you'll meet later in this book (see page 195). Some are able to accept what has happened, while for others this can take years.

It's normal to move backwards and forwards as you face up to your experiences (see diagram on page 70). At times it might feel overwhelming, and stepping back for a bit is your body and mind's way of managing this. It might feel like two steps forward, two steps back, but just looking at what has happened and allowing space for it is making progress.

It can be helpful to remember as you work through this book that progress is not a straight line. More recent thinking suggests that it is circular. Feeling good and struggling are not separate but intertwined. You might be struggling, then you feel better, but you don't just stay there; it swings round to struggle again. You are constantly moving around the circle, but as you do, you learn and grow from your experiences. When approached in the right way, negative emotions can help to build resilience, increasing your ability to cope in difficult times so that you move forward stronger.

There will be difficult days, when it might be harder to keep new insights clearly in your mind, but progress is always happening. Remember, it's OK to have ups and downs; often it's the challenging days you gain the most from. Each setback is another chance to learn and grow. You'll get quicker at noticing when you fall into old habits and patterns and better at knowing

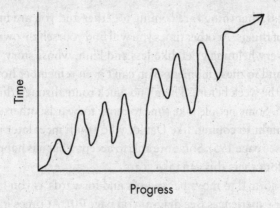

The path to progress

how to pull yourself back out. On the stuck days, make it easier for yourself – just think of one small thing you can do.

When you're close up to things, it can be easy to miss what's changed. To counter this, keep track of the small ways you are progressing. You could try taking a few minutes before you go to bed to think back over your day and remember three good things that happened – things that went well, any progress you've made, something you enjoyed or were grateful for. This lets you look at what you are doing instead of focusing on what you're not. When you focus on what you are not able to do, it leaves you stuck and shifts you to the negative, bringing your mood down.

I know this is easy for me to say and harder to do, especially when your emotions are turned up loud, but when you manage it, it moves you into a completely different mental state so you no longer feel stuck. It puts you back in control and helps you build confidence. The more you note down the things you are doing or that are going well, the better you will feel.

They can be small – making time for a hot drink, reading a chapter of this book – or of bigger importance – confiding in a friend or trying something new. You'll probably find it varies. Write them down. This is important. You may want to get a small notebook just for this purpose, or you can track them using your phone notes or an app. Then at the end of each week, look back and remind yourself of all you've done. Making notes will give you a chance to gain new perspectives and consider alternative ways of thinking about what has happened and about yourself.

TWO ROOMS

I think about the movement between good days and bad as two rooms with an interconnecting door. There's the 'good room', where we like to be as much as possible. This is where we are when life goes well and we are managing; when we feel capable and connected to others. The room next door is the 'struggle room', where we go when life feels unmanageable and we are threatened with negative emotions like anxiety, fear, frustration or anger.

The good room plays an essential role in our survival; positive emotions like happiness, joy and gratitude broaden our minds and open us up to new possibilities and ideas. It also builds our personal well-being resources, social, intellectual and physical. Like an animal stocking up on food before hibernation, we draw on these resources when we are in different emotional states to maintain well-being. When we're in the struggle room, we are in threat mode. Our mind constricts and focuses on the threat, real or imagined, limiting our ability to be open to new ideas and other people or to build our resources.

In each room, we think and feel differently, and when we're in one room, it's hard to remember that the room next door exists. In the good room, it's tempting to imagine that all's well, and that we are safe and will never come to any harm, but this can lead to us denying parts of ourselves or repressing negative emotions. For example, trying to be always patient and calm is impossible and can push us back into the struggle room. When we're in the struggle room, we feel overwhelmed and our problems can feel insurmountable. This can overspill from what we're currently facing into other areas; for example, we might end up generalizing and feeling that everything is wrong in our life.

Ideally, as you work through this book, I want you to try to keep the door open. This is hard, but it's important to remember that both sides exist. Moving between these rooms is part of life and how we process our experiences. We want to use the good room to shore up our resources, but we also need to remember that the struggle room exists and that negative emotions are a normal response to difficulty. We won't be there for ever; in time we will move back to the good room.

STEP 1: CARE

Step 1 puts you in the best place to start. It's important to take care of the basics so you have a solid foundation on which to begin this work. Ensure you are getting enough sleep and give yourself time to rest. Make sure you are eating the right amount and the right sort of food to fuel your body, and that you are staying hydrated. These are the essential components of feeling physically good. Having enough energy in the tank makes a big difference to how you feel and puts you in the best position to move forwards.

THE IMPORTANCE OF HOPE

To help you through this period, it's essential to find hope. It can be the smallest spark or flicker of light in the darkness, but this spark will open you up to a different future with new possibilities ahead. I want you to make an active decision to be hopeful. As difficult as things feel right now, they won't always be this hard. You can make the changes you need and find the strength within you.

Hope can be a catalyst for change. Research shows that it seems to mitigate the negative effects of trauma. Kerrie Glass, a researcher at the University of South Carolina, interviewed 228 survivors of Hurricane Katrina. She found that people with higher levels of hope had lower levels of distress and fewer symptoms of PTSD. David Berendes and Francis Keefe at Duke University surveyed 51 patients with lung cancer and found that people with greater levels of hope, regardless of the severity of their cancer, tended to have less depression and fewer physical symptoms such as coughing, pain and fatigue.

Hope is stronger than fear; it motivates you, inspires you to make changes and allows you to think differently. The alternative, hopelessness, is understandable, but from here it will make it very difficult to succeed.

When I talk about hope, I don't mean forgetting what's happened or no longer caring that you have lost someone. Or wild optimism and trying to think positively when you don't feel positive at all. I'm simply asking you to allow yourself to believe things can get better. This hope must be rooted in the importance of 'doing', such as working through the chapters in this book, coupled with a realistic understanding of the situation and a confidence in your ability to face it and to keep trying when things are tough.

LETTING OTHERS IN

To help you through this journey, relationships are key. Ensure you have support in place and that the people around you are those who are rooting for you and your hopes; who will encourage you to move forward and reach your goals, walk beside you through difficulties and foster hope within you. Knowing that people are there for you and that you have support protects you from experiencing more intense distress.

When you're going through your toughest times, often no one else is aware, but knowing that even one person will always be there for you will make a huge difference. Social support – physical and emotional comfort from others – is shown to provide a buffer to the emotional effects of trauma and other negative circumstances. It is proven to protect some people from mental health problems and is a predictor of post-traumatic growth. A block to this is keeping the trauma secret, something that is linked to the worst outcomes.

A review of 77 studies examined the risk factors related to PTSD and found that a lack of social support was one of the strongest predictors of PTSD. What's interesting is that it is the trauma survivor's *subjective* perception that support is available that most strongly predicts their emotional well-being. It is not about how many people there are or how much they are doing; what's key is that it feels helpful to you. This highlights the importance of finding the right type of support to move to growth – trauma has a way of showing you who your true friends are. It's about quality, not quantity, so be careful who you let in. Someone you can count on and who you enjoy being with. A friend who makes you smile but who will also be there when you need their support. This is vital to getting through trauma.

In their excellent book *Supersurvivors: The Surprising Link Between Suffering and Success*, David Feldman and Lee Daniel Kravetz reviewed the research on social support: 'According to dozens of studies, the people in our lives really matter...believing that someone is by your side – someone who makes you smile, but also someone you know you can count on when you need support – is one of the great secrets to supersurvival.'

Often, we feel alone or that no one cares, but it's difficult for others to care if they don't know what's happened. There's never a good time to talk about these things, but it's important that you do, so friends can be there for you. If it's easier, text in advance and say you need to speak about something. Or send an email telling them what's happened. People don't naturally ask deeper questions; they aren't expecting that something has gone significantly wrong. If you say you're OK, they believe you.

In therapy, people often tell me that they feel like no one understands, and there is a truth to this. When you've experienced trauma, people don't always know what to do or how to act. They hurt us and let us down, but they don't mean to – and if they do, they are not friends.

When you've been through something that they themselves haven't experienced, some people won't be able to fully get it. Friends might worry they will open up the topic when you don't want to, or feel uncomfortable talking about things. It is easier for them to put it away and move back into their normal lives – remember, their mind wants to keep the world as a good place, where bad things won't happen to them. This can leave you feeling misunderstood, or more lonely and withdrawn from others.

Good friends will hopefully know how to support you without being told what to do, but even with the best of intentions, people can get it wrong. They might try to cheer us up when really we want to have a good cry, encourage us to talk when we feel all talked out, or leave us feeling criticized rather than accepted for what we're feeling and what we're going through.

To overcome this, tell people what you need. It might feel hard, but people are happy to help if they know how and feel they are being useful. Even though you might hope that the other person knows what you need, no one is a mind reader. It works much better when you let someone know what you're looking for.

If I've had a tough day and I tell my husband about it, he might start offering me brilliant advice on what to do, but it can feel like a real clash if I just want to be heard and understood. If I'm feeling like this, what I now do is let him know in advance what I'm looking for. I might say to him, 'I just need you to acknowledge this is rubbish too', while at other times I might actively seek out his advice.

It might not feel like your job to do this, but it really helps if you can make others feel more comfortable with what you're going through. You can do this by offering them concrete ways to help: you could ask them to support you with your coping strategies; phone you once a week to check in; or text you every few days. If they say they can come over, let them know if you just want them to sit with you or if you're looking for advice.

I think it's helpful to recognize that although others might not fully understand *exactly* what you're going through, they still care about you. It's not that they don't want to understand; in most cases they are doing their best to try to, and they can still be there for you even if they don't completely get it. The only way for them to begin to understand is if you are able to share your experiences. This means approaching rather than withdrawing. As hard as it is when you're feeling like this, what you need is connection. To feel part of something. To feel supported in what you're going through.

Therapy is also something to consider as an additional support in the aftermath of trauma. A good therapist is trained to walk alongside you on part of this journey and having someone supporting you who is not directly involved can make a big difference. They can provide a safe space to go through the more frightening aspects of your experience, which can be difficult to deal with alone; and therapy can provide a chance to reflect, re-evaluate and rebuild your sense of self. I know this both because of the work I do in my clinic and from my own experience of receiving therapy.

In the next story, you'll meet siblings Jess and Finn, still very much in the early stages of their grief after their mother, Sue, died. Sue lived in the village I grew up in. She was a wonderful woman and gave her boundless energy and enthusiasm to so many activities in our village and beyond. If she thought something needed to be done, she made sure it happened. She was always cheerful and positive, even when faced with a difficult life and her final illness. Quite simply, she was the glue that stuck people and activities together. As the plaque on her memorial bench in North Waltham churchyard reads: *Like a sunflower she lit up our lives.*

JESS AND FINN'S STORY: DEATH OF A LOVED ONE

JESS

Mum was always such a positive person. She told us everything that was going on right from the start. The first I heard was that she had found this lump and that she was getting it checked. I thought it was nothing to worry about and it would be fine.

Mum rang me straight after the biopsy, as soon as she heard the news, and told us that it was cancer. She was eventually diagnosed with aggressive anaplastic thyroid cancer, which has a 10 per cent survival rate for a year. I went to one of the early appointments and met all of the nurses, the nutritionist and the consultants. We knew then that it was very likely to be incurable.

When she went into the first major surgery, the doctors said they'd only take it out on one side of her thyroid, and if they found it on both sides they would do the second part another time. But Mum said no, whatever you find, take it all out. And that's what they ended up doing.

Afterwards they said that if they hadn't taken it all out then and there, she would have only had four weeks more to live. We actually got seven months with her, which was precious. Mum threw a little party to say goodbye near the end. All the way through that year she said, 'I was only going to have four weeks, so it is all a bonus.'

I was in the final part of training to be a midwife when it all started. When she was on treatment and had the radiotherapy, life, as much as possible, went on as usual. Mum came up to visit a lot and I went home loads.

The one thing that I hoped for that didn't happen was that she would see me qualify as a midwife. She said to me, 'Don't you dare drop out of uni, don't you dare let this affect your future.' She died before I qualified, but she would have been so proud of me. I know that.

It was all too easy, being at uni, just to pretend it wasn't happening. I'd reached the craziest part of the course and it was all a bit surreal. After she started having chemo and she became unwell, it became very difficult, as it is hard to see your mum like that. The course helped, as I had been training to be a carer, and I channelled that part of me – I cared for her as much as I could. It was good to feel useful.

She kept us informed fully. We couldn't be protected from it; we knew what to expect and what was going on. It would have been far harder if she had just suddenly died and it had all been a total shock. We were given time to adjust by her.

Mum had always been open and honest with us, and that continued through the experience. It meant that we could plan for what happened afterwards. We've got a list of things that Mum left us that we should do. We have to go camping every year, for example. She would say to us that we're lucky that we've got time to talk about death and talk about what to do when she's not here. She would say people that get hit by a bus don't have that.

Although we knew Mum was very ill, she went downhill very quickly. I was at my boyfriend's flat in London and got a phone call saying I had to go to the hospital straight away. When I got there, she was in so much pain, but she was lucid. I was there with her when she died. She told us how happy it made her that we were all there. All the family came up to say goodbye and support me and Finn, my brother. I could tell Mum was so pleased to see that. I wouldn't have wanted it any other way.

Straight after she died, I didn't cry for a week. I wasn't really processing the trauma. I spoke to a counsellor and she assured me that was normal, when it happens so suddenly. Only the day before, I had spoken to my mum about what I was doing that week. When it happens like that, I don't think your brain can quite keep up. The numbness lasted for a short period, and then it went the other way and I was incredibly emotional the whole time. When I finished my shifts, I would burst into tears. Not because of anything in particular, but just because everything was so overwhelming. But you have to keep going and then start again the next day.

It took a while, but the balance came eventually, where I can be sad about it but get on with life. I still have those moments when I want to talk to Mum about stuff and then I realize that I can't. It's got harder as I've got to the end of uni and started doing nice things, like looking for a flat to share with friends or having celebrations. These are the things that I would have always shared with Mum. I wish she could be here to see it all.

The best way for me to deal with it in the early days was to keep working and keep myself distracted. People wanted me to take longer off university, but I wanted to qualify and keep myself busy. Mum would have wanted that too. I started running as well – that is one of the key things that has really helped me, even now. I will go for a run and I can direct my thoughts, clear my head and think things through.

University was tough the whole way through. I was in my second year when Mum got ill. The first year had been during COVID-19 lockdown. And in the third year, I was dealing with the loss. University wasn't a great help – I struggled to get exceptional circumstances. I missed a lot of hours as I had to be with Mum. In the end, I worked extra-long hours to get my minimum amount of time on the ward logged. No one thought I could do it, but I did.

Apart from university, everyone else was so supportive, even the midwives I was working with at the hospital. At the beginning, I thought it would be easier if I didn't tell people, so I could be treated normally and things could just carry on. But actually, it was nice when people knew; just knowing they were aware was comforting. Small things, like just being asked if I was OK, or because I could talk about Mum and they understood the context.

Initially, I did find it hard to talk to people about it. You don't want to just walk up to people and tell them out of the blue. Although I am pretty good at that now! It made me realize who I was close to, who I wanted to talk to. I never realized how many people I had around me that I could turn to for support. It's rubbish that something bad had to happen for that to become clear, but it did make a difference.

A lot of people don't really want to talk about it. They ask you how you are doing but they don't really want to go into the detail. You soon understand who you can talk to. I have a friend who is a midwife who is 26 and her mother passed away when she was 20. We've become very close. On my last day at the hospital we went to this field nearby and we had a celebration and talked about it all. She told me it gets better over time.

Afterwards, whenever something went well or something nice happened, I would feel guilty. That went on for a while. And when people would talk about the little things that bothered them, it would wind me up – it still does on occasion, especially if they are moaning about their parents. I understand it's relative, I used to do it too. But you learn to appreciate what you have when you lose something so special to you. It makes you value other things more.

I used to call Mum on the way home from work to tell her what I was doing. It was weird walking home and not having that. You feel like you're the only one this ever happened to, but then you meet people who have experienced the same thing. That helps.

At first when people came into the ward to have their baby and had their mums with them, I felt really sad that I wouldn't have that. But then I had one lady who came into the delivery suite and told me her mum had passed away the year before and it was really lovely to share that experience with her.

I don't think I will ever get over it. And I don't think I ever want to. Obviously you deal with it better, but I don't ever want to feel less sad about it. It still catches me by surprise sometimes. I was in theatre for a C-section and one of Mum's favourite songs came on, and I felt like I would burst into tears. Before Mum died, she said that she would watch over me, and now I like to think that it is her reminding me that she's there.

In some ways it has made me a stronger person. I know that I am resilient. I am also much more aware of other people. When you have had something happen to you like this, so many people tell you about what has happened to them. Sometimes it's things that you never would have imagined. It makes you realize how many people go through things. That you need to be compassionate to others and look out for them. Life is never as simple as it looks.

One thing that particularly helped with the grieving process was that I got a notebook and I started writing letters to Mum about what was going on. For the first month, I wrote to her every day. I don't do it as much now, but if something big happens, I will get the notebook out and write it down. So often I think, 'I wish I could tell Mum this or that', and this is a way of doing it. It feels like I've got it off my chest. If I'm thinking, *I wonder what Mum would think about this*, once I've got it written down on paper, I know what she'd think.

Work has also been a constant, a release. If I've got a day on the delivery suite, I will start at 7 a.m. and finish 12 hours later. I'll be with a lady and totally in their world. You don't have time to be inside your own head. You do need those times alone so you can process it, but it is also nice to be away from it now and then. You can't just sit around feeling sad all the time.

It does feel so unfair. Mum was such a good person and such a positive person for so many people, but she died quite young. We've never been a very religious family, but Mum would say everything happens for a reason, even near the end. It made me angry, as I couldn't see how that was fair. I know I must put aside that feeling of unfairness now, as there is no answer to it. I'll never understand it, but I accept it.

I definitely try to be positive and value the things I have, as well as the time I spent with my mum. At the start of the year, I got anxious about life, thinking that literally anything could happen at any moment to take it all away. But now I've gone the other way and have decided to take any opportunity I can to *do* life. To enjoy it.

It's shown me what's important. I feel like a different person in some ways – going through something like this makes you grow up. You don't get that chance to go home to your mum and completely stop and relax. There is always a reminder that things are different. I'm lucky that I'm close to Finn and to my boyfriend's family and to my stepsisters, who have been amazing, so I can find places to simply veg out and be comfortable, but it's obviously not the same.

I just try and make so much more time to see my family now. People I really care about. I used to get worked up and upset about small things, like my hair or small stuff, and I just don't feel the same way any more. I don't waste my time on things that I don't enjoy. Everything I do needs to have a purpose, even if it's just that I really enjoy it. I try to be true to myself and think about what's meaningful to me.

When Mum was diagnosed, she went through her social media account and she deleted all the people she didn't really care about, because she couldn't be bothered to keep them all updated. She wanted it to be about the people she loved. I want to live my life like that now. Life really is too short.

Most things you are upset about can be fixed. There is some action you can take to make things better. But this cannot be changed and there is nothing I can do. You have to live with that and work out ways to get by. You will never get to be the previous version of yourself again. You have to build yourself up from nothing. You have to learn how to live your life without being really, really sad all the time. It's a slow process, but it is happening.

When I look back at her life, she did all the things that made her happy. It was hard for her at times, of course, but she didn't let that get in the way of living the life she wanted. I think about that a lot. I want to live like that too.

FINN

My mum was always good at telling me and Jess what was going on. It was the same from the very first appointment, when they had no idea what it was. As soon as she was diagnosed, she told us.

Initially we didn't know how aggressive the cancer was, but we soon realized. I was at college then, but it was right during the pandemic so I was mostly at home isolating and I went for a run. When I came back and knocked on the door to be let in, she couldn't get up as her breathing had got so difficult. It had spread to her throat. We knew then how scary it was.

At the beginning they thought it might be operable, but they also knew they only had one shot to get it out as it was so aggressive. After the operation, they said there was a chance they'd got it all, but it soon started to spread. Then they knew there wasn't a lot they could do. It was more about slowing it down.

Our Mum being so open with us made it much easier. She would tell us how she was feeling. We didn't have to second-guess anything. I trusted her. When I was younger, I was with Mum in a lift. I was scared and Mum said to me, 'You don't have to be worried unless I am worried.' I've always remembered that. And that's how it was during the whole process. It gave me much longer to deal with it and process it as I was around the whole time at home and able to get my head around it. I was able to support her and drive her to hospital appointments. Jess was at university, so it was all much more of a shock for her.

When Jess first went to uni, it was very quiet in the house as she had always done all the talking. But me and Mum became very close then. We had a whole year together before it happened.

Me and Jess are a team. We speak to each other quite a bit, but I tend to handle things better on my own, whereas Jess likes to talk things through with other people. I'm a very quiet person. I deal with things internally. It took me a while to speak to people around me, but it's nice knowing that people know.

As long as I can remember, it's just been me, my mum and Jess. So we've always had to crack on and do stuff. Every summer holiday we've been doing the child-minding with Mum. We've always been quite self-sufficient. Both me and Jess can do a lot more than most kids of our age. I've got a friend from uni who is 21 and has never done his own washing. I feel like Mum set us up so well.

Apart from family, the dogs have been the biggest help to me. They can just be there. Taking them for walks has been great for me and it gets you out of the house. Home still feels like home, even without Mum. The dogs are still there, so it's not an empty house. One thing that I started doing just as Mum got her diagnosis that has also helped is going to the gym. Now I do powerlifting. It is something I do every day.

I just keep doing what I've done before and what Mum would have pushed me to do. When I went back to uni, it would have been easy to stop working and dwell on what had happened. But in my second year my grades actually improved. I try and do what she would have wanted. She knew what I was capable of, and I don't want to let her down. I still hear her voice all the time, giving me advice.

Other people expected me to be really upset about it and outwardly emotional. That made me feel as if I had done something wrong. It was always more physical for me. When we got a phone call saying we had to come back that weekend, I could feel it in my throat.

I'm not over it, but I am used to it. I haven't tried to avoid anything as I know I can't. I need to accept it and not ignore it or let things build up. I had to embrace it in a certain way. Things that I do, I put more effort into. The only time it all really caught up with me was when Jess qualified and I knew how proud Mum would have been.

I'm still doing what Mum would have expected us to do. She always used to moan at me for leaving the bathmat on the floor. Now I hear her telling me to pick it up. If I'm ever sitting around at uni when I should be working, I can hear her telling me to get on with it. I want to do it for her.

MY THOUGHTS

Jess and Finn live in the village where I grew up and their mother was a childminder to my sister's children. Their story shows the importance of having a coherent understanding of your experience in order to process trauma; and how the same event can affect us very differently, both in the moment and as we work through the stages of grief.

Different experiences

While Jess and Finn were both adjusting to the same situation, their experience and the way they dealt with it differed. We know that it is not the event itself but the way we interpret it that determines how we feel and cope. Jess and Finn's experience highlights that there is no right way to adjust to trauma. Only what's right for you.

The phases of grief

Jess and Finn moved through the phases of grief in different ways. Finn had a chance to slowly adjust, as he was living with his mum for the whole time and was able to reach acceptance sooner. He also stayed in the family home and kept things the same, which meant that in many ways his mum was still very much with him and he still felt her presence in his thoughts and surroundings. This perhaps meant there was less change to his meaning framework.

Jess had to be away at uni and kept working as she was training to be a midwife. This helped give her some distraction and normality as a way to deal with what had happened, allowing her to move between the first four phases of trauma in a healthy way. Then the week after her mother's death, she was numb, in the shock phase, unable to cry. Her brain couldn't keep up with what had happened but as reality hit, Jess moved to the overwhelm of phase one: outcry.

Jess described poignantly the loss of her previous life and her naivety, initially losing trust in the world and understandably struggling with its inherent unfairness. At first she would be struck by the full pain of the trauma again in familiar moments – such as when she'd normally call her mum for a chat. In time, she was able to put her meaning framework back together and found a balance between feeling sad and being able to focus on life. Learning to live alongside grief.

I think of grief as a hole inside. It is always there and always part of you, but you slowly get used to it and can step around it. You don't get over the loss of someone you love so deeply, but you do slowly learn to live with it, and in time you can think of that person without only feeling sad.

Coping and feeling

How we feel in response to an event and our coping strategies also differs. Jess felt the emotions of what had happened as tears and upset, while Finn felt them very physically. Jess coped in more outward ways – talking to trusted others, showing her emotions. I loved Jess's idea to write letters to her mum. Writing is a brilliant way to verbalize how you're feeling and process what is going on. Finn was quieter and preferred to handle things on his own, making sense of things internally and relying on the dogs, who didn't ask questions but who gave him familiarity, comfort and care.

Both Jess and Finn used physical activity as a way to cope – Jess running and Finn doing powerlifting. Having something that brings routine and structure gives stability and makes life feel more predictable. They continued to work hard and do well at uni and work, which was a source of stability and feeling good. They also found a way to feel useful and play an important role in their mum's care.

A sense of coherence

Both Jess and Finn told me how important it was to be well informed and involved in their mother's illness. There were no secrets or surprises, and this gave them time to slowly adjust. While nothing can prepare you for a loss so great, being aware of what to expect and what was happening allowed Jess and Finn to adapt their meaning frameworks gradually, knowing they would lose their mother. The initial shock of the diagnosis gave way to time together and a chance to support each other and their mum.

Having an understanding of what is going on allows what we call in psychology a sense of coherence. It's a way to bring order to a chaotic situation. We need to develop a coherent narrative to process what's happened and put it away. Sue was upfront from the start, but sometimes a wish to protect others can mean people don't share the full details of what is going on. This can lead to a mismatch between what we're feeling and picking up on (the fear, upset and pain of a terminal cancer diagnosis) and what we're told. Even when it's a difficult situation, outcomes are better when your feelings and experience are consistent.

Facing up to death

I was really struck by how well Sue prepared Jess and Finn for her death. She accepted what was happening and talked to them about dying and what she wanted them to do after she had gone. This meant they were able to face up to it together and there were no questions left unanswered.

In addition, Sue's mindset that the time they had together was a bonus (after the initial operation) meant she was able to positively reframe the experience. This was a gift to her children that gave them space to see all the positives they could gain from the time they had left with her. They could prepare for the future together, even though she wouldn't be there.

When I spoke to Jess and Finn, I could see that so much of Sue lives on in them. They both have her positive approach to life and have taken onboard her lessons, from working hard and finding a purpose to being true to yourself and making the most of life. I know she would be incredibly proud of them.

KEY TAKEAWAYS

- There are five phases in working through trauma; and we commonly move back and forth between stages.
- Progress is not a straight line of improvement; we grow and learn from our experiences.
- Keep track of the small ways you are progressing and read back through what you have written each week.
- Moving between the 'good room' and the 'struggle room' is a way to process and learn from our experiences.
- Negative emotions are a normal response to difficulty.
- Make sure you look after yourself and seek out hope and support.

4

POST-TRAUMATIC GROWTH

'That which does not kill us makes us stronger'
– Nietzsche, *Twilight of the the Idols*
'You can't get rainbows without some rain'
'Seeing the dark lets you see the light'
'Every cloud has a silver lining'
'The darkest hour is the hour before dawn'

Intuitively we know that hard times can lead to positive changes. Although it can be difficult to reconcile that something so destructive can ultimately improve your life, trauma can be the beginning of a new chapter and a springboard to transformation.

When we read stories such as the ones in this book, we often think of the person as extraordinary for managing to not only get through their experience but thrive. I know I was in awe of the people who told me their stories. But you do not have to be special to get through trauma – post-traumatic growth is not unusual or an experience that only happens to those who are lucky. We can all overcome unimaginable difficulties and survive. I hope knowing this can give you something to hold on to as you go through your own hard times. Distress and growth are not separate, but part of the same process.

In this chapter I will introduce you to post-traumatic growth and the process that occurs in order for us to move forward.

WHAT EXACTLY IS POST-TRAUMATIC GROWTH?

The study of trauma reaches back to at least the First World War. Historically, the focus of research has been how we respond to trauma; considering trauma as a trigger for extreme psychological and physical problems (such as PTSD) and looking at how to help sufferers back to psychological health. In more recent years, scientists and clinicians began to look at the ways in which critical life crises offered possibilities for positive personal change. Research now shows that growth experiences in the aftermath of traumatic events far outnumber reports of psychiatric disorders.

One landmark piece of research discovered that people who endure psychological struggle following adversity can often see positive growth afterwards – this the researchers named 'post-traumatic growth'. They found that these difficult experiences can lead to an enhanced appreciation for life and how to live it, improved relationships, spiritual development and a greater sense of compassion for others who experience difficulties.

Since the term was first coined in 1996 by Richard Tedeschi and Lawrence Calhoun, there have been decades of research confirming that the majority of trauma survivors report some degree of positive change following adversity. It can put us back in charge of the direction our life takes. It can bring a shift in our priorities, opening our eyes to the choices we make about how we want to spend our time. It can show us our strengths and teach us what we are capable of. It can deepen our relationships, improve how we relate to others and increase empathy. It can help us to look outside of ourselves and give back. It can be a reminder of what life means to us and open our eyes to a fuller view, so we appreciate the day-to-day and make the most of the good times. We say to ourselves that we could never cope if something terrible happened, and yet somehow we do.

Alongside the academic research, history and storytelling are littered with examples (just consider the common sayings at the start of the chapter) demonstrating adversity to be a long-considered part of human existence. Not all growth is obvious – changes can be internal and private – but what is key is perceived growth. The evidence shows that people who reported and maintained post-traumatic growth over time were less distressed. Studies show a link between greater perceived growth and lower emotional distress as well as better physical health. It is time to see that trauma is common, but so too is positive change.

PROGRAMMED FOR GROWTH

In evolutionary terms, this makes sense. The human brain has been designed over millions of years to be shaped by experience. This means that we are hardwired for growth. We are always striving to adapt to our environment and are constantly changing and evolving. This push to make sense of what happens to us and to learn from it is innate and occurs even if we do not experience trauma. If we had been knocked down by difficulty, we would not have lasted long as a species.

We can see this movement towards growth in the way that we often seek out struggle in smaller ways. Pushing ourselves to take part in a challenge, like entering and training for a 10km run, going for a job promotion, doing an evening class or taking up a hobby. When you think about these things, it is easy to see that growth is not meant to be comfortable. When you step out of your comfort zone, you are pushed out of autopilot and into uncharted territory. You learn new skills, and this will stretch you, but that is a good thing.

New experiences, new hobbies and challenging yourself on a regular basis are massively important for maintaining good mental health, personal growth and self-esteem. Working towards and reaching your goals is brilliant for confidence. It gives you a sense of purpose and a feeling of fulfilment. When your mood is higher, you are more likely to succeed at making changes in the other areas of your life that you wish to tackle.

When we experience trauma, it heightens this process. Trauma rips open a gap in our meaning framework and this creates a tension. The tension is the pull between our long-held beliefs and this new information. When trauma challenges our whole belief system, we feel a strong emotional urge to close the gap. We need to resolve the tension between what we thought we knew and how we see life now. Our brain hates being in this unsettling in-between place.

Post-traumatic growth happens when we make sense of what has happened and close the gap. Closing the gap is not something we choose to do, though it can become conscious. It is a human drive rooted in our biological make-up. As much as we might wish to retreat or give up, our whole being wants resolution, and it is in this struggle that we naturally move toward growth.

Post-traumatic growth does not happen in the absence of emotional distress. When firmly in a post-trauma situation, we will struggle as we try to get to grips with what has happened and find a new way to live. Letting go of what we know can be a painful process, but it is only when we review our beliefs and find a new way to fit things together that we can move forward and close the gap. It is this resolution that determines how we will come out of the experience, and it is only by doing this that we grow.

When we manage to close the gap, we have better outcomes: increased well-being, a sense of mastery, meaning in life, greater personal autonomy, self-acceptance, improved relationships and the ability to seek further personal growth. It is possible through this struggle with adversity to come out the other side stronger and more philosophical about life.

MIND THE GAP

To conjure up this push to resolve on a much smaller scale, think about what it is like when you are watching a film or reading a book and trying to work out who the murderer is. When you start the next episode (and the next) of a series because you *need* to know what happens. Or when you are sitting in a traffic jam with no idea why you have stopped or how long you'll be there. In each of these scenarios, your brain does not have all the pieces of the puzzle so it cannot resolve the tension. It is only when you know what happens that you can relax. It is like this for trauma, but magnified – no wonder it feels so unsettling when this gap is created.

We are motivated to reconcile and make sense of what has happened in a way we can hold in our mind. It's a bit like fitting the pieces of a jigsaw together. When the pieces are all in place, we can see what the picture is, making it easy to put away. Our brain is the same: it wants to resolve things and know how it all fits together. This feels more comfortable and means we can file it away without it pressing upon us.

Initially our brain just does not know what to do with this new information; we are in shock. Our natural defence is to try to stick to what we know. Our brain wants to incorporate the new situation into our original meaning framework (repairing the house). It is understandable that we try to cling on to our old life and the security it used to bring us. A benevolent and meaningful world is a far nicer place to be. The loss of our naivety can feel like ripping a comfort blanket away, but people who try to hold on to their pre-trauma worldview are more fragile and easily hurt. It leaves them in a position where they will be easily knocked again when difficult things happen. This approach to overcoming difficulty does not lead to post-traumatic growth.

When we cannot fit what has happened to us into our meaning map (see page 43), we have to start all over again in our thinking (rebuilding). Abandoning the ideas we had about ourselves and our life is painful and brings emotional upheaval and distress. It is being in this space that creates many of the symptoms of trauma. We feel haunted by what has happened, and are constantly confronted with past events – rumination, nightmares, flashbacks, fear, anxiety, shame or guilt.

To genuinely move on, we need to confront this new information and change how we think about our lives. This is the push to resolve. It can feel incredibly painful as we do this. It is scary to look at our beliefs and say they are wrong. Life no longer seems meaningful, and it can feel like everything we thought we knew is a lie.

This is a normal and understandable consequence of going through trauma, and is part of re-finding our way. As we grapple with what has happened, we must remember that most people *do* adapt well over time, and this can be a turning point for change. Discomfort can be a trigger to growth, and going through this process can make us stronger.

When our losses are great, it can be difficult to acknowledge any positive changes. We will always be connected to the things in our life that have hurt us, but when we start to manage the effects of what has happened and to change what's happened from simply defining us in a negative way, we leave space for growth.

Research shows that distress and growth can co-exist. They are not in opposition, but are two separate independent dimensions of experience. When we look at and feel our distress, we also create space for growth. We can use what has happened to confront truths about ourselves and our lives. This can lead us to learn new things about ourselves and what we want. Finding a way through these experiences can bring a deeper confidence and a new-found sense of making the most of life.

Trauma is a complex issue. It brings together so many different feelings. We like to believe that things are black and white, but few things are all bad or all good. Trauma challenges our assumptions about how the world works and our place within it and brings to the surface questions we might normally ignore. What do I want from my life? Am I living the way I want to? When life seems long and there's so much to do, it's easy to ignore this voice. Trauma reminds us that we only have one chance at life.

Trauma is destructive and lays everything bare, but it also allows you to look at the foundations of your life and choose how you want to rebuild, with the benefit of what you have learned about yourself and what you want from life.

WHY DON'T WE SEE THIS WITHOUT ADVERSITY?

Despite the natural impulse to grow, at times this drive can be stunted. We can become so caught up in the daily grind that we stop seeing the beauty of life and just get through the day, the week, the year, putting off happiness for another time, not fully conscious of life and all it has to offer.

This desire to stick with what we know is linked (again!) to our brain and its mental maps. We have a natural desire to be consistent and are most happy when all our beliefs and values line up. Our brain prefers things to be as expected, and as we saw in Chapter 2, it does its best to keep it that way. When information fits our framework or we are in situations we know, we can run on autopilot, a place our brain likes to be. It takes up less energy, frees up mental space for other things and feels easier as we know what to expect.

When everything fits and there are no surprises, we experience less internal discomfort. Familiarity feels safe. Routine and order also fit with our core fundamental assumptions. We spend much of our lives in this comfortable state, but it brings with it some problems.

To stay in autopilot, our brain needs external inputs to be reasonably constant. In simple terms, this translates to a life in which we prefer to know how things will be and where we can follow the same patterns and habits. The situations and experiences we encounter fit our mental map and we file them away without paying much attention. This is why weeks can feel like they go by in a blur. There is little to take notice of or deeply consider.

We go through the same routines, take the same routes, see the same people, engage in the same behaviours, without really looking up and thinking what we want from life. I am definitely guilty of this. I have a favourite mug for my coffee, I like to sit in the same seat at breakfast and I have a preferred spot on the sofa. I follow the same routine most weeks; I even eat the same breakfast and lunch most days! There are many good things in the familiarity, but it can also impact us negatively in subtle ways. It is like driving a well-known route; it is so easy to follow that we might stop taking notice of what's around us. We know exactly where we are going and we always end up at the same place.

When things are not quite as we expect or we have to do things in a different way, it pushes us out of autopilot and can leave us with a sense of discomfort. It opens up a small gap of uncertainty and puts us in that unsettling in-between place that our brain dislikes so much. Being in this space can leave us feeling vulnerable, as we struggle with not being able to do things so easily or dealing with the unknown. This is even harder when our capacity is full.

Stepping out of autopilot can feel unsettling. We like what we know, which is why we can find even small changes hard (don't ask my husband what I'm like when I get a new version of a computer operating system). No wonder it can feel tough when we face bigger issues.

I'll give you a simple example of something fairly inconsequential. Despite there being multiple routes to Brighton Marina, wherever possible I stick to going along the seafront. This route frequently takes longer, as the traffic can be slow, but I tell myself that I prefer this way as I get to see the sea. While this is partially true, the real reason is that I feel nervous at the thought of driving through town, as I don't know the route so well.

By taking the familiar route, I am probably only losing ten minutes on a bad day, but when we think about this in the wider context of our lives, we start to see how many things we are doing that mean we miss out on a better alternative. Whether in small ways, like my drive, or in more significant ways, we have little motivation to change things. We put up with 'good enough' and rarely review what is working for us and what is no longer serving us so well.

When we stay in autopilot, we can end up living half a life, ignoring the fact that this life is all we have got. Slowly, over time, our inner and outer lives become out of sync. The life we are living no longer matches up with what we truly want. We might be stuck in a job that is driving us into the ground, a relationship that is not fulfilling our needs. We plaster over the cracks, ignoring things that are not quite right, and in some cases we are no longer sure what we want from life or who we are. We prefer the certainty of potential misery to the uncertainty of the unknown.

TRYING TO ELIMINATE DISCOMFORT

When I do take the town route to the Marina, it is always much easier than I expect, and I have a chance to remind myself that although it feels a bit more stressful, I can do it. While the idea of things being different can be scary, it is rarely as bad as we imagine. The trouble is that we have little opportunity to remember this.

In many ways, modern life has become a quest to eliminate discomfort. There is very little that we have to wait for (that unsettling in-between), so we do not have the same opportunities to tolerate discomfort and get used to it.

When you think about how things used to be for those of us who grew up in the seventies and eighties in the UK, so much has changed. In those days, there were only four TV channels, and even on those channels there was not always something on. We watched TV live and had to sit through the adverts, we used Ceefax to look up the sports results, and we usually had to wait a week before the next episode of our favourite show. We had to make phone calls on a landline, and if no one was in, we would leave a message or try later. This also meant the risk of speaking to your friend's parents or sibling, who you might not know. We had to post letters and then wait for the reply.

When you met up with people, you had to make a plan and stick with it, and if someone was late, you had no option but to wait. If you wanted to buy something, you had to go into town and hunt around the shops to find it. This meant waiting for the bus, or driving and finding parking; then often when you got there it was sold out or not in stock and you had to either wait for it to be ordered in or put up with something else. When I started driving, I used to have to print off directions and read a map. I frequently went off course and then would struggle to find my way back. Even in my early twenties, if I wanted to check my emails, I had to go to the library or an internet cafe, or wait until the next day at work.

It is a truism, but it is one worth repeating. Everything is instant now. We do not even have to leave the house if we want something. If we search long enough online, we can generally find exactly what we want and even get it delivered the same day. We have hundreds of TV channels, can fast-forward through adverts and watch episodes one after the other; we can access the internet and other people 24/7. We can surround ourselves with people who hold similar views. Even when we are stuck in traffic, our phone can tell us for how long and offer an alternative route. As a result, we are not confronted by uncertainty or challenged much on our views.

We are rarely in that unsettled in-between place, even in lesser ways. Avoiding change and discomfort in all these small ways and trying to keep tight control of life gives us little practise when a bigger change happens. Rather than trying to eradicate uncertainty and inconvenience (which is ultimately impossible), it is much better to gain experience of these things so we learn to tolerate and manage them, and gain greater confidence in ourselves. We have a chance to see that the discomfort goes away when we do this, and that we do not need to have a perfect plan or know exactly how things will go to enjoy something.

WAKING UP TO LIFE

Trauma is often described as an awakening. The power of a traumatic experience, the depth of feelings and the shock it can bring shake things up in a way that is rarely possible otherwise. Before trauma, we can become so comfortable in autopilot that we end up sleepwalking through life. It is only when we face struggle that we start to think about an alternative.

Life before trauma and life after trauma can feel like two different worlds. To some extent, our pre-trauma life is really life in denial. We hold a naive view in which we believe we are exempt from pain and suffering. When we experience trauma, it confronts us with existential truths, but in a strange way this can be freeing.

It awakens us to the life we are living, but it can also awaken us to the life we want. This can link us back to our natural motivations and desire to grow – a chance to live again and live differently, waking us up to life and all its future potential. These experiences allow us to notice and value things that we might not have seen before and lets us look with fresh eyes at what we want and what matters most to us.

Adversity is not something any of us would seek out, but it sometimes allows us to view our life from a wider perspective, giving us a new way of seeing things and a new way of seeing ourselves. Imagine you are on a mountain. Until now you have been standing halfway up, believing that you are getting an accurate picture of life. What has happened can take you further up the mountain to a higher vantage point, where you will have a far better view and can see the world as it really is.

Trauma is like an explosion in our life that forces us to take a new perspective. We cannot control the explosion, but we can choose how we piece things back together. We can use what has happened to come back to life. It is a chance to stop, look up and decide the direction our life will take. It is a chance to see opportunities we might have previously missed and bring into sharper focus what is important to us. The job we do, the way we live our life, how we spend our time and who we spend it with. Not according to the rules set by our parents or peers, but following our own heart and what is right for us.

It can be a wake-up call to become true to ourselves and think about what we want from life. It is only by letting go of our old existence that we can begin to consciously choose how we want to live now and to look at what makes life worth living. This allows us to dismantle our beliefs and goals and, in time, slowly build new mental maps that are aligned with what we truly want.

KEY TAKEAWAYS

- You do not have to be special to get through trauma; we can all overcome difficulties and survive.
- People who endure psychological struggle after adversity often see positive growth afterwards.
- Post-traumatic growth happens when we make sense of what has happened and close the gap between what we thought we knew and our life now.
- Adversity can allow us to see our life from a wider perspective.

Part Two

WORKING THROUGH TRAUMA

5

LOOKING AFTER YOUR BODY
(STEP 2)

Understanding how our body works and how our emotions express themselves within it is a key part of overcoming trauma and looking after ourselves. In this chapter we're going to be looking at the mind–body link, including the neuroscience, to understand our reactions when we experience adversity and stress. In many ways we're only just scratching the surface of our understanding of how our body and mind interact.

When we understand what's going on physiologically in our nervous system it makes sense why we react and behave as we do, and this understanding moves us towards recovery.

TRAUMA AND THE BODY

The mind and body are intimately linked. Intuitively we know this, as when we talk about feelings we link them to our body, for instance, 'feeling sick to my stomach', 'my heart sank', 'it gave me goosebumps', 'gut-wrenching', 'heartbreak', yet sometimes we forget just how physical our emotions can be.

Depression can present itself as a loss of energy and motivation, such as feeling tired, struggling to sleep, aches and pains, our body feeling heavy, no appetite or sex drive. Anxiety symptoms include increased heart rate, rapid breathing, sweating, trembling, feeling sick, weak or tired. If you have ever experienced a panic attack, you'll know how strong these symptoms can feel in your body, and that they are not imagined.

Emotions really can feel painful, and numerous studies have shown that when we experience emotional pain, the same neural networks in the brain are activated as when we feel physical pain. Although there is not an external reason for the pain, like a cut or a hot stove, the experience of emotional pain is the same. It really does hurt. I think we also forget how exhausting emotions can be. Think about when you go to the cinema and watch an emotive film – you feel tired afterwards, even though you haven't moved.

Though we typically think of the brain telling the body what to do, the body also guides the brain. A simple example of this is when you imagine your favourite food: your mouth starts to water and your stomach reacts. You feel it physically, even though there's no food in sight. This connection also works the other way: we might feel hunger, and this makes us think about food.

When we think about this for trauma, it's easy to see that we experience the event physically too, and this physical response can be a reminder of everything that happened. As we saw in Chapter 1, there is a long list of physical sensations that are felt both during and after traumatic events. Trauma pushes us over-capacity and this can leave us stuck in hyperarousal – phase 3 of trauma, intrusive re-experiencing – or lead to us becoming detached and dissociated – phase 2, numbness and denial – but what exactly is happening in our body to cause this?

To understand, we need to take a look at our evolutionary history, the purpose of our emotions and the neuroscience of how they function in our body. Bear with me, I'm summarizing a complex system that we still don't fully understand, but if you take only one thing from this chapter it is to remember that our body's response system is not directly within our control.

A BRIEF EVOLUTIONARY HISTORY

When we think about the purpose of emotions, we first have to think about this in evolutionary terms. The human brain is the product of many millions of years of evolution, based around one simple goal – survival. We were designed to function in a world where there was always danger, no second chances and we had to rely on others to stay alive. Rather than think through a problem (something we didn't have time for if we wanted to survive), emotions delivered a smart solution. This meant that a focus on threat was necessary.

We're highly social beings, and early humans needed to live together and get on in a group to ensure survival. Being cut off from the group would have resulted in death. The group also supplied care and support and helped to regulate emotions. This means we have a deep need for social inclusion – we feel rewarded by positive social interactions and hurt by negative interactions. Positive interaction with the same individuals within a framework of long-term and stable care is a fundamental human need, and in addition, the need to belong is integral to self-development.

That need for a sense of belonging is still an innate need within us, and relationships are still key to our health and happiness. Research shows that a lack of social support is as bad for you as smoking. Social isolation is associated with heightened risk of disease and early death, whereas warm and supportive relationships have long-term benefits for health and longevity. Connection is key – relationships are what give meaning and purpose to our lives. When we think about our emotions and our behaviour, it is all linked back to the goal of survival.

POLYVAGAL THEORY

Stephen Porges' polyvagal theory describes how the autonomic nervous system has evolved to keep us alive. It helps us understand how our experiences of safety and connection are directly shaped by our nervous system.

The autonomic nervous system is constantly scanning and receiving information from the environment for cues. It operates using neuroception, picking up information in the environment and evaluating it on a neurobiological level. You may not realize it, but in your daily life you read thousands of social cues in the environment, constantly observing and interacting with the world and other people. This means that your body is actively alert to threat.

Neuroception lets us distinguish whether a certain situation, person or place is safe or dangerous. This all happens outside our conscious awareness, meaning safety is not just registered at a conscious level as a thought; it is also registered at a bodily level.

The autonomic nervous system responds to external and internal stimuli through three biological pathways each with its own predictable patterns of response, and they follow a hierarchy. In evolutionary order from newest to oldest they are:

1. *The ventral vagus*, our social engagement and connection response. This is the newest, at 200 million years old.
2. *The sympathetic nervous system*, our mobilization response. This is 400 million years old.
3. *The dorsal vagus*, our immobilization response. This is 500 million years old.

The vagus nerve helps us with neuroception. It connects our brain, heart and gut and is bi-directional – carrying information from our body to our brain and from our brain to our body. It takes its name from the Latin word for wandering, and is thought to have the widest distribution of nerves within the human body. It has two branches, the dorsal (back) and the ventral (front), and is a critical part of our brain–body connection. It is involved in the expression and management of our emotions.

The vagus nerve essentially feels out situations and sends information about the state of the inner organs to the brain.

- *The ventral side* responds to cues of safety in our environment and interactions. It supports feelings of physical safety and being emotionally connected to others.
- *The dorsal side* responds to cues of danger. It makes us feel less connected to others and in a state of self-protection. If it senses extreme danger, we can shut down and feel frozen.

Social engagement mode

If the autonomic nervous system concludes that a situation is safe, the vagus nerve tells our body to relax, and this engages the parasympathetic nervous system to calm the body. In this mode we feel connected, grounded and secure. This is sometimes called the self-preservation zone, or restoration zone, as it conserves energy and supports health, growth and restoration. In this mode our heart rate slows, blood pressure returns to normal, breathing deepens, muscles relax. We tend to sleep well and eat normally. Digestion takes place so we gain energy and nutrients, our immune system is healthy and wound healing takes place.

In this nervous system state we enter what Stephen Porges calls the social engagement mode. In evolutionary terms, this is the newest part of the system and evolved only in humans. In this state we feel connected to and relate to other people. We feel a sense of contentment and are open and curious about life. We can feel empathy, joy, playfulness and love. We feel present in what we are doing and safe. Our face is expressive, we more easily understand and listen to others and emotionally relate. The more we connect, the more we feel heard and understood and the more we feel loved, appreciated and validated. Clearly this is a good place for us to be, and in the next chapters I'll be sharing strategies to help you stay in this zone.

Threat mode

If we sense something in our environment that is dangerous, we shift to threat mode. The vagus nerve sends a signal to the sympathetic nervous system, and the arousal system prepares the body to react – and remember, this is registered at a bodily level; we are not yet aware of the danger on a conscious or cognitive level. It takes only one tenth of a second to notice threat and unpleasant situations. Our body reacts automatically to what it perceives as dangerous; the conscious thought comes later.

We know this mode as fight-or-flight. Activation hormones such as cortisol, adrenaline and norepinephrine are released to fuel the body and brain so we are ready for action: to get up and run or to fight off the danger. We're likely to be in this mode during trauma and in phases 1 and 3 post-trauma.

This response affects nearly every organ in our body. We feel an adrenaline rush, and are restless, agitated and anxious. Our heart rate increases, the airways widen to make breathing easier, stored energy is released, our muscles strengthen, and digestion and other bodily processes that are less important for taking action slow down. Our muscles may feel tight, hands clammy, stomach knotted, and our facial expressions change. All hyperactive states that we link to stress.

This response system means the body and brain are brilliant at detecting threat, but since our brain is unable to distinguish between a real threat, such as a tiger, and a perceived threat, like the daily stresses we encounter – negative thoughts, a troubling memory or a future worry – we react to everything as if it is life-threatening.

In this state we experience the world differently; being in this mode changes our reality. The world becomes threatening and we become overly alert to any potential problems, or we might want to escape and run away from our situation. It is much harder for us to engage our rational brain in this mode, and we do not have access to higher conscious states like planning. It reduces our attention and there is no room for love, nurture or care. We are more likely to misread social cues, for example seeing a neutral face as angry or jumping to negative conclusions. We don't sleep as well, we are more prone to nightmares and are sensitized to pain. It can leave us feeling frazzled or out of sorts. We really do think and behave differently. This can add to our problems and make recovery harder.

Freeze

Polyvagal theory highlights that there is also a third state: freeze. If our nervous system believes we are in a life-threatening situation we cannot get away from, we shut down. This response is the oldest in evolutionary terms, and is much more primal. In this state we might look outwardly calm, but internally we have a sense of feeling trapped, out of body or disconnected from the world. We can feel numb, dizzy, dissociated, nauseous, hopeless or ashamed. We might have difficulty getting our words out, and our facial expressions are flatter. In this state we do not feel capable and have no sense of agency; we are likely to withdraw, sleeping more or finding other ways to escape how we are feeling.

In this freeze state, we often don't have a clear memory of what happened. We are not downloading memories we can come back to. This explains why our memories of a traumatic period are often hazy. We might be in this mode during trauma and in phases 1 and 2 post-trauma (see pages 63 and 64).

THE IMPACT OF TRAUMA ON THE NERVOUS SYSTEM

When we experience stress, our sympathetic nervous system is activated, and when the threat passes, the parasympathetic nervous system kicks back in so we can return to the self-preservation zone, or restoration zone, releasing acetylcholine to slow everything down. The body and mind work best when there is synchrony between the two branches.

- *The parasympathetic nervous system* is the body's brakes. It calms our body and is involved in a vast array of crucial bodily functions, including control of mood, immune response, digestion and heart rate when we are at rest.
- *The sympathetic nervous system* is the body's accelerator. It activates our body so we can prepare for fight-or-flight, our immediate physical reaction to stress.

When our autonomic nervous system is functioning well, the parasympathetic and sympathetic nervous systems work together, and this helps us to manage our daily stressors and challenges. Stress is a normal part of life, and in the right amounts it helps us grow and adapt.

Thanks to survival of the fittest, our nervous system has evolved to be easier to switch on than off. It is a natural and adaptive response – better to be safe than sorry if you want to survive – but one that doesn't work so well in modern life, where there is always plenty to respond to.

How we live now differs massively from how we used to, and modern life can be unrelenting. We have 24/7 lifestyles, with societal stressors, work stress, long commutes, marital and family pressure, poor sleep, artificial light, noise and less exercise. It's no wonder things can sometimes go wrong. Left to its own devices, our brain will consistently misinterpret the signals of the 21st century. These constant multiple stressors keep us in sympathetic activation, and our body cannot return to equilibrium.

When we experience trauma or chronic stress, this is amplified. It hijacks our nervous system, and when our autonomic nervous system is out of sync, we are thrown off balance. Our body's surveillance system goes into overdrive, wired for threat, and this skews our ability to scan our environment for danger cues. Like an overly sensitive car alarm, we might read as dangerous signs that would be seen as neutral or benign by others.

Stress hormones continue to be pumped out to deal with the threat and we stay hyperreactive. This is because our parasympathetic nervous system cannot kick in, and we can become stuck in either of these activated states – fight and flight or freeze.

When we think about what's going on in our body, it makes sense that the response becomes so physical and that this has an impact on how we think and behave. The symptoms we experience in reaction to chronic stress or trauma (see page 30) are the result of being stuck in this activated mode. Understanding this helps to normalize these symptoms and builds on Stephen Joseph's recognition that experiencing a response to trauma is a normal and natural reaction.

Although the danger has passed and we might rationally know that we are OK, emotionally our brain hasn't got the message yet and stays stuck in threat mode. This might be in response to a physical sense of danger (neuroception), or we might be replaying the trauma in our mind.

With our nervous system activated, we are unable to return to our pre-stressed state and so our body cannot recover from stress. We know that things feel too much, but we still keep going. This takes a toll on us physically, emotionally and mentally, causing a long list of problems such as poor sleep, difficulty concentrating, loss of appetite, feeling constantly on edge, a sense of dread, sexual dysfunction, IBS, eczema, chronic pain, a persistent cough, migraines, psoriasis, agitation, oversensitivity to sound or touch, and panic attacks. When we can't sustain activation, we then shift into shutdown.

Our body is not replenishing itself. It can't concentrate on digestion or repair, compromising our immune system. We are social beings, but being in these states makes it harder to connect to other people, as we're more likely to see them as threatening.

In these dysregulated states, we are using up all our energy staying on high alert in a survival state of hypervigilance. This interrupts our ability to regulate our nervous system responses and therefore feel safe in our body and our relationships.

HOW IS THIS HELPFUL TO ME?

Understanding how our nervous system functions and why it can become dysregulated brings an awareness of what is going on in our body. Polyvagal theory provides us with a physiological and psychological understanding of our autonomic nervous system and highlights that stress reactions take place outside of our conscious control.

Instead of judging ourselves for going into these defensive fight-or-flight and freeze states, we can see that our nervous system *puts* us into these states. It doesn't run it by us first and check that we agree. When we understand that this is how we evolved to get to safety, we can begin to find compassion for ourselves.

I find this really helpful in understanding why, on the days I'm feeling more stressed, despite promising myself I'll stay calm, I don't have the same levels of patience as I might wish. A good example of this is the school run. If I have no time pressures, I feel more relaxed. When the kids are slow getting ready (which they are every day), I can be rational and remember that's what kids do, and that in the grand scheme of things it doesn't even matter, as in all the years they've been at school, we've only been late once. On these days I can remain calm as I help them get ready. I know this is the best approach to get out of the door on time, and that we all prefer it when the day starts like this.

Despite knowing this, on the days when I have to get them to school by a certain time (extra stress) or I've got an important meeting or talk (things outside my comfort zone), I tend to be more easily annoyed and irritable when they are slow. I'm more likely to forget things and have less empathy for any problems that arise. Even though I really want to be caring and stay calm, and know rationally that getting annoyed slows everything down, it isn't always enough to change my response and means we leave the house on a bad note, which is something I hate.

Understanding how we react to stress lets me see that it is not that I'm not trying hard enough; it's that my brain and body are more taxed and this makes everything else more difficult. In the stressed zone I can have the best of intentions, but if my body is wired to threat and I can't get into the social engagement mode, it's a different playing field. Like trying to play tennis with a watermelon instead of a ball. It's going to be much harder. You're trying to play the game by the same rules, but everything has changed.

Wanting to do better and rationally thinking about how to do this is not going to work, no matter how hard I try. I need to focus on bringing my body out of this activated state so I can think and behave in the way I want to. I also need to predict when these situations are likely to happen and try to make it easier for myself – leaving more time, getting ready the night before, or being kind to myself when things inevitably do go wrong.

OVERCAPACITY

We can now understand how experiencing trauma pushes us into the sympathetic nervous system and means we run on threat mode. We are overcapacity in terms of our ability to cope, but this is also because we are overcapacity at a physiological level and our body has to use up excessive energy, making it much harder to regulate our emotions. Just when we most need our body and mind onside, our reaction to such high levels of stress means they do the opposite. It's very difficult to feel safe in the world if you do not feel safe in your body.

Understanding why the nervous system becomes dysregulated and recognizing that stress reactions take place outside our conscious control helps us to normalize these behaviours and shows clearly why it is so hard to do the things that will make you feel better. It's crucial to remember that these responses are not voluntary – our nervous system puts us into these different states.

When you're in these modes, a rational conversation with yourself or good intentions will not sort things out.

This explains why we are more reactive and find ourselves responding disproportionately to stresses in our life, and why it is harder to feel engaged or connected at these times. When we're stuck in our head or our body feels alive to threat, it is hard to keep up with the basics. We can lose track of who we are and what we're feeling. It is difficult to engage with the things that matter to us, to care about what we're doing, to take in our surroundings or find enjoyment in the day-to-day. Our emotions colour our thoughts, so when our mind tells us stories of all the bad things going on, rather than challenge it, we just believe what it says. And as much as we need the support of others, it is difficult to engage with them and trust in them when we're in the threat zone.

It also explains why other things can go wrong – poor memory, clumsiness, leaving our key in the lock, forgetting to turn the hob off – so we end up creating more problems for ourselves. We don't have the same access to higher-level thinking, organization and planning at these times. It's hard to make good decisions when we're in fight-or-flight or freeze.

When we're overcapacity, we don't have the space for doing things that aren't within our normal routines. That's why doing anything more than the basics feels overwhelming, making it much more difficult to do the things we know will make us feel better. So if you're finding it hard to begin to put the strategies in place as you go through the next chapters, cut yourself some slack. It's not because you don't care enough or you're lazy or no good at this. It's because of everything that is going on in your body and mind.

Take a moment to think about the different states you inhabit. When are you in social engagement mode, threat mode or freeze?

Which one do you spend most of your time in and what impact does this have on you?

STEP 2: LOOKING AFTER YOUR BODY

In step 2, I'll be teaching you to feel safe in your body again. To give yourself the best chance of overcoming trauma, you need a healthy nervous system that is in equilibrium. Your sense of self is anchored in your connection with your body, and when your body feels safe, you feel safe. It gives you more capacity, increases energy and allows you to feel connected to others. It also allows you to access higher states of thinking so you can problem-solve and think about how you want to move forward. All things you will need in order to overcome what has happened to you.

To do this, you need to go back to basics and bring your body out of the threat zone. Using the bi-directional link between your body and mind, you can focus on your body to make yourself feel safe again and begin to process your emotional pain. When you listen to your body, you can start to understand the information it is sending you and learn how you respond to things. This is a foothold into helping you regulate your emotions and feel calmer, enabling you to move back into the social engagement mode. Once you are in this mode, you can begin to think about phase 4 of trauma – working through (see page 67).

TUNED OUT

I know this is not as simple as it sounds. When you've experienced prolonged stress or trauma, the relationship between mind and body is a complicated one. People often tell me they feel scared of their body and what it might do next. It sends so many signals that feel dangerous or threatening, and these symptoms can also be an unwelcome reminder of what's happened.

It's understandable that we begin to disregard our feelings and become disconnected from the messages our body is sending us, but this means we lose the ability to listen to it or understand what the feelings mean. Or we can become overly tuned into it, amplifying everything we're feeling inside. This leaves us feeling very anxious and is likely to lead to panic attacks.

This then becomes part of the problem – we have stopped trusting our body. If we can't identify what the physical sensations mean, then we can't work out what is going on inside our body and we can become out of sync with ourselves. Or if our internal sensations are so overwhelming that our body feels unsafe on a daily basis, we can't regulate ourselves or give our body what it needs, making it difficult to take care of ourselves, to eat the right amounts or get the sleep we need.

I commonly see this in my clinic: despite numerous signs that things are not right, people struggle on. They can even become so used to running in these hyperalert states that they seek them out. They power through tiredness with caffeine, sugar or exercise when what they need is rest. It is all too easy to respond to emotional fears with food, zone out in front of screens, or dull anxiety with alcohol.

Even though you might be ignoring the physical sensations, it doesn't stop the fight-or-flight or freeze reaction in your body, which in the longer term can lead to migraines, back pain, fibromyalgia, eczema, psoriasis and chronic pain. Often it's the physical symptoms that people focus on, and before they have seen me, they have seen their GP or specialists. While this can be helpful, these symptoms are the expression of an underlying problem, and the best way to deal with them is to look at the cause. In this case, the cause is your body being stuck in activation.

Sympathetic activation is a message that all is not well, and if we choose to, we can use that message as a signal that we need to look after ourselves. If we ignore it, the body often just shouts louder until we *have* to listen.

When my kids were little, they would come to me with the tiniest of cuts, barely visible to the human eye, and tell me how painful they were. Initially I made the mistake of not taking it seriously, and tried to reassure them there was nothing to worry about, but I noticed that the harder I tried to convince them, the more their response escalated. Trying to dismiss the feeling or be rational in response to it just made it come back stronger. Eventually I realized that the more seriously I took it, the quicker they were able to forget about it. If I had a good look, gave them a hug and empathized with how much it hurt, they felt much better.

It's like this for our body. When we recognize and acknowledge feelings, we allow them to pass. It sounds strange, but ignoring them keeps them blocked. And remember, these reactions are outside our conscious control, so a rational conversation won't help. When we notice how we're feeling and observe and acknowledge our feelings without judgement, we stop the cycle, giving ourselves a chance to experience the emotion and work through it. It is this that leads to recovery and growth.

TUNING BACK INTO YOUR BODY

Tuning into our body is known as interoception, an awareness of our subtle sensory body-based feelings. Our brain uses the information about the way our body feels as clues to our current emotional and physical state. This can be conscious or outside awareness, and gives us valuable information. At its most basic level, it lets us notice when we're hungry or tired, or that we need the toilet.

It can also help us tune into our emotions, recognizing when we feel butterflies in our stomach or sweaty palms before doing something that makes us feel anxious. If we are aware of the constant changes in our inner and outer environment, we have a better chance of managing them. When we are dysregulated, our body signals can alert us that our internal balance is off. This can motivate us to take action to restore the balance and help our body feel more comfortable. For example, eating if we feel hungry, putting on a jumper if we feel cold, or seeking comfort if we feel sad.

Greater awareness helps us to become less scared of our emotions, so we can learn to regulate them and express them more easily. When we tune into how we're feeling, we can work out what our body needs and look after it. This helps us develop emotional intelligence and feel in control of our lives. It also helps to create space between feeling and reacting, so we can choose how we want to respond, making us less reactive. This enables us to self-regulate, and when our body feels safe, we can move back into social engagement mode, putting us in a much better position to overcome what's happened and move forward.

In the next section, I will help you to get to know your body so that it doesn't scare you any more, and in the long term to build to a point where you trust in it again so you can make changes at a bodily level. To do this, you need to learn to listen to your body and discover ways to make it feel safe again.

We'll do this in stages:

1. Getting to know your inner experience and learning to tolerate the different feelings and sensations.
2. Learning to link these internal sensations to your outer experience.

3. With practise, you can then begin to tune into your body, allow yourself to feel and change your emotional state.

Part 1: Getting to know your body

Becoming more aware can sometimes feel scary, as you start to notice new feelings and their effects on you. You might feel overwhelmed to begin with, or even feel a loss of your previous unawareness – it can feel like being in a new country, with different customs and social norms. Be aware of this and take this stage slowly – just try it for a minute and build up gradually so you can learn to tolerate and understand your feelings.

Being still can be hard. If it feels too much, it is too much. Stop and try something different before coming back to this. I once treated a man who was highly avoidant, and when he tried the body scan, a strategy I outline later (see page 285), he went straight into panic mode, as he had finally tuned into the anxiety in his body. When you are in fight-or-flight mode, it can be difficult to get into your body and stay there. I've tried to put the exercises in order of what's easiest, but it is personal to you. Try them all and see which work best.

I want you to start by tuning into your body and noticing how it is reacting. It can be helpful to make some notes afterwards and to keep track of any triggers when you're out and about. Being in tune with yourself lets you get to know yourself better, and is a good way of understanding yourself and where you are with things.

- Notice and describe the feelings in your body. Are you aware of any physical sensations – muscle tension, pain, tingling, heaviness, aches, pain? How is your body reacting?

- Where are you feeling the sensations? In your back, stomach, chest?
- Next, I want you to befriend the different feelings: hello, butterflies; hello, tiredness. Acknowledge them without judging or needing to fix or change them. You could use the body scan exercise (strategy 1 in the toolkit at the back of this book, see page 285) to do this.
- Notice the impact on your body of being in different environments. How does your body feel when you are relaxed at home? How does it feel when you are at work or with other people?
- Can you observe yourself in the different states: social engagement, fight-or-flight and freeze?
- Are there any environments or situations that trigger you into the threat zone? Can you notice any patterns?

When you're conscious of your body's signals and attend to them, you can begin to acknowledge how you're feeling and understand what your bodily sensations are telling you. Most importantly, you notice when things are harder and can bring in compassion and understanding at these moments – looking after yourself and giving your body what it needs. The better you get at understanding your body's reactions, the better chance you have of keeping yourself in equilibrium.

You can also begin to learn the situations that are likely to trigger threat mode. This lets you predict in advance how you'll react to something, bringing it into awareness so you can be more conscious of how you are feeling and what you might need. If you know you have a busy or difficult week, you could make those closest to you aware that you might be stressed but it's not personal, and ask for their support. You might try to get to bed on time so you have enough sleep, or use one of the exercises in the next chapter to look after your body.

Part 2: Bringing context to how you're feeling

To build emotional intelligence, the next step is to simply begin to label your feelings. To feel and interpret the different physical sensations in your body as a way to understand what you are feeling. When you name your physical sensations, you give them context, and integration can take place (something you'll also be doing when you tell your story in Chapter 9). This makes the emotions feel less intense and helps you to recognize the relationship between the physical sensations in your body and your emotions.

Finding the right words to name feelings can be hard initially. It's a bit like learning a new language. Be patient with yourself. In time you'll get better at knowing your cues and triggers. You will slowly learn to recognize and name the physical sensations in your body and interpret what they might mean. You might recognize that an upset tummy, body tingling or feeling light-headed signal nervousness, and identify that you're about to do something out of your comfort zone. You can also work backwards – if you know you're feeling nervous, work out which bodily sensations go with it. If you're feeling angry, sad, overwhelmed, do the same.

As you get to know your body better and the different physical presentations of stress and anxiety, try to give them more context and make the feeling more specific to what's happening. Instead of thinking, *I'm anxious*, think, *I'm anxious because I feel unsettled adjusting to all these changes*. Once you start to know your body, you can begin to predict situations that you might find more challenging and prepare in advance.

Try these ideas out:

- Notice the physical sensations in your body. Get to know your cues and triggers. Learn to recognize and name the physical sensations and what they might mean.
- Ask yourself, 'Why am I feeling like this?' Think about what you're doing, where you are, who you're with, what's just happened or what you are about to do.
- Build on this and start to work out how different emotions feel in your body. What does anger feel like, happiness, sadness, anxiety, guilt, shame, calm?
- Try to identify any sensations that you associate with relaxation or pleasure.
- What happens when you simply slow your breathing or take a deep breath? Or when you drop your shoulders, unclench your jaw or stretch?
- Use your breath to get to know your body. Can you feel your breath inside you? Notice how it expands your body when you breathe in. Can you feel it in your back, filling your sides? Can you breathe into tension and notice it soften?
- Can you notice strong physical sensations? Can you change these?
- Give the feelings context – what's happening that might be having an impact?
- Think about how these feelings influence you. Be aware of how they are causing you to act. Is this a choice or a response to the emotion?
- Think ahead about your week and what might be stressful so you can be aware in advance and plan the best way to manage.

Noticing where you are holding tension or your responses to what you're doing improves emotional regulation and means that you shift from ignoring what's going on internally to listening to it and hearing what it has to say. You can also start to see how these feelings rise and fall, that anxiety doesn't increase for ever, that it's normal to move into your sympathetic nervous system when you are busy or more stressed, but that you can come back out of it and into your body once that period has passed.

CARING FOR YOUR BODY

You don't need me to tell you that looking after your body will help you feel better. Yet it is one of the hardest things to put into action. This is especially true if you're overstressed and overworked, which is actually the time when you need it most.

Often people overlook work with the body or give it less priority as it feels too simplistic. I know that I have been guilty of this in the past, but I've learned through experience, both professionally and personally, that it makes a *huge* difference, and resistance can sometimes be a clue to what you need.

Looking after your body is an easy route into changing how you feel. It can also help you to release the stored-up physical effects of stress and trauma, and this is the first step to processing the emotional pain you are carrying and to help your body feel safe. When your body feels safe, autonomic regulation works more smoothly, you can get back into the restoration zone and this also puts you in a better place to engage with the changes you'll be making in the following chapters.

Looking after your body needs to be non-negotiable. Not just as you recover from what's happened, but for the rest of your life. It is a crucial part of feeling your best. If you want to have good emotional and physical health and build your resilience, you have to work at it. It takes daily effort, but it is so worth it. These practices are proven to make a difference, and the time you give to them, even if it is just a minute or two to start with, will make a huge difference. This happens on multiple levels:

- When you stop and make time for these things, it means you are thinking about and caring for yourself. Prioritizing yourself and thinking about your needs is essential to feeling better.
- It is a simple way to change your mood. You are helping your body to feel calmer, and this calms your mind and moves you from feeling stuck.
- There are so many gains to looking after your body, from improved mood and stress management to brain growth.
- It will help you build a better relationship with your body so you can trust in and listen to it again.
- It will give you time out from your day to step out of what's going on and check in with where you are, giving you a chance to see other perspectives.
- It will help you to develop a greater understanding of yourself and a greater awareness of how you feel, giving you more choice in how you choose to respond.

In this chapter, I'll introduce you to a few of my favourite strategies (the full details are in the Strategy Toolkit at the back of this book, see page 285) to look after your body and find inner calm, so you have a repertoire of methods that you can use in response to how your body feels. And in the next chapter, I'll be thinking about the importance of exercise.

The strategies in this book are just an introduction. Think of this as a life-long project of getting to know yourself better and seeing what works for you and your body. The techniques that you enjoy and that work for you might change over time, but the main aim is to follow your heart and do what you enjoy most as a route to looking after yourself and feeling good.

Think of it like a menu of options so you know what works when, whether it's calming your body through breathing or yoga, or physically expressing sensations through exercise. If I am feeling stressed, I'll make time for exercise. I know from experience that it's the quickest way to change how I'm feeling, and it puts me back in control. I always make time for a walk on my lunch break. Even if it's only 15 minutes walking round the park, I know it will set me up for the afternoon, and that being outdoors is a great reset. If I'm really busy, I might just take a minute to pause and look out of the window into my garden and take a deep breath. If I'm feeling really overwhelmed, I might use the butterfly hug exercise (see pages 286–287) or a grounding exercise (see page 288). It might sound like a lot, but the benefits are huge, and once you get into a routine, it makes it much easier.

The key is to start small. Aim to do one thing each day – this is much better than doing a long session every few weeks – and whatever you choose, ensure it is doable. Try linking it to something you already do, like brushing your teeth or making a hot drink, or set yourself a reminder to tick off each day. You could even get someone else involved so you have extra accountability. You can then gradually build new habits. Small steps are the best route to lasting change. Even if it is just looking out of the window at nature and seeing how the wind blows the leaves on the trees.

It's also important to continue to take care of the basics so you are in the best position to take the next steps. Keep hold of hope. Let others continue to support you. Make sure you are getting enough sleep (if this is a struggle at the moment, the exercises will help). Give yourself time for rest, stay hydrated and eat well, so you are taking care of your body at a basic level.

TRACK HOW YOU FEEL

In our house, we often say, 'Don't knock it till you've tried it'. I want you to apply this saying to the strategies you will try out. Trying to avoid judging things that we have no experience of is applicable more widely in our lives too. It's fine not to do something, but we have to have given it a go first. Our natural response is to stick with what we know. It's easy to count ourselves out of things because we fear them, or because we get stuck in our routines and the comfort that brings, but this approach is so limiting.

I am certainly guilty of this. I always thought I wasn't a yoga person, until I tried it in my late thirties, and now it is a point in my week where I catch-up with how I'm feeling and recentre. There are so many things I've done this with that now I wait before I judge and try not to rule anything out. As a result, many of the things I enjoy most at the moment are things I have only recently tried.

When you start with these exercises, I want you to track how you get on and write down the strategies you enjoy. Our mind is good at tricking us into *not* doing things. When we're not feeling good, the last thing we feel like doing is looking after our body, but this is often a sign that it is exactly what we need. Record how you feel before and then again afterwards, so you begin to see the difference it makes. Holding on to this is key to doing it the next time.

Trying new things opens up your world, boosts confidence and teaches you more about yourself. It's also a good way to increase tolerance of being in the unsettling in-between place that your brain tries to keep you out of. But while I'm all for trying new things, I also believe that you should always reserve the right to change your mind. If it's not working for you, don't keep going just because you said you would. Stop and try something different. It's going with what feels right for you at that time that will make the difference.

Breathing

Breathing is a direct link to our parasympathetic and sympathetic nervous systems. In fight-or-flight mode, our heart rate increases, our breathing gets shorter and shifts into the chest, and our muscles tense. Reversing this reaction with a slow breathing technique shifts us out of the stress response, activating the parasympathetic nervous system and bringing us back to calm and safety. Even better, breathing exercises have been proven to decrease stress, increase optimism, improve sleep, reduce pain, decrease anxiety, lessen impulsivity and strengthen immunity. Even one deep and slow breath can feel calming (see page 286).

Bilateral stimulation

Research suggests that bilateral stimulation can shift us out of fight-or-flight or freeze. The practice increases communication between the left and right hemispheres of the brain. Studies have shown that there are numerous benefits to bilateral stimulation, including better anxiety management, increased happiness and self-esteem, higher levels of creativity and enhanced performance. A great place to start with bilateral stimulation is the butterfly hug (see page 286). It's a calming and grounding exercise for when we're feeling anxious, stressed or stuck in our thoughts, and it only takes a couple of minutes to do.

Grounding

When we are stressed, we can experience an overload of feelings and thoughts, our body and mind races and it can be difficult to switch off. When we feel a sense of overwhelm, it can be helpful to try to ground ourselves in the present moment. We can use our senses to do this. Holding a stone in my pocket is one of my favourites. See page 288 for some more suggestions.

Thought leaves

Mindfulness simply means maintaining a moment-by-moment awareness of our thoughts, feelings, bodily sensations and surrounding environment. Acknowledging them but not getting into or judging them. Thought leaves is a brilliantly meditative exercise to try, especially good for getting to sleep (see page 289).

A breath of fresh air

Getting outdoors can make such a difference to the day and is a natural reset (see page 289). When we spend time in nature, evidence suggests that our parasympathetic nervous system is more likely to be activated, and our stress recovery response is faster and more complete when compared with exposure to built-up environments. Life satisfaction is higher for people who live near nature, and research shows that exposure to soil bacteria (*Mycobacterium vaccae*) is a natural antidepressant, activating brain cells that improve mood, reduce anxiety and facilitate learning. If the exercises above feel too much, try just stepping out of your front door. Walking is also great bilateral stimulation. I feel very fortunate to live by the sea and next to the South Downs; you can't go wrong whichever direction you head in, but the sea never fails to remind me how small I am and to put things in perspective.

KEY TAKEAWAYS

- The mind and body are intimately linked; we experience traumatic events physically too.
- Understanding how your body works and how your emotions express themselves within it is a key part of overcoming trauma.
- To give yourself the best chance of overcoming trauma, you need a healthy nervous system that is in equilibrium.
- Greater awareness of our emotions helps us to become less scared of them and to regulate and express them more easily.
- Looking after your body is an easy route to changing how you feel.

6

WHY EXERCISE IS
THE HOLY GRAIL

There is an overwhelming amount of research on just how brilliant exercise is for both your mind and body. It can make a profound difference to your life and it is something that should be part of everyone's week. If you want to save yourself a few minutes of reading, the key message in this section is that exercise is a life-changer!

Exercise is a fail-safe strategy for managing your mood and it is one of the best routes to good mental health. It is proven to make meaningful improvements to how happy we feel – we're all familiar with the runner's high – and depending on our exercise of choice, it can make us feel joyful, intoxicated or mellowed. We generally feel these good effects only 15 minutes after starting. It has the ability to exhilarate and relax, counter depression and dissipate stress, and provide stimulation and calm. If there was a drug that had the same effects, everyone would be taking it. It works on multiple levels: brain, body, thoughts and emotions.

When life feels out of control, it can be good to have a simple activity to focus on and complete that is under your control and straightforward, and where you can see progress and improvement.

It gives you a tick in your day, puts you in a better mood and brings a sense of achievement when you complete it.

Having time in your week that isn't about work, chores, other people or being productive is important, and success in one area can spill into other areas, increasing confidence, self-esteem and your ability to cope. It can help rebuild identity and it can be a great link to other people if you join a group, giving you a sense of belonging and a chance to make new friends. And unlike everything that has happened to you, it does respond to the rules of life that you used to believe.

- When life feels overwhelming, exercise is a guaranteed way to take back control.
- It has a cause-and-effect nature – if you work hard at it, you do improve.
- If you develop a routine, it can bring structure and stability to your week.

When you are stuck in a feeling, it can be difficult to think your way out of it, as your mood colours your thinking patterns. If you feel anxious, your thoughts are anxious; when you're feeling low, everything seems hopeless. Exercise, however, lifts your mood, taking you out of your current situation so you can return with a fresh perspective, helping you step back from ruminative, anxious or angry thinking and providing distraction. Changing how your body feels can be a physical way to discharge feelings, and it can also bring some normality back into your life. Remember how Jess used running to help get her through her mother's cancer diagnosis and death (see pages 80–81). I think about it as a way of disrupting the feelings, shifting you out of autopilot and putting you back in control.

There's something about letting your thoughts tick over without actively looking at them that untangles things. It can also be a way to physically express how you're feeling and provide a temporary distraction. Running off anger, cycling away sadness, dancing out anxiety. The rhythmic pace of exercises like walking, running, cycling and swimming also brings in the bilateral stimulation that we've already seen can make such a difference to how we feel. In hard exercise, you breathe more deeply, activating the sympathetic nervous system.

It's also a brilliant way to rebuild a positive relationship with your body. It reframes strong bodily sensations so you begin to feel them without fear. Rapid heartbeat, breathlessness, dizziness and tight chest from overexertion can be something to feel proud of and lets you see that being in these states can't hurt or damage you, so you learn to trust your body again.

EXERCISE AND RESILIENCE

Exercise empowers you – when you feel strong in your body, it spills over and helps you to feel strong in your life, something we will see in Sophie's story later. When you push your limits, you have a chance to see what you are capable of. If you didn't believe you could run 5km or swim in cold water and you manage to, it translates to other areas of your life: 'If I can do that, what else can I do that I didn't believe I could?' It's also another great way to build up experience of moving into that unsettling in-between place and back out of it.

Winning the mental battle to exercise, reaching your goals or coming back from injury teaches you to overcome difficulty in smaller ways, building mental strength. You will also learn to overcome the temptation not to bother or to give up, and get better at moving into calmer states. When I don't feel like exercising, instead of debating whether to do it or not, I just go for a walk, run or bike ride and tell myself I can always turn around and come back if I want to. I've never turned around once I've started and I don't think there's ever been a time I've regretted it. Every time you think you can't do it and you overcome the feeling, you also have a chance to see that you can.

Exercise also increases your stress tolerance. A small amount of stress on your body lets you bring yourself in a controlled way in and out of the stress response. This means that your nervous system gradually gets used to handling moderate levels of stress, increasing your ability to cope and teaching you that you can safely manage discomfort. Getting used to feeling and managing discomfort in safe ways is a much better option than spending your time trying to avoid it, which can stop you engaging in and living your life. Doing this increases resilience and your ability to recover from stress.

EXERCISE AND THE BRAIN

When we exercise, move vigorously or break a sweat, it kick-starts a complex chemical and biological process that causes immediate and long-lasting changes in the brain and makes it easier for the brain to grow new neural connections. More intense activities raise the levels of glutamate and gamma-aminobutyric acid, which boost mental fitness and regulate emotional health.

Aerobic exercise and strength training have been shown to stimulate the growth of areas of the brain involved in emotional processing, including the hippocampus, which is known to be reduced in size in people with anxiety and depression.

They have also been shown to reduce inflammation, which has been associated with a range of mental health difficulties, and oxidative stress, which can damage the body's cells, proteins and DNA. This can contribute to ageing and may play an important role in the development of a range of conditions such as diabetes and heart disease. Researchers at UCL tracked 152,978 participants in the UK Biobank study aged 40–69, over seven years. They found that people with the lowest combined aerobic and muscular fitness had higher odds of depression and anxiety.

Biologically, any movement that gets us out of breath teaches our body to deal with stress more effectively as it mimics the stress response. Heart rate and adrenaline increase and all the main bodily systems – endocrine, muscular, cardiovascular, nervous, respiratory – are working and interacting with each other much more than when we are resting.

FIND WHAT YOU LOVE

We all respond to exercise differently, so it's important to find what is right for you. You will rarely feel like doing the exercise beforehand, so choose something that you really enjoy. The more you love it, the easier it will be to convince yourself to do it.

Like pretty much everything, you can have too much of a good thing. Be careful of using exercise to always escape your mood, or overexercising, which can leave you feeling stressed and anxious. It's something to enhance your life, not a pass or fail. Try to find the balance between building a routine and making it so strict that it adds to your stress. When you move your body out of the threat zone, you might also notice that you feel emotional. It unlocks a different part of you that you can't get to through thinking alone.

Brainstorm a list of activities you want to try and find what works for you. If you don't enjoy an activity, try something else. It can be the obvious ones – an exercise class, running, cycling, swimming – or just dancing round your kitchen, skipping or roller-skating. The rhythmic flow of exercises like yoga and dance can have a pacifying effect on the mind, decreasing the number of stress receptors in the brain. Just swaying, spinning with your arms outstretched, can elicit joy in 8.5 minutes! Music and dance together can bring even bigger drops in cortisol levels, regulating your immune system and making you feel relaxed and at ease. I also love listening to music when I run.

Yoga might sound like a stock response, but it is a brilliant way to link the body and mind, moving you into a slower zone and shifting out of the threat zone back into safety. It brings an awareness to the body. It lets you check in with how you're feeling so you can listen to what your body has to say before gently changing it.

It incorporates breathing, opening up, stretching and releasing tension. It's not seeking an endorphin high as a way to change your state; it's gently moving how you feel, finding out where you are and connecting with your body. I often leave my yoga class feeling quite spaced out. When you do yoga, you are being mindful – you have to be in your body to do it, and when you're focusing on your movements and trying to stay balanced, there's little space for worries or stresses to come in. Warrior pose really is a good pose for worriers!

I'm not going to run through all the research and benefits or the different things you can try, as it will take up the whole book, but I will tell you my own story to encourage you and explain why I believe it is well worth incorporating exercise into your week.

CYCLING

It's never too late to start something new. I didn't get on a road bike until just before my fortieth birthday, and if you had told me that I'd become someone who loved cycling, I would not have believed you. It definitely wasn't a case of love at first sight. I always thought the Lycra was a bit much, and if I'm honest, I was slightly judgemental about cyclists, but it's not an exaggeration to say that cycling has changed my life.

It all started when after yet another running injury, I bought a bike on whim. When I started, I was *terrified*, but after calculating my price per use for one go, I felt like I couldn't give up. I hated clipping in, and I felt so low down on the bike that at first I didn't even dare signal for fear of falling off.

On the first two rides I did fall off, as I didn't manage to unclip my feet before stopping. The second time I took my husband out with me (he was a softer landing than the road). I told myself that I'd do ten rides, and if I still hated the clips, I'd go to normal pedals. I managed the next six rides without falling off. I was starting to feel pretty good about clipping in, and then on my eleventh ride, I fell off again, right in front of a group of builders.

It wasn't just clipping into the pedals that caused me problems. I'd feel nervous before I went out, with multiple trips to the loo, and then once I was on the bike it took me about 20 minutes before I could enjoy the ride. Each time before leaving I'd question my sanity in continuing to bother, but by the time I got back, I felt alive! Out in nature, enjoying the amazing scenery on the South Downs.

I'd also panic about getting lost – I have no sense of direction, so my ability to find my way is non-existent – and the stress of trying new routes felt strangely crippling, but I got such a sense of achievement when I managed it. I would go out really early before the kids woke up, as the roads were quiet (traffic was something else I was afraid of), and I wouldn't sleep well the night before. But each time I did it, I was exhilarated by the end of the ride. I felt myself improving and had a growing sense of satisfaction.

After a year, I plucked up the courage to join a cycling club, and this introduced me to a wonderful group of women. I felt a sense of belonging, and I loved that I wasn't 'work me' or 'mum me' when I was with them. I was just someone who liked cycling. I've made some amazing friendships with people I might never have met otherwise.

Trying something new and improving at it – getting out on my bike, even when I didn't feel like it, finding my way on a new route, getting quicker, overcoming my fears – has helped me grow stronger both physically and mentally. I've done things I never thought I'd be capable of, and this has given me greater self-belief and shown me a strength in myself that I had lost touch with. The pattern of feeling like I couldn't do it and then managing to, helped me feel better able to cope with what the day or week threw at me. Managing to grind my way to the top of a steep hill in record time translated to grinding through other difficulties in my life and achieving success.

When I'm having a tough week, I get on my bike. It's a way to sort through what's happening without looking directly at it, giving me space to think over everything and positively shifting my mood. Somehow being out on the bike lets me sift through things and gain perspective, or gives me new insights and ways to think about what's going on. At other times, I think of nothing except the route and the views. I zone out, mindful in the present.

The time on my bike is a space in my week just for me; it's become part of who I am. When I am on my bike, I'm not answerable to anyone else or thinking about what anyone else needs. It gives me the most incredible sense of freedom, something that can be hard to come by in adult life, and somehow it has helped me to remember myself. The part that believed in myself, that was courageous and strong. The part that did things my way and strove for the things that mattered to me. Trauma took that part from me. When I lost my meaning framework, I lost my trust in life and other people. Cycling has given it back to me.

I wish I'd discovered cycling before I was 40, but I'm just grateful that I persevered. It's opened up a part of my life that I didn't even know about before. Exercise doesn't need to take over your life or become an obsession, but it's amazing what can come from trying something new, and what it can lead to.

Listening to your body and looking after it is key to understanding yourself, as you'll see in the next story. I first met Sophie in 2015, when she was referred to me for therapy after being signed off work due to insomnia and anxiety. Over the time I've known her, I've witnessed her completely change her life. Her courageous approach to everything she does is incredibly inspiring, and it's amazing to see how she has not just turned her own life around, but is now helping others as a self-worth coach and with her Move and Inspire online yoga platform.

SOPHIE'S STORY:
HIDDEN TRAUMA

I was 15 when I first experienced insomnia. It was quite sudden. Throughout my childhood my dad had suffered from cancer. First when I was 10 and then again when I was 16. Quite rightly, the focus was on him. I used to tell myself, insomnia isn't going to kill you. I didn't want to make a fuss, with him being so frail. I didn't want to admit I had a problem. I did go to the doctor about it, but they really didn't help and it was minimized as an issue. My insomnia wasn't taken seriously, so I didn't take it seriously.

At the time, I had a great friend at school who was very depressed – in a really bad place, self-harming and not able to get out of bed some days. I would often try to look after her and help her. I would look at her issues and my father's issues and compare them with my own. I told myself that I was fine. After my dad was in remission, he was still very weak from all the drugs and had a suppressed immune system. We had to be really careful. If we were ill, we couldn't go near him. Sometimes at Christmas I couldn't be with him because I had a cold and couldn't risk him getting it.

In my early twenties, I started to suffer from increased anxiety and the sleep problems continued. My father also had cancer for the third time. Increasingly, I felt the need to control everything and achieve as much as possible (although at the time I had no idea I was doing this). I continually put pressure on myself to get good grades, to go to a good university, to get a great job. Again, I didn't realize it at the time, but I was doing all of this because deep down I didn't feel I was enough.

I got a job in TV and started climbing the ladder quickly. From the outside, everything was going well: I had a boyfriend and a 'glamorous' job (in reality, working in TV is anything but glamorous). Looking back, I was coming at life in such a different way to how I do now. Success meant something very different to me back then. But even though I had the life I apparently wanted, sleep had become a huge problem, it felt like a monster that I was scared of every single night.

I was always exhausted. I would have panic attacks at night. I would wake up thinking I was having a heart attack, as I had no understanding of what my body was trying to tell me. I had terrible stomach problems and awful night sweats – so many physical problems with no clear cause. During that time, I started to take sleeping pills, which I became addicted to, and I would also drink alcohol to get myself to sleep. Thinking about it now, it sounds crazy that I was doing that, but it really was just my way of surviving and it became my normal.

It all came to a head when I was 29. I'd had about 72 hours of no sleep and I had got myself into a complete state. The TV work was so full-on then. I'd been working 90-hour weeks starting off a show and not really sleeping. In that industry, it wasn't that unusual – everyone was in a heightened state, drinking coffee from 5 a.m. We'd all be running on adrenaline and energy drinks.

I'd just started a new job and we had commenced filming that day. I remember feeling like I was in a trance. I'd had years of very bad sleep, by then, but this was at a new level. One of my roles was to look after the actors. I remember getting them to the set and I just couldn't get into work mode. The line producer came up to me and said, 'Sophie, this isn't you. Are you OK?' I'd been masking it for years, but it was now becoming obvious. He said, 'Whatever you need to do, go and do it.' I called my mum in tears feeling totally helpless and she told me to go and see a doctor straight away. I even looked up how I could check myself into some type of sleep or mental facility – I felt so desperate. I managed to get an appointment, so I left work and was driven straight there by one of the staff drivers as I wasn't in a state to drive. I left my car in the car park as I thought I was going to go back to work the next day. It never occurred to me that day would be my last day on set.

I remember that appointment so well. The doctor started asking me questions about what was going on, but not just about the sleep. I think it was the first time in about 14 years someone had actually said, 'How are you?'

I had gone to see a therapist in my early twenties, but he was no help. He put me on amphetamines in the mornings to try and kick off my body clock and get me to sleep in the evening, which didn't work at all. No one had tried to get to the root cause of my sleeping problems. I was unkind to myself and very self-critical about it all. I blamed myself completely. I felt I had no reason to be sad and I was ashamed that I couldn't sleep and for the problems I felt I was causing everyone. Although I didn't see it as shame at the time – I didn't even realize what shame really was.

I talked to the doctor about going back to work the next day, but he told me there was no way this could happen and that I was very ill. It really hit me then that I had to take this seriously. At that point I couldn't really understand what had happened, as it had been such a gradual thing. It had always just been a case of taking a different pill and carrying on. For the first time, I was signed off work.

The next week, I called my line producer and quit. I started seeing a psychologist twice a week. It was a massive help, but I found it hard to talk about myself and felt so guilty. But I found the empathy I received really useful. It was only then that I realized that being a little girl with a dad with cancer and then not sleeping properly for so many years had been traumatic.

I ended up on four pills – two to get me to sleep and two to keep me asleep. I was only supposed to be on them for a short time, but I was on them for a while. I didn't feel very good on them, almost hung-over, but it was the lesser of two evils, as staying awake with bad anxiety was worse for me – I would get myself into such a state. After doing a lot of therapy and other work on myself, I finally came off them in 2018. I don't take them now. It has been a huge change.

Moving away from TV was scary but liberating. I felt very unqualified, as I had never had a job outside of film. I battled with feeling like a failure, being unemployed, feeling not worthy. I was seeing myself as a victim. What I realize now is that so much of my energy up to then had been spent on achieving. Now I try and do things in a different way, with a more loving approach and a different language. I know I am worthy whatever I am doing. I have redefined what it means to live a successful life – and that's to live a life that feels true to me, not a life that fits society or other people's expectations of me.

At that point, when you are so broken, it is just baby steps. My psychologist asked me to write down all the good things I had done each day. Some days it was something as simple as doing a food shop. But I started to see myself as a valuable being, even if I wasn't rushing around on a TV set.

I had two words in my head – health and happiness. My dad had told me when I was younger that these were the two most important things in life. I used to be very sporty when I was younger, but due to the pressures of TV and the sleep issues, I hadn't done any exercise for a while. The first thing I did when I stopped working was get fit. I started doing yoga with my cousin in the garden and I was awful at it. I could hardly bend at all, but I was kind of intrigued by it, so I started going to classes. I was full of anxious energy and I suddenly had all this time on my hands, so I began doing two classes a day.

Yoga had a huge impact on me, so I decided to train as a yoga teacher. It's hard to get a yoga business off the ground, as there is not a lot of money in it, but I started doing everything I could. I was flyering to publicize my business, teaching classes wherever I could, seeing private clients. I started to realize that I was determined, I was brave, I was strong. I also began to realize I was incredibly positive. I'd had this negative inner voice for a long time, but now I saw that wasn't the real me. I believe that positivity is an integral part of who I am, but it is hard to get in touch with that when you haven't slept for 72 hours.

Now I understand that there are two different sides to us all. There is an inner guide that comes from a place of love and is nurturing – this is your truth. The other side is based on the survival mechanism, full of ego and fear. But when you don't understand that, you can't help but listen to the voice that is loudest.

I got the yoga business going, although I took on way too many classes and ended up burning out for a second time. When I get anxious, I have a tendency to become a workaholic. I didn't realize that then, and so again had put far too much pressure on myself to achieve and lost my voice for three weeks. I had a camera put down my nose to look at my throat and was told there was nothing wrong with my voice physically; it all had to do with stress. All my emotions had lodged in my throat. This seems to be a pattern when I am heading in the wrong direction – my emotions take over and I lose my voice. As a yoga teacher, not having a voice forces you to stop, which was probably a blessing. It taught me a lot. Now my work is looking after myself, not trying to be endlessly productive.

I had always really wanted to get married to my boyfriend, but it took him a long time to propose. While I was doing the yoga thing, he finally did, but then only a year after the wedding, we ended up separating. It was such a shock that the relationship had broken down. I was totally invested in it. By then I had done so much work on myself, I was in a very different place, and I think we had started to go down slightly different paths. He was so proud of me, but we had both been in TV and I suddenly had all this freedom and wanted to do other things. My feeling about what success was now had become so different. The way I wanted to live my life felt very different to my life when I was an assistant director in TV, and that changed things for us.

No one goes into a marriage thinking it is going to fail. I was so committed to it. When that path doesn't happen, you can either sink and drown or look for a path with a whole new story and a new ending. At the beginning of our separation, I was so shocked by what was happening that I was in a place where I was constantly trying to fix everything. I was trying to control it all, but I couldn't. I had to accept that. That was part of why I ended up in Bali.

It was just before the pandemic. I decided to go to Bali to work for three months and ended up getting stuck there – although willingly stuck. Moving to Bali felt so good, so freeing, so liberating. It was an adventure. It gave my life a new perspective. I had always wanted to live abroad, so now, with this new life ahead of me, I finally took the leap.

Initially, before committing to moving there, I went for two weeks and had the best time. I knew I didn't want to be in London; it represented everything about me and my ex-husband, so it felt too painful to stay there. I wanted to take my work online and I couldn't afford a studio in the UK, so going to Bali was a way to grow the business. It was such a change in the way I had been living my life – I went from having my own flat to living in someone's spare room.

There was an ability to be selfish in a way that I hadn't been selfish before. My break-up was so painful that I had to do something for me. The reaction from friends and family was mixed. I realized that me making these different decisions felt threatening to other people who had gone down a more conventional route. I had always wanted to move abroad, but I had always felt scared. Looking back, it was so brave!

It was the start of a powerful healing journey. I really looked at myself and realized that so many of my problems in life were down to my lack of self-worth. I no longer live my life feeling unworthy. When you have the understanding that you are living your life in fear, and that the fear is the part of you making decisions, you can spot it and deal with it. But when you don't, your fear becomes your reality. When I was younger, I didn't know any different. I didn't know that a shaky feeling with sweaty palms wasn't normal – I just thought that was how things were.

Moving to Bali, I felt so alive. I was listening to music the whole time – joyful, happy music. Before, I had indulged in sad music when my dad was ill, but uplifting music became very important to me as a way to heal. I tried so many different things. I had guitar lessons, was singing a lot, I learned to skateboard. If I move back to the UK in the future, I want to bring that Bali way of living with me!

I realized I was looking for a sense of purpose. I now know that if I am in a difficult spot, a really good way to help myself is to help others. When the pandemic happened, I found I could help people get through their difficult moments with my work. I started to teach others about wellness and about healthy boundaries, dealing with codependency and how to live a thriving life. Don't get me wrong, I still struggle with stuff. But I have such a clear understanding of who I am, what I want and what drives me, plus I have so many amazing tools to keep moving forward no matter the pain or the struggle. It feels so freeing and expansive to be able to live like this.

Whatever happens to me, I know that these last couple of years in Bali have been life-changing. I've been able to grow in so many different ways. For so long, I wouldn't let myself think I had the possibility of another life. We are so conditioned to settle. The scary thing is to do something new, to not settle. I had only felt like a failure in the past because I had strayed off the path that was taught to me as a child – get married, have kids, buy a house…I know now that even though my life doesn't look like that, I can still have an incredible life. It's not the external things that really matter, but instead the energy you choose to show up with.

A few things were of particular help in moving on from the trauma of divorce. Walking was great. It became a part of my routine. I would just walk on the beach listening to podcasts so I didn't have to be in my head. A sense of belonging has also been really important. I found two amazing friends in Bali. We all arrived just before the borders closed and ended up spending so much time together. Having professional advice has been very helpful to me, particularly in the beginning. Journalling has been a large part of the healing process too. I did some online courses to make it really structured. Pen to paper, not typing it up. Inspiring others has been great – I've really enjoyed going on podcasts, for example. I asked the guy who I did my online courses with if I could go on his podcast, and he said yes! (And I know that if he had said no, that would also have been OK. It showed me how willing I had become to just put myself out there.)

The language I use to talk about myself and how I describe things has changed massively. I used to start sentences with 'this might sound stupid' or 'correct me if I'm wrong'. People used to compliment me and I'd bat it away. I'm not the finished product and I don't have to be – I have let go of perfectionism. There are lots of things that are unresolved in my life, lots of things I still want, but the most important thing is that I fully love myself. Sometimes I think society frowns on us celebrating ourselves; it's seen as arrogant. But being able to tell myself that I love myself is more important than caring what others think.

It is healing to be in the emotion, to feel it, to actually process it. But the story we tell ourselves can't leave us as a victim; we have to find an empowering inner dialogue, which takes time. We need to allow ourselves to grieve, but also we need to realize that grief is not linear. The old me accepted things into her life that she would never accept now – by raising my self-worth, I have raised my standards, which allows me to live a life that feels more in alignment with what I actually want. I still love the old me – that has been part of my process of healing. I accept her mistakes, and love her for all the ways she went wrong.

I still feel fear, I still have my anxious moments and I still occasionally have trouble sleeping, but I know I have a firm base now. I can short-circuit it and stop my mind from spiralling out of control; I can accept that life isn't always going to be good and then move on.

I used to have such a rigid structure of what I thought life should be. I had always imagined living with my ex-husband, in the house we were supposed to have bought, with a baby. And that life was ripped away from me so suddenly. It was incredibly hard. But my life now is so much more expansive in a way I could never have imagined. I know I am going to have many more tests in the future. I know I am deeply sensitive and emotional – something that I now can see is a superpower. I realize it's OK to feel all my emotions and choose how I react, rather than feeling powerless and controlled by each and every emotion I have.

When I first slept for the whole night without drugs, I cried the next day it was so emotional. I realized that I could do it, that I could actually sleep. When you don't even have the hope that you can sleep a whole night through, it can feel very dark. The difference between taking a pill to sleep and sleeping naturally is massive. When you take a pill, you don't have agency. But I can sleep now without them and that has been a huge and important step for me.

Through my work I can see that so many people are struggling. So many people are in an unsustainable situation. I can see that it's hard to live a life that is driven by love and truth rather than fear. But it is so empowering if you can do the work on yourself to build your self-worth, because I believe that when you do, everything changes. My relationship with myself is so much more loving. I feel that everything is possible now. I trust myself and I have faith that I will have an incredible life. I am already living an incredible life!

MY THOUGHTS

Sophie was referred to me for therapy by her GP. Her story shows how trauma can manifest physically and the importance of the mind–body link. It also shows that when our experience isn't what we imagine as a 'typical trauma', it can be harder to see it for what it is.

Physical expression of emotional pain

In therapy, I often find that people can be unaware of how difficult things have become. They keep going and going until it becomes impossible to ignore. Because they are not conscious of the impact of their situation, their experience is expressed at a bodily level – the physical expression of the anxiety and stress is a result of being in the unsettling in-between place.

Sophie's insomnia became progressively worse, trapping her in a vicious cycle. All those lonely hours awake at night opened up more time for thinking, and night-time thoughts tend to be when we are at our most anxious. These anxious thoughts set off the fight-or-flight reaction in our body, making it even harder to sleep. When we sleep less, it has a knock-on effect on our day, negatively impacting on our mood and making it difficult to find energy or motivation. Polyvagal theory gives us an understanding of the ongoing impact of our autonomic nervous system being stuck in activation, and we can see this play out in Sophie's story. The long-term build-up of problems coupled with an overwhelming work schedule meant it got to a point where her body literally forced her to stop.

Mismatch between messages and experience

Sophie tried to seek professional help, but no one picked up on what was going on. The message she was given was that there was nothing wrong with her apart from some difficulty sleeping. No one looked underneath at the underlying cause. The mismatch between how she felt and the reaction from professionals meant that she couldn't make sense of what she was going through or process her feelings. And as no one else took what was going on seriously, Sophie didn't take it seriously herself. This is something I'll be looking at in more detail in the next chapter. Sophie also minimized what was going on, as she compared it to the situation of her childhood friend and her father.

Our work together

Therapy was a chance for Sophie to share with me what had happened, to tell her story and put everything together. To be heard, but to also make sense of her experience and to take action. Looking after her body, reviewing her past experiences, learning new coping strategies and re-evaluating how she wanted to move forwards.

Looking back to look forwards

Sophie had always looked up to, and idolized, her dad. When someone we love encounters serious illness, it changes our view of the world and our trust in life. Sophie's meaning framework, that her dad was strong and invulnerable, was fractured. As a child, you don't consciously register a change, but from one day to the next you have a different view of your world. Not having that same security can change things at a level you aren't even fully aware of. You pick up on what is said and the unsaid – seeing her dad going through such a serious illness, the fear that he might die, his fragility; at times he was so weak she couldn't be in the same room as him. It was important to help Sophie understand her situation differently. To realize that feeling anxious when your father is diagnosed with cancer is natural. To acknowledge how scary it must have been to see him go through that and the impact on the family. I think it was perhaps harder for her to see how difficult things were as it was all wrapped up in a good home life with loving parents.

My job was to validate what Sophie had been through and give her a new perspective on her experiences. To explain the impact of these experiences and why it was understandable that she had got to a point where she was no longer able to cope. Looking at what has happened is in no way about blaming; it's about gradually building a new understanding. Sophie needed to realize that it wasn't a problem with her, but a situation that was incredibly difficult to cope with.

Coping well

Therapy was a place to explore what had happened so Sophie could begin to look at things differently. By looking back, she was able to build a new, coherent understanding of what had happened and understand why she felt like this. Psychoeducation helped explain the impact of not sleeping on mood and showed Sophie the link between thoughts, emotions, how you feel physically and behaviour.

This gave space for me to gently show Sophie how misplaced her self-criticism was. I remember after the first few sessions pointing out to her how often she put herself down. It had become automatic, but pointing it out meant she could question whether it was helping or hindering her and develop a more compassionate internal voice instead.

Therapy was also a chance to build new coping strategies. To manage her anxiety, Sophie would try to fix and control. But the more she did this, the less in control she felt. She learned not to show others that she was struggling or to let her guard down, believing this was a weakness. As a result, others saw her as someone who coped well and it meant she was unable to access the support she needed. Our work was acknowledging that these coping strategies were understandable, but they weren't working. Instead we focused on building an inner well of confidence and self-belief that could give Sophie a more stable view of herself. I could see an insightful, determined, kind, intelligent and strong woman sitting in front of me, and I wanted her to see herself as I did.

If you have low self-esteem, it's common to rely on external validation to feel good about yourself. Praise and positive feedback are great in the moment, but you need to be able to internalize them, to build an inner measure of how you're doing. Otherwise, you'll only ever feel as good as whatever you're doing now. I think about it in terms of how tennis seeding is done – you're not rated solely on your last game. Often we feel everything needs to be right about us to be acceptable, rather than recognizing that we're all flawed. No one's perfect; that's what it means to be human.

Looking after your body

Sophie's yoga allowed her to tune back into her body and begin to trust it again. She also started to notice her warning signs – when she felt something in her throat or lost her voice, when her stomach was upset or unsettled – and realized that this meant she needed to look after herself.

Telling your story

Bringing an awareness to Sophie's experience was a large part of the work. Sophie was missing so many pieces of the puzzle that she couldn't make sense of what was happening, and it continued to press on her. Telling her story and feeling the emotions connected to what had happened made them less frightening and painful. Putting all the pieces of the jigsaw puzzle back together and matching up Sophie's feelings with her experience allowed her to lay the trauma to rest (as you'll see in Chapter 7).

Becoming yourself

Therapy also gave Sophie space to think about what she wanted, rather than what others wanted or expected. She began to listen to her inner voice and to re-evaluate how she would move forward in her life. To think more about her values and find a way to work that felt meaningful and that mattered to her. Slowly I watched Sophie get to know herself again.

Ongoing learning

Since completing therapy, Sophie has continued on this journey of learning. She has found a freedom in the way she lives, knowing that she doesn't have to have it all worked out. She has learned that she is a positive, capable person, living a life aligned with her values. I feel incredibly fortunate to have met Sophie and to have walked the first part of this journey with her.

KEY TAKEAWAYS

- Exercise is a life-changer; it can lift your mood and give you fresh perspective.
- It empowers us; when we feel strong in our body, we feel strong in our life.
- It increases our stress tolerance in a controlled way and teaches us that we can safely manage discomfort.
- Exercise boosts mental fitness and regulates emotional health.

LOOKING BACK TO LOOK FORWARDS (STEP 3)

7

Y ou have now completed the first two of the seven steps: care, and looking after your body. Getting the basics in place and helping you to understand and feel safe in your body will increase your capacity and put you in a better position to move through the next steps.

In this chapter, we will be moving on to step 3 – looking back to look forwards. In this step I will help you understand the effects of your childhood and how these might have shaped your meaning framework and coping strategies. To overcome trauma and better understand your current thoughts, feelings and behaviours, we first need to go back in time.

STEP 3: LOOKING BACK TO LOOK FORWARDS

In this step I want you to review your history as a way to understand and get to know yourself better. Family environment, family dynamics and the way your parents raised you combine with your personality and your experience of the world to shape your framework of beliefs (Chapter 2) and give you a sense of who you are. This means that what you learned as a child influences how you see and experience things now, and these childhood experiences shape your approach to life and provide clues to why you think and act as you do. As you go through this section, I want you to think about your own childhood and how this might be influencing the coping strategies you use.

Until I had children, I really underestimated the part that personality plays in development, but when you're around babies and children, you see how differently they arrive into the world. My three children each have very different personalities and approaches to life, despite being raised in broadly the same way. Nature and nurture are not separate – each has an impact on the other. Your personality type interacts with your experiences and influences the world's response to you. But nurture clearly plays a role too.

When we're born, our brain isn't fully developed and we come into the world ready to collect information from our environment. The transfer of information in childhood mostly takes place through everyday interactions, and our parents play a role in what we learn about ourselves, both directly and indirectly. Children tune in to the subtle and not-so-subtle messages they are given, which influence how they think about themselves and the world around them.

LEARNING TO REGULATE OUR EMOTIONS

This process starts from when a baby is first born. In an ideal world, the parent acts as a container for the baby's emotions and feelings. When the baby cries, their carer reflects their sadness, soothing them, helping them regulate their emotions and begin to trust that their thoughts and feelings are understood. Through this interaction, the baby also gains an understanding of what they are feeling. If a parent is attuned with their child and in touch with how they're thinking and feeling (both positive and negative), it can help them to regulate their emotional and physiological state.

It's easy to see this process when we think about how we react to babies when we're with them. We tend to shift to baby talk, changing our tone of voice and matching it to what we see in the baby. If the baby is smiling, we smile back; we might compliment them: 'Who's a clever baby, who made you so gorgeous?'. If they're crying, we console them, changing our tone to match their mood: 'Oh dear, what's the matter? You're feeling sad.' We also change our movements, bouncing a happy baby up and down, and slowing our movements if they're tired or sad and bringing them closer to us.

As a child, you need things to match up to make sense of them. Maybe you fall over and graze your knee, and when you go to your parent upset, they give you a cuddle and say, 'Oh goodness, that must have hurt, are you OK?', reflecting the feeling back to you and containing it. You learn: this hurts, it's taken seriously, love and care help it to go away. You feel something, the parent responds with a reaction that fits, and you come to understand that this feeling is worthy of a response.

This awareness of ourselves as reflected back through the face and mind of the other is central to all psychological growth. As a child, our mind literally grows and develops through being thought about, empathized and attuned with. When this happens, we feel responded to and somehow encompassed in that care, helping us to understand our own and other people's experiences. This helps us to build both a psychological and emotional understanding of ourselves in relation to others. These experiences also mean that we are more likely to be securely attached to our parent, another protective factor for getting through life.

When parents get it right (and no parent manages this all the time), the child learns to regulate their emotions. If we can understand our emotional experience, it helps us make sense of ourselves and others as well as events in our everyday life, making the world easier to navigate. It helps us to form better relationships, which are protective to our health. It enables us to understand or predict other people's behaviour and reactions and adjust our own accordingly. If we can see things from someone else's perspective, our relationships will run more smoothly, making it easier to get along.

WHAT IF THERE'S A MISMATCH?

Unfortunately, not all upbringings are 'ideal'. If you were cared for by someone who did not have the mental space to pick up, take onboard and be sensitive to how you were feeling, or if your feelings were ignored or a different perspective was imposed on you, then you will have a very different experience of the world. This might be unintentional – like Sophie's experience. Or your world may have been either lacking or, more seriously, neglectful, traumatic or abusive, making it difficult for you to develop a secure attachment. When you think about a child with these experiences, it's clear they will have a very different start to life, and explains why childhood trauma can have such a damaging impact.

As a child, you're dependent on your caregiver and you can't just leave the situation. Your only option is to change your response so that you don't lose the attachment. To do this, you have to tune out from how you are feeling, and as a result you begin to dismiss your own emotional needs. You might shift to fawn mode and become an expert at reading your carer's mood, tuning into their feelings and needs over your own as a way to try and keep them happy.

Imagine you fall over and are upset, but this time when you go to your parent they become annoyed at you or tell you to stop crying: you learn to suppress your emotions. Maybe they tell you off and blame you for what happened: 'What have you done, why do you always get into these scrapes?'. You learn that you are to blame when things go wrong. If they are too busy to stop and listen, you learn not to burden other people with your problems. Or maybe they start telling you about how bad it is for them: you learn to put others' needs before your own. Perhaps your parents try to make you feel better by telling you it's not so bad, or worse, to stop being ridiculous – then you minimize how you feel. In all these scenarios, it is hard to match up how you're feeling inside with the response you are getting.

You might also learn coping strategies from those closest to you through modelling – this is when we observe and imitate. If your parents modelled good coping strategies, such as making time for self-care or exercise, taking time to step away when they were feeling overwhelmed, verbalizing how they were feeling or finding compassion, then you will learn to do these things too. You have to see it to be it. If they regularly blew up when stressed, you are more likely to find yourself angry when things are difficult. If your parents frowned on emotional expression and never showed their feelings, you are likely to suppress and ignore your emotions. If you had a parent who kept going regardless, you will find it hard to stop. Or if you had a parent who always kept their needs at the bottom of the pile, you are likely to be more self-sacrificing.

Whether you come with a cut, emotional pain or a problem in your life, or you just want to have your experience and views heard, if there is a mismatch between what you experience and what you see or hear reflected back, it is very difficult to make sense of and process your feelings. As a result, it can be difficult to recognize your own needs as valid or prioritize yourself. Just like your parents, you stop taking it seriously.

This can make it harder to be in touch with, and sympathetic to, your own or other people's feelings, and you are more likely to distrust your emotions and tune out from what you're feeling. It makes it difficult to rely on your instincts or understand people. It also puts you at greater risk of future problems, such as mental illness, substance misuse and even cardiac disease. Our start to life can have a big impact.

LEARNING ABOUT OURSELVES

The messages we receive as children also teach us about ourselves and others' expectations of us, building our personal belief system. These ideas and opinions come from those closest to us – parents, teachers, siblings and friends. The things they say and do and their way of relating to us and others lay the foundation for many of our beliefs, values and attitudes. Our parents' views, for obvious reasons, are particularly important. These beliefs tend to be centred around ideas of self-worth, achievement, acceptance and loveability.

When we are children, our thinking has not yet matured, so these ideas are taken as 'the truth'. We tend to accept what we are told and conclude that this is an accurate view of the world. We rarely think that others might be wrong or ill-informed, and we have very limited opportunities to check out these ideas or ask others their opinion.

History, society and culture can also heavily influence us. An example of this is showing emotions. This is still not something everyone feels comfortable with, and there are multiple layers to it: our own personal comfort or discomfort with showing emotion, our family's beliefs – such as seeing emotion as a weakness – and cultural or societal norms (for example, the saying 'boys don't cry'). Added to all this, there is a generational impact – often in older generations, mental health is still more stigmatized.

In short, early messages have a lasting impact. It's as if they are set in concrete, solidly embedded in our brain, making them much harder to change as we internalize the views held about us. These form our self-view and filter into the way we speak and relate to ourselves. Negative messages can hurt all the more when they come from our parents – they see us every day, know us inside out, and their opinion matters. As a child, it's impossible to know that this is one person's view and that this person may not be a good judge.

It can be helpful to reflect on the problematic beliefs we hold about ourselves as a result of our experiences. Disproportionate responses – when our reaction doesn't fit the situation – can provide clues as to what these beliefs are; they can be a link to another time we were made to feel this way. This can happen without us fully realizing, like a key that unlocks an old emotional experience or a particularly sensitive spot, linking us back to the past and making us feel vulnerable.

This is especially true if we have avoided the past and have not dealt with previous issues – they keep coming back to us in the present. Imagine your parents always teased you when you made mistakes. As an adult, making a mistake can cause you the pain of the situation coupled with a link back to the old emotional experience. You might make a mistake and your friend sincerely tries to comfort you, but because of this link, you misread their compassion for sarcasm.

In these situations, it can be helpful to pause and think: *Am I reacting to what is happening currently or to my old beliefs and thoughts?* Most common are feelings of being ignored, not cared for, worthless, not good enough, unappreciated, not seen or heard. If something feels very personal, it's often a sign there might be something else going on. What are your sensitive spots?

REWRITING THE FAMILY SCRIPT

Our experiences can be more predetermined than we realize – we repeat what we know. In psychology, the way a family acts and behaves is often called a family script. Our own experience of being parented can create internal working models of what it is to be a parent, and how we behave and interact with one another in our family.

Replicative scripts are when we repeat consciously or unconsciously these family scripts. We might consciously choose to continue with the family scripts we saw as positive, such as Christmas traditions, but we may also repeat scripts we do not wish to pass on, such as hiding feelings, self-criticism or not communicating with others when we're feeling bad. When we feel stressed, we are more likely to fall into these old patterns, because these were the dominant scripts of how we were parented.

I was incredibly fortunate to have caring, engaged parents, but growing up there was little sympathy for illness, unless you were at death's door. I vividly remember my sister getting measles and my parents moving a TV and a bell into her room so she could ring if she needed anything. This was unheard of in our house, but it did take hallucinating and a sky-high temperature for something so monumental to take place!

Illness only counted if you could prove it. No one stayed off school unless they were *really* ill, and if you did stay off and my parents weren't completely convinced you were ill, you had to spend the day in your bedroom. My friend's mum used to bring her peanut butter on toast in bed – this seemed like utopia to me.

Both my parents worked and my mum was self-employed, which left little leeway for things like illness. I don't think I've ever known my mum take a day off. As a parent myself, I now understand the juggle of work and family and the difficulty in trying to work out what is a true illness and what is a response to not having practised your spellings for the weekly test (something I was frequently guilty of as a child!).

If you weren't taught certain skills in childhood or given a healthy road map of how to cope, you can develop blind spots that you unwittingly pass on to the next generation. But looking at these experiences can be helpful to understand your own reactions. When I first had children, I found that I was not naturally sympathetic to my kids when they were ill. My automatic response (which I feel bad admitting to) was that it felt like an inconvenience. If there wasn't an obvious indicator that they were ill, I would assume they were faking.

Without any experience of sympathy for illness, I had no practise at this response. The inconvenience and mistrust of being ill was something I had grown up with and internalized. I had to actively notice this and learn to respond differently. At first I said the right words even though I didn't always *feel* sympathetic. I also made a decision to believe what I was told, rather than be suspicious. In time, I noticed that I not only said the right thing, but also felt the right response of sympathy and compassion.

While our responses from childhood can operate automatically in our adult lives, we can overcome this by bringing awareness to these things. When we catch the automatic reaction, we have a chance to decide how we want to respond.

HOW TO TAKE THESE IDEAS FORWARD

When we understand this, we can see that how we act and behave is not just what we choose in the moment. Our past influences our present. These experiences feed into how we think about ourselves and how we act and behave in our life now. It is only in observing and paying attention to our reactions that we can truly see how big a part the stories of our own lives play when we interact with others.

It can be illuminating to see the subtle and not-so-subtle impact of our experiences and how this shapes our view. To think about our own family scripts and to see biases and prejudices play out that we were previously unaware of, and how our preconceived ideas and judgements can inform our views.

Looking back at your history is not about blaming anyone; it's about understanding yourself better, questioning whether your beliefs are helping or hindering you and whether they are right. When you really know and understand yourself, you put yourself in a much better position to overcome difficulties in your life. What you come to believe about yourself – except for the more obvious negative messages – is not anyone's fault.

In many cases, though by no means all, your parents were doing what they thought was right for you, based on their own experiences of being parented. Parents are also human, have their own history and are not immune to getting this wrong. Understanding this is another way to distance yourself from their view and acknowledge that they might not be correct.

I'd like you to reflect on the following:

- Were there any significant events or experiences in your childhood that had an impact on you?

- Are there any situations that trigger a disproportionate response in you? What is the feeling in these situations. Do you feel ignored, not cared for, worthless, not good enough, unappreciated, not seen or heard, or something different?
- What were the family scripts you grew up with?
- What messages did you receive as a child about emotions?
- What messages did you receive about self-care?
- What influence if any do you think these messages had on you?
- How do they affect you now?
- What do you want to let go of?

By understanding the different impacts of all these factors, you can again begin to have an awareness of them. It is also so important to have compassion for yourself – you do not choose the family you are born into or your start in life.

Accepting that everyone has these unconscious biases is the next step. Once you're aware of the different beliefs you hold and how behaviours can play out, rather than responding automatically, you have a chance to question them, to decide whether they are right for you now and to make an active choice rather than letting past experiences drive your decisions. Corrective scripts are when we consciously choose to do things differently. They are a way for us to 'correct' the mistakes we felt were made by our parents or previous generations. This is called rewriting the family script.

THE MANY PARTS OF YOU

One way to get to know yourself better is to begin to understand the different parts of your personality that characterize your reactions to events. These parts are often more apparent when you feel stressed or are struggling. In schema therapy they are called 'modes'. The healthy adult mode, the child modes, the parent mode and the coping modes.

The healthy adult mode is the part of you that thinks and behaves in a healthy and compassionate way to yourself. It is the part that is nurturing, kind, rational, responsible and validating. It balances emotion with reason when making decisions, and knows how to set limits and cope in healthy ways. This mode is the best place to be when navigating difficulty or facing life's challenges. In therapy, the aim is to strengthen this mode and develop healthy coping strategies in response to your emotional needs. We'll be looking at how to do this in the next chapter.

The childlike modes – the vulnerable part, the angry part or the more impulsive part – react instinctively to situations. This is a more threat-based response as opposed to the healthy adult mode, which uses logic, thinks more rationally and understands nuance. These younger modes often hold difficult emotions like shame, guilt, sadness, loneliness, fear and anger. We might also have learned problematic ways to manage emotions – the coping modes. Or carry with us critical or punitive voices from childhood which can be demanding of ourselves and others and can contain the negative messages and treatment we may have experienced growing up. These different modes link to different emotions and memories, which is why something from the present can give us a feeling from the past.

When we feel vulnerable or experience strong emotions, our more problematic modes can come to life and it becomes harder to regulate our feelings. It's also common for them to come to the surface when we are busy, tired or low on capacity, as these things push us into the threat zone and make it harder for the healthy adult to bring a more rational approach. We want to listen to all our different parts, but to also be aware that they don't always have our best interests in mind. This is particularly important when we are in a heightened state. When I'm pulled into an angry, childlike mode, I often think of it as a small child stamping their feet. When I do this, I can begin to distance myself from what I'm feeling and slowly bring in a more considered response. I can also begin to think about what that part of me might need. There's always a reason for these reactions. Triggers for me are things like stress, tiredness, feeling unappreciated, being too busy and feeling under pressure. By dealing with these issues, my childlike parts are less reactive. What we require at these times is care and understanding, not self-criticism or demanding we do better. So, we can think about what this childlike response is trying to tell us and what we might need. Where possible, it's important for the healthy adult mode to step in, bringing regulation and stability. I imagine the healthy adult mode, walking hand-in-hand with our more vulnerable parts.

Humans are complex. We might prefer certain parts of ourselves, but it is the combination of each part that makes us who we are. When we acknowledge our different modes, we can begin to identify which part of us is reacting and think about the best way to manage how we are feeling based on this.

Harjeet, one of my clients, named her punitive mode Sergeant Major Harjeet. Sergeant Major Harjeet was demanding, critical and set incredibly high standards for both Harjeet and anyone close to her. It wanted everything to run perfectly and didn't care what it took to achieve this impossible standard. This meant that Harjeet never took care of her needs and often became upset with those around her for not having the same approach.

When she realized how this part operated and how it linked to her father and his expectations when she was younger, it became easier to see it for what it was. She recognized that it had developed to find a way through feeling vulnerable and afraid and to try to regulate things that felt wildly out of her control. But over time it became her approach to everything. She never stopped to think about how she was feeling or what she truly needed.

Externalizing this part and naming it made it easier to see when it was around, and to understand that this was not all of her or how she wanted to be. Instead, it was a bully that sapped any joy from life and made it impossible for her to look after her own needs. It pushed her too hard, made her less compassionate to those she cared about and was never satisfied with anything she did.

This awareness let her look more objectively at her situation. She slowly began to see that Sergeant Major Harjeet told lies and did not have her best interests at heart. Over time, she realized that when she was in Sergeant Major Harjeet mode and became angry or irritable, it was because she felt vulnerable, stressed or anxious. Often the root of this was things in her past or present she hadn't allowed herself to properly look at – something we'll focus on in the next chapter – rather than anyone else.

First came awareness, then a recognition of the impact. In time, Harjeet learned to speak to the different parts of herself. To think why she might be feeling a certain way, to work out what else might be going on and to consider different perspectives. Most importantly, she became more compassionate towards herself, and this also filtered into her relationships with others.

It can be helpful to externalize your different parts and the thoughts they have so you can see them as separate from you, rather than all of you. Just because this part tells you that something is true doesn't mean it is true; thoughts aren't facts. There's always more than one perspective. When these thoughts and feelings come up, think about the different possible explanations there might be. The better you become at seeing these different parts and how they act and behave, the better you will become at making active choices about what you want. Notice what the part is like and what triggers it:

- How does this mode present itself?
- How old is it?
- What is its tone?
- What does it expect of you, from others or from life?
- What situations are you more likely to see it in?
- Can you see it as an image?
- Can you name it?
- Where does this part come from?
- Is it helping you or hindering you?

LOOKING AFTER THE DIFFERENT PARTS OF OURSELVES

When you know your different parts, their personalities and characteristics, you can understand why and when they tend to be around, meaning you can understand yourself better. When you get better at identifying the different parts of yourself in action, you have a chance to think about what else might be going on. Knowing them won't make them disappear, but it will let you tune into yourself and what you might need.

If you do fall into the old modes and patterns, it can be helpful to think afterwards whether the response is giving you what you need. Think about when anger helps and when it hurts. Anger is a natural and usually healthy emotion, but if you become stuck in it, it can be destructive. It might feel good in the moment, a chance to feel powerful or to move you away from feeling vulnerable, but in the long run it isn't solving your problems, it's creating more. If you meet everyone else's needs and never speak up, then you can't look after yourself and you're likely to begin to resent the people you're close to.

When you see these parts in action and step back from them, you have a choice. It can be helpful to pause, think about where this might be coming from and bring in the wider picture of what is going on. Remind yourself that thoughts aren't facts. This lets you make space to be curious about what is going on and reflect. It is also important to find the unmet need within you, such as a need for care, understanding, rest or validation.

Over time, you can use the healthy adult mode, its wisdom, strength and rational approach, to begin to talk to the other parts of yourself and care for them. It's important to look after the different parts of yourself and develop a relationship with them. What are they saying? How can you respond and make them feel better? What do they need? The younger parts don't respond so well to rational argument. I always imagine a real child. What they need is compassion, connection, physical touch or the body-based strategies from the Strategy Toolkit (see page 285) that calm and connect. Every time you choose the healthy adult mode, you are priming new pathways in the brain. The more you do this, the stronger the pathway becomes, so that this choice gets easier and easier to put into action.

I appreciate there is a lot going on to gain awareness of and that this is hard when these things are not all within your direct control. You are influenced by your body and by your childhood experiences, and both of these are at a level of awareness that you are not always conscious of. It takes hard work, but in time you will begin to understand yourself and your reactions. It will positively impact you on so many levels: how you feel about yourself, what you see yourself as capable of, your relationships and self-compassion. Building a good relationship with yourself is the best investment you can make.

KEY TAKEAWAYS

- Your childhood experiences shape your approach to life and provide clues to why you think and act as you do.
- The messages you received as a child taught you about yourself and others' expectations, building your personal belief system.
- Our experiences can be more predetermined than we realize: we repeat what we know.
- Understanding the different parts of your personality that characterize your reactions to events can help you to get to know yourself better.

8

COPING WITH TRAUMA (STEP 4)

When we experience trauma, we do our best to find a way to cope with what has happened to us. In this chapter I'll be looking at common coping strategies that can cause problems, and I will help you move from avoidance to active coping to give you back a sense of control in your life. To move forward, you need to start to face up to what has happened, deal with how you are feeling and manage your situation as best as you can by taking action.

Before we begin this chapter, make sure you have completed steps 1 to 3. You need the basics in place – good nutrition, good hydration and decent sleep – and the coping strategies that work best for you before you move to the next stage.

AVOIDANCE AND DENIAL

You may remember that numbness and denial is one of Horowitz's five phases. When something awful happens, the sheer incomprehensibility can make it difficult to take onboard and can leave you in a state of disbelief. Combine this with the flood of emotions, thoughts and physical sensations, and it's understandable that you try to push it out of your mind and avoid the pain of what's happened.

This type of denial gives you a chance to come to terms with events at a pace that is manageable for you – it's too much to deal with all at once. It allows you to keep functioning while slowly giving space to what's happened so you're not feeling constantly overwhelmed.

Avoidance can be helpful initially, but it becomes a problem when you actively keep yourself in this state. Difficult emotions are experientially important; they let you know that a situation is having a negative effect on you and direct you to change. Excessive avoidance of feelings is associated with higher levels of mental illness and lower quality of life.

Avoidance might block the past and make life more tolerable, but it blocks the future too and shuts out the things that can bring you pleasure or joy, stopping you from being fully alive. It leaves no space to think about how you're feeling. It prevents you from dealing with your problems and can keep you feeling distressed and confused. This stops you processing what's happened and makes it difficult to talk to others and gain support. It can put a strain on your relationships and leave you feeling many of the emotions you're trying to avoid. It also means there's no room for reframing, acceptance, forgiveness and all the things you know will lead not only to you feeling better, but also to growth.

PROBLEMATIC COPING STRATEGIES

When it comes to trauma or emotional upset, many people try and cope by ignoring what's happening, and this is what I see most often in my clinic. I'm going to run through a list of the most common problematic coping strategies. I want you to think about which of these you are using and whether you are trapped in certain coping cycles that are leaving you feeling worse. As you go through this list, it is important to find compassion for yourself and what you're dealing with.

- Self-medicating to anaesthetize your feelings – alcohol, drugs, sex, food, screens, shopping, exercise.
- Distraction – online, news, keeping busy, overwork, never sitting still.
- Denial – consciously or unconsciously avoiding the issue.
- External validation – perfectionism, people-pleasing, social media, overwork, constant busyness.
- Self-sabotage – risky or destructive behaviours such as self-harm, an affair, getting into bad relationships, self-medicating at problematic levels.
- Not taking responsibility for what you can do or seeing yourself as a victim of what has happened, leading to feelings of resentment, blaming, anger or rage.
- Rumination – the stories we tell ourselves, going over what has happened, thinking about what we could have done differently, hindsight, questioning why.
- Avoiding reminders of the event.
- Self-criticism and self-blame.

I'm sure you don't need me to tell you that these coping strategies do not work, and although they may give you a brief reprieve, they have a kickback effect, amplifying your problems. This is because you are treating the symptoms rather than the cause.

This list is not about shame or blame. When you experience trauma, you must find a survival strategy to get through. All these coping strategies make sense in context – they allow you to switch off from the overwhelming sensations in your body and the fearful thoughts you experience after trauma. Many of these strategies have been with you since childhood, which means they can operate without you consciously choosing them.

You're not thinking about whether it is a good choice or not, you're just doing your best to manage the overwhelm you are experiencing. Or if you are stuck in a long-term difficult situation, you might turn to avoidance to escape mentally. Added to which, when you are stressed or overcapacity, you can become more rigid and inflexible, making you cling to these routines even more. You do what is easiest, rather than what is best for you, and it becomes harder to think about doing things differently.

Avoidance makes everything more difficult, using energy and taking up mental space, filling the pan with water. You become more forgetful and your sensitivity is raised so that you are easily tipped over the edge by small things that wouldn't normally bother you. Or you may find that you can just about keep it together at work, but that things catch-up with you at home, boiling over into angry outbursts.

You might be able to outrun your problems to begin with, but they will keep following you until they become impossible to ignore. You then have to ramp up your avoidance strategies in an effort to escape them – more alcohol, sleeping pills or risky behaviours. It's tiring running all the time, and ultimately there's no escape.

In the long term, avoidance can actually increase symptoms and distort the situation. My wonderful colleague Dr Anne Lane compares avoiding emotions to trying to push a beach ball under water. Holding it down takes effort and energy, and when it does get away from you, it bursts out of the water more strongly than before.

AVOIDANCE IN DISGUISE

Avoidance can also show itself in more subtle ways. When you ignore your thoughts and feelings, they do not go away. It's like a game of whac-a-mole; they just pop up in a different place and your reactions to day-to-day things might become disproportionate.

This happens with or without trauma, but due to your reduced capacity, trauma amplifies the effect. When you ignore your emotions, they can become displaced on to something in your daily life or a past memory. For example, getting stuck on minor daily problems that are solvable and within your control, or becoming disproportionately stressed about things you wouldn't normally worry about, rather than allowing the bigger worries to come through. This provides a hook to hang the emotion on.

Anger and rage are another form of hook. They are often a secondary emotion, protecting you from your vulnerable feelings of fear, upset, hurt or frustration. How you are feeling is no longer the issue; other people or things are: if they just got *that* right, or *this* hadn't happened, you'd feel fine. This is another emotional cover-up.

When I'm more stressed, I find this happening in many different ways. I feel more sensitive to the kids making repetitive noises. I can be more irritable with my husband, picking up on things he hasn't done. Or stuck on bigger hooks, like health, worrying that normal tiredness or illness is something more sinister. In my clinic I frequently see distressing hooks showing up as health anxiety, panic disorder or OCD.

Problematic coping strategies – drinking, overeating, self-sabotage – all do the same. Thinking about, doing and regretting these things takes up so much mental space that you stop thinking about the real issues.

When you're stuck, it's hard to see it for what it is – avoidance. Although you don't feel good at the time, in some ways it is a convenient distraction from your real concerns. These displaced emotions tend to have a clear outcome and are often fixable, compared to bigger worries, which are more uncertain and harder to resolve. You're trying to change how you feel internally with an external change, and this gets in the way of looking at how you're actually feeling and doing something about it.

Take a moment to think about what your hooks might be. If you become more aware of your reactions and learn what your hooks are, you can use this to your advantage to gain greater awareness of how you're feeling and what's actually going on inside you. This allows you to make a conscious choice, rather than just reacting. Once you are more aware of these hooks, you can become better at noticing when you get pulled into them, which gives you a chance to do something to look after yourself and the issues that are really troubling you.

THE SECOND ARROW

Thích Nhất Hạnh, known as the father of mindfulness, used the analogy of the second arrow. If you are shot in the arm by an arrow, it hurts a lot. If you are shot in the same place by another arrow, the pain is not twice as bad but ten times. Imagine the first arrow is the difficult time you've been through and the impact it is having on you – physically, mentally, emotionally, economically and socially. The second arrow is your reaction to it. You can't avoid the pain and suffering the first arrow causes. You do, however, have a choice in how you react, and can prevent yourself from getting shot a second time.

You'd hope that once hit by the first arrow, your mind would jump into gear and start supporting you. Sadly, it does the opposite. It tells you it's futile to do anything about it, and entices you with all the things that leave you feeling worse. Problematic coping strategies like self-medicating, self-sabotage, withdrawing, worrying, over-checking are all second arrows, adding to your problems and making them harder to resolve.

The good news is that everything you have done up until this point puts you in the best position to let go of these problematic coping strategies. You have to put new strategies in place before you take the old ones away, otherwise no matter how hard you try, it will not be possible to implement changes. There's a reason that it's hard to let go of these problematic coping strategies; not because you're weak or you're not trying hard enough, but because they serve as a survival strategy to help you through the immediate aftermath of trauma. It's only by changing your approach and bringing in new, healthy coping strategies that you can let the old ones go, turn off autopilot and break the cycle.

You now have a choice. Paying attention to your reaction and doing the things that make you feel better can prevent you from getting shot a second time. It's important to keep in mind the positive choices you can make, even when things are very difficult. It's this we'll be looking at next, so that you can learn to take control and look after yourself and your emotions.

STEP 4: COPING WITH TRAUMA

In this step, I want to help you understand and listen to your emotions and take action where you can. The key to coping well is avoiding the second arrow, and this requires flexibility. Telling yourself you have to cope in a set way or do certain things at certain times turns it from self-care into boot camp. Don't exhaust yourself in an attempt to do everything. Remember, it should feel like an addition to your day. It's good to have a loose structure, but make sure you listen to what you need. If you're exhausted, it's not the day for a long run. These strategies are meant to make you feel better. Give yourself permission to feel, sleep, rest and live alongside overcoming trauma.

Before we move on, I want you to note down the strategies that you have found most helpful so far. Think about which work best for you and the situations in which you have found them most useful. Writing this down gives you something concrete to come back to when you need.

FEELING YOUR WAY THROUGH

Many of us have trouble tolerating our emotions, even pre-trauma. We do our best to avoid uncertainty and are fearful of the discomfort that comes with so called 'negative' emotions. In therapy, people often fear that if they look at these feelings they will be overwhelmed by them; fear of fear can create an anxious cycle, where we begin to fear feeling discomfort. This gives us little experience of regulating our emotions and discovering that we can manage.

The first step to looking after our emotions is simply to allow them, rather than trying to fix them or make them go away. It's understandable that right now we may be feeling a range of emotions – anxiety, upset, hopelessness, anger, resentment or despair. Even when we're living well, there is no avoiding discomfort. Emotions are messages helping us make sense of what is happening. It is right to feel sad in response to loss, to feel anger if we have been wronged, or anxiety if we are worried. This is not something we ever want to lose, as it would make us a machine rather than a person.

I always think feelings are a bit like clouds; they're around for a while before moving on. Although you might prefer what we term 'good' feelings, all feelings are valid, and experiencing the full range of emotions is what makes us human. When you have darker feelings, remember that how you feel does not necessarily reflect how things are. You are not your feelings, and you have a choice about how you react to them. Remind yourself that these feelings are not permanent and that the sun can break through.

It's also important to be careful of creating stories around your feelings. Emotions colour everything with that feeling, so don't just follow them blindly (e.g. I feel bad, so things are bad). When I'm tired, overwhelmed or struggling, I often find myself thinking that I'm getting things wrong. That I need to change the way I work and live. That if I do this, I'll feel fine. In these moments, I'm back to believing that if I just do everything right, I can feel good all the time. But I'm kidding myself that there's a way to avoid these feelings, and by getting caught up in questioning my life, I lose time and energy and always end up feeling worse.

When I recognize that these feelings mean that I'm having a bad day, that I'm tired or finding things hard, the response is completely different. I can acknowledge that I've got a lot going on and it's OK to feel like this. I can remind myself there are always days like this, but they don't last. I can look after myself better. I can seek support from others.

Rather than seeing myself as at fault or to blame in some way, I open up a completely different view that is supportive and nurturing. It might not bring me out of the feeling, but it stops me sinking lower into it and seeing my life in a way that isn't helpful and doesn't match up to the reality of what's going on.

When we stop ourselves from being pulled into creating a story about where our emotions come from, we shorten the life cycle of the emotion and have a chance to see that our feelings pass, just like those clouds. We can also use everything we have learned about our body to understand what it is telling us. Fight-or-flight, freeze, hormones, muscle tension, breathing. When we listen to our body and what it is telling us, we can take care of it in the way it needs.

The aim is to allow feelings and create a space between the feeling and your reaction. When you bring awareness to what's happening, you give yourself a choice. Pausing can give you space to sort through your feelings and choose how you wish to respond, so you can try to do the things that you know will help you, rather than feeling worse. Seeing this choice stops you responding in the old habitual ways.

Every time you manage a difficult situation or difficult feelings, you have a chance to see that you can do it, and this creates new neural pathways in your brain. It's a bit like a path across a field; every time you take this new path, you carve it out more firmly, and in time it becomes easier to take this path over the older one.

TAKE ACTION WHERE YOU CAN

Taking charge of what you can is one of the most important steps, and this shines through in every story. Active coping is the opposite of avoidance, letting you concentrate on doing something about what's happened. This is the final focus for step 4.

Active coping means taking ownership of your situation and choosing how to move forward with a determination to live again. This is particularly important if you are feeling lost or you are in a situation that needs to be changed. Taking action puts you back in control. It's important to do this alongside feeling your way through. If you're too focused on getting everything in place, you may not give enough room to how you're feeling.

The action you take will be individual to you and can take many different forms. Taking action could be addressing any practical problems that need to be solved; making sure you are looking after yourself and doing everything you can to get better; confronting the things you've been avoiding; making a plan of how to move forward; or setting yourself future goals and working towards them.

I hope the stories in this book will provide you with ideas of the different ways you can take charge again. Akemi coped by focusing on her pregnancy and her four-year-old, and thinking about what she would need for the new baby; Sophie left her job, retrained and ultimately moved to Bali; while Naomi (who you'll meet at the end of this book) took an active approach in her treatment: exercising, journalling, eating well and looking after herself, as well as giving herself space to think about what she wanted if she was to die, getting her affairs in order and updating her will. Dealing with the practicalities allowed her to put her fears of death to one side and focus on getting better.

To think about this, ask yourself 'What can I do about my situation?' Note down anything and everything you can think of. Is there anything you've been putting off doing? Are you avoiding going to certain places or doing certain things because of the trauma? Alongside this, write down all you are already doing – for example, listening to and looking after your body, allowing your feelings, reading this book, letting others support you – so you can see all the active ways you are helping your situation.

It can be helpful to take a day-by-day approach and to have a realistic view of what you're facing, rather than being blindly positive. When you think, *What can I do today?*, it opens up possibilities that feel doable. When you take action, you are also engaging with hope. You believe things can be different and that change can happen. It also puts you back in control of your situation, and this helps to regain a sense of control in your life.

RECLAIMING YOUR LIFE

When we go through difficult times, it can close us down, and I often think about how our world shrinks at these times. We want to protect ourselves from ever being hurt again. We might become withdrawn, disconnected, doing only the essentials as everything else feels too hard. We are reluctant to go out, socialize or pick up the phone. We lose interest in the things that used to bring us pleasure and joy. It can be hard to trust others or take risks. When times are really difficult, it can be hard to even get out of bed in the morning.

This approach keeps us in a holding pattern and stops us from re-engaging with life. But we can't just stop living as we wait to come out the other side of trauma. It's important to reclaim our life. To step out of autopilot and simply surviving, and to step back into really living. To tune back into our wants, needs, ideas, hopes and dreams.

I'll be focusing on this in the final chapters, but this is also another part of taking action. It's really important to reintroduce the things that matter to you. Take time for the things you enjoy. It might sound strange, but your normal routines and interactions are part of what makes you feel like you. What can you reintroduce to your week? Do anything small that gives you a sense of normality. It can also be good to book in things to look forward to.

WRITE IT DOWN

Journalling is a great habit to get into and a way to bring everything in this chapter together. It will help you get to know yourself and your emotions and give you space to think about what you can do and the progress you are making.

Writing offers a whole host of benefits. Writing about how you're feeling and problem-focused coping stops emotional suppression, facilitates reflection, lowers psychological distress, improves well-being, helps you to sleep better and is proven to be good for your health. If you're finding it hard to talk to others, writing can be a good alternative. Just 15 minutes a day can make a difference. Studies have shown that expressing a ratio of around 3 to 1 positive to negative emotions can improve well-being and resilience, and that displaying positive emotions more broadly in your life can enhance relationships, improve health, relieve depression and broaden the mind.

I want you to try this out and set aside 15 minutes each day to write – choose the same time each day, as you'll be more likely to stick to it. Make sure that you are in a safe space, where you can step out of your life, as if you're speaking to your own personal therapist. Write about anything that comes into your head – thoughts and feelings, practical steps you want to take, things you're pleased with, steps you've already taken or difficulties you still wish to overcome.

Checking in with how you're doing is also important. Progress happens gradually. Like growing taller, you don't always notice it, especially if you're still reeling from what's happened, but noticing and writing down how far you have come is vital. When you go through trauma, it can leave you feeling that you're not coping or that things can never get better, but this is not the truth. Change is always happening, and although it might not be a straight-line graph, you learn from every step and are never back at the start. It's also helpful to remember that even when things are good, we all have ups and downs. When you look at the full view of what's happening, it will give you a fairer view of where you are.

Reflect on what you've done so far and anything that goes well in your day. You might note down what you're grateful for, compliments, or things that aren't bothering you as much. You could write about your relationships, increased capacity, a good night's sleep or any moments of internal or mental peace. It can be helpful to record the times you feel your best, the practical things you're doing, or what enables you to do the things you need to. You could reflect on all you've managed to cope with or the ways you have noticed yourself coping better. Or it might be how you have managed difficult days, doing things even though it's hard just getting out of bed. It all counts!

When you start to focus on growth, you have a chance to view yourself differently and to see all of yourself again. It will boost your confidence, reminding you of all you are doing and helping you keep track of change. Make sure you reread what you've written so you can really take things in.

In the next section, you'll meet David Richmond CBE. It was a privilege to speak to David and have the honour of hearing his story, which he told with great humility. It is an amazing example of active coping. David's determination meant that he not only kept his leg, he went beyond what was expected. Due to his incredible focus on his rehabilitation, he now walks without a limp, and can swim, cycle and run. He took ownership of his situation, engaged fully in his recovery and didn't dwell on whether it would work or not. He took a step-by-step approach and worked with what he had, rather than what he wished he had.

DAVID'S STORY:
WOUNDED IN BATTLE

I was the commanding officer of the UK Battle Group in Musa Qala, Helmand Province, Afghanistan. It was June 2008, and we had just cleared the Taliban out of a village and had reset ourselves prior to heading into the Green Zone to clear them from there too. We were about to move, and the security patrols had been called back in, but unbeknown to us, one was followed back by four Taliban fighters.

They started firing from around 70 metres away. The mistake they made was they all fired on automatic, which meant only the first shot was accurate from that distance and the rest were all over the place. They only managed to hit one of us, and it was me. The bullet hit my leg and completely shattered my femur.

I had been in Iraq twice and Northern Ireland lots of times, so I knew what the risks were, but I never focused on that or went out on duty thinking it would happen 'today'. It is in your mind that you might get shot or blown up, but you do all that you can to mitigate against that. That's all you can do – it is your job and comes with the turf. That's what the armed forces are for. If there isn't likely to be a firefight, you wouldn't send the army.

After I was hit, I quite stupidly hopped around for a few seconds – my leg was just hanging loose by that point. Another round came right past my right ear and another to my left, so I fell to the ground. I was lying with my head down a slope and my leg up the slope, and because of the weight of my body armour and helmet I couldn't sit up. I was also lying on my first aid kit so couldn't get to that either to do anything about the bleeding.

For a couple of seconds it was utterly painless, and then it became the most agonizing thing I could have ever imagined. I went through the whole tunnel vision thing; everything disappeared into the distance and it became staggeringly painful. A couple of guys crawled out to get me into cover while others returned fire. They grabbed my shoulders and pulled me behind some armoured vehicles. That was even more painful as my leg was just bouncing around, pulled along behind me.

They did some immediate first aid and fashioned a splint out of a stick they had found somewhere – it was much longer than my leg so it stuck out at the end. The consequence of this was that all the guys running around during the firefight were falling over it, pulling the splint and jarring my leg each time.

The doctor appeared and started to do some work on me; most importantly, he gave me a large amount of morphine. Next thing I knew, he'd pulled out a bone saw, and in my increasingly drugged-up state I thought he was going to cut off my leg. As he went down to do it, I closed my eyes, and then all he did was cut off the end of the splint.

My number two, the battery commander, stepped in to take command of the group, and he pretty seamlessly picked up the whole thing. It had been a year of preparation and training to get that group together. We'd prepared a lot for the scenario by investing in our deputies, so it was very gratifying to see it work so well, though emotionally it was hard to be taken away when I thought I should be in command.

I still felt a responsibility to lead the team, even though I couldn't and was about to be flown away; that was one of the toughest aspects of the whole thing.

I was flown back on a helicopter to Camp Bastion, our main base, where I was sedated with ketamine and then taken straight into surgery. I don't remember much from that journey, just flashes as I was going into the hospital.

I came round in the recovery unit. They decided that although there was a lot of damage, they could postpone the decision of whether to take the leg off or not until I was back in the UK. I was flown back to Birmingham the next day – I have a vague recollection of that journey, but not much, as I was on a lot of medication. I do remember announcing my arrival at the hospital by promptly being sick in the ambulance. It turns out I have a bad reaction to morphine.

My family met me there. My wife had had the 'knock on the door' the previous night to say her husband had been injured. My girls, 11 and 13, had grown up with a dad in the military being away and doing exciting stuff. They had just got to the age where they had started realizing what risk that exciting stuff entailed. The schools were brilliant, but it was hard for them.

I remember my younger daughter's face when she first saw me in the hospital bed, looking extremely worse for wear. She was terrified. That is etched in my memory and brought home the impact this would have on everyone around me. It's not just the wounded person's life that gets turned upside down, it totally changes life for everyone else and there is a trauma impact on the wider family too.

It is a proper emotional roller-coaster and your family ride it with you. There are some things you can never get back. I was an active dad who loved going out with the girls on bikes or kicking balls, but for a long period of time I couldn't do that, and by the time I could, they had mostly grown up. It was extremely hard on my wife – for two and a half years she was the only one who could drive, and she had to constantly take me back and forth for surgery and X-rays.

At the beginning, I didn't understand how bad the injury was. I thought I would be up and walking in six months, but it ended up being four years of surgery until I was fully discharged. The option when I got to the UK was 'on or off'. But you only ever get one pair of legs, so I really wanted to try and keep it. If it had come off, it would have been taken off right up at the top of the leg.

At no stage did it cross my mind that the reconstructive surgery was going to fail. Although apparently there was quite a long period of time during which recovery wasn't certain, and if it hadn't worked, they would probably have amputated. The consultant who did the reconstructive surgery said it struck him that I never looked back, only forward to getting better. That was helpful in so many ways, but the downside was I didn't listen to people telling me to slow down, which came back to bite me towards the end of my rehab.

I didn't have any PTSD, fortunately; I've been lucky. There were times when I could picture it all over again, but it tended to be for a purpose. I could have agonized over the day itself, ruminated over should I have done this or that, but I couldn't see the point in looking back. It happened. Don't waste your energy over 'what if?'. I've always been like that. I've seen people who couldn't look forward after something like this and it is hard for them. It can be agonizing.

What's coming tomorrow is important; what happened yesterday has already been. What you can control is how you go forward, especially for something like an injury – the investment you make in your recovery and the effort you put into your rehab. The only person who can do your rehab is you. It also helped to engage with the medical staff and understand the things I needed to do to be well in the longer term.

My philosophy was that it was my leg, my future, so I had to do everything I possibly could. Was I the model student? No – I still went out and had a curry and couple of beers. But I got myself as fit, strong and healthy as I could. When it comes to operations, the stronger you go in, the stronger you come out. It is frustrating, but you need to accept it for what it is and push it as far as you can, sensibly. You need to work with what you've got, not what you wish you had. You can't blame anyone else. I had an amazingly supportive family. My wife was an absolute Trojan during the whole thing.

When I was in Headley Court, the former defence rehabilitation centre, I was conscious that as a patient, I was the senior officer there, and I felt a pressure to show myself as a role model. No one put that pressure on me, but I felt that I had to lead by example, even in a hospital bed. It was at Headley that I began to realize that my recovery was going to take a while. Your journey back from a serious injury is not a linear one, I had one major setback that put me back a year.

The reconstruction required that I have various large things surgically attached to me. In the end I had nine surgeries, with each being a major multi-hour event. Each one took a lot out of me and things didn't always go according to plan. The first surgery took so long that the consultant couldn't do the leg breaks. After two weeks in hospital and another two at Headley

Court waiting for the swelling to reduce, I was readmitted to have my leg broken above and below the wound site. Two weeks after that, I had to go back for an X-ray, which I did every two weeks for a long time. There was good and bad news; the good news was that I grow bone very quickly; the bad news was that the bones had healed over. This meant that when I turned the screws of the Ilizarov fixator, a ring-like brace used to treat damaged bones, nothing happened. So I was readmitted the following weekend to have the breaks done again. The whole experience of having the Ilizarov fixator was painful – turning the screws especially. And the process of having it removed was especially so.

After just under a year, I finally had the fixator removed, and after getting around on my unclad leg for a day, I noticed that my femur had bent. So I had to go back to hospital and go through the whole thing again: having my bone broken, another fixator attached, and a return to turning screws four times a day to straighten it all up again. This set me back by a year. I needed to get myself mentally ready for that one. The finish line kept being moved, which was mentally challenging. The common phrase is that rehab is a marathon not a sprint. But that's not quite right. In a marathon, you've trained for it, you know the course and how long it is; you know where the finish line is. But in rehab, you probably never intended to be there, you don't know the course, and it isn't a set distance; there are lots of unknowns, and that can be mentally as well as physically challenging.

While I was still injured, the army promoted me, so I was made a full colonel. They didn't quite know what to do with me, as I was relatively senior, so in the end they kept giving me jobs. I was made the chief of staff of the Land Warfare Centre, which is a busy job at a big teaching and research institution. I was having to fit all the work around the rehab. I lost a huge amount of weight as my body focused all its effort on my leg, and I was so tired. I thought, 'I am doing my army job, I am trying to be a dad and husband and I am trying to get over this bloody injury – I can't keep on doing this.'

I eventually phoned my boss and said, 'I need to step back from the role, as I am only at work half the time because of my injury and nobody is getting the best of me.' I don't think the army knew how badly injured I was; to be honest, I didn't really know myself. I had to admit to myself that I needed some time to get sorted. I think people around me could see it, but they knew I had to decide for myself. When I made that decision, I felt a huge sense of relief. Looking back, I should have stepped away from work much earlier, and focused on getting better, rather than trying to bring rehab, job and family together.

As I was getting nearer to the end of my leg being fixed, I had to decide whether to leave the army or stay in. I'd joined up to go and do stuff. I either need to be in something or out of it, not hanging around on the fringes. If I wasn't deployable, I would have been hanging on the fringes. I'm sure they would have found something for me to do, but not something I really wanted to do, so I decided to leave. It would have been the easier option to stay, but I believe that the army is a place for fit, young people, not for someone who is essentially holding on to a slot that could go to someone else.

I was the most senior officer to be seriously wounded in Afghanistan, so I got wheeled out to speak at a lot of events and meetings. That also helped me to process it. The more you talk about it and make sense of it, the easier it becomes. The experience I went through now feels part of who I am, although it doesn't define me – that is important. I'm happy to talk about it and help others who are going through similar things.

When I look around the cohort of people I know who were injured in Afghanistan and Iraq, the successful ones since leaving – and I'm measuring success in lots of different ways – have never let it define them. They've used it go on and refocus on something else, whatever that means for them. The ones who have struggled are those who can't detach themselves from what has happened. Although I can understand the difficulty in doing it.

I never considered taking my leg off. It was my leg and I had to take ownership of it. I didn't dwell on whether the operations would work or not. I always placed my faith in the surgeons and staff to do the right thing. I just concentrated on the next achievable step. Sometimes you don't always make that step when you want to. You generally go upwards, but it's not always a smooth climb.

Following my accident, I wanted to play with the girls again, to be active in a sporty way and continue to serve. I managed the first two and chose in the end not to do the third. The reason I can walk around reasonably normally is because I worked really, really hard. There were days when I felt sorry for myself, but I got back on it. I didn't see the benefits of all that hard work immediately, but I do now.

One year after my last surgery – which was an absolute beast – I entered an Ironman triathlon. I needed to prove to myself I could do it. I have no quads on one leg, as they were cut away, but I can still run, just with a bit of a limp. I look back now and think, *What was I thinking!* I'd swum the distance before in training, but I was unprepared for the bike and the run, as I could only do limited training. I gritted it out and pushed myself, somehow, and got to the end. It was a mental marker that showed I was through my recovery. It all adds to the bank of resilience.

After the army, I went straight to Help for Heroes and became the director of recovery services. I was responsible for the four recovery centres. It was great, a brilliant opportunity. At that point, Help for Heroes was transitioning from being a fundraising and grant-giving charity into also being a service delivery charity. I was asked to set up their recovery services and I had a great six years with a superb team. I met some wonderful people, learned an awful lot and had the opportunity to contribute to helping many people when they were going through a tough time. Being wounded is a great leveller – whether you are a general or a private, you are all together in hospital. You form some great relationships with people in hospital and at Headley Court who you probably would never normally have met. You give each other shared support.

After that, I had a portfolio career where I did things that interested me – such as para sport, leadership and veterans' recovery services. Then one day I had a call from Johnny Mercer MP, who asked me if I would be interested in helping him set up the Office for Veterans' Affairs, so I joined the civil service for 18 months to do that. When I left, they asked me if I would be the Independent Veterans Advisor, giving independent advice to ministers. I get out and about around the country, meeting people, hearing from them and working out what works and what doesn't, and feeding that information back to the government. This will come to a natural end at some stage, so we'll see what comes next. I'm not a long-term plan maker; I like to see where life leads and what comes to find me. I never had a life master plan.

I loved my time in the army and would do it all again in a flash. I'd always wanted to do it, right from when I was a little boy. But weirdly I never missed it once I left. I occasionally think about how my life would have been different if I had stayed. I think I had a chance of going up a rank, maybe two. From a different perspective I'm glad I left ten years ago and met those challenges then rather than going through it now.

Headley Court was important in my recovery, as there were always other people around, many in far worse states than me. Sometimes it was hard, it was overwhelming, and I had to take a break from it, but it was fantastic support. What I found as I went through my time at Headley was how differently people are wired. Everyone is shaped uniquely. There is a big difference between an RAF air traffic controller and an army corporal. Everyone comes with different baggage and personalities.

Peter, a good friend of mine, says that injured soldiers who are struggling come with their own combination lock – you don't know what the combination is and neither do they. You need to keep trying different things, and when you find the right sequence, the lights come on. For some it is engaging with sport; for others it might be the arts. But there are common threads in all recoveries that are helpful: taking ownership, accepting what has happened, looking forward rather than backwards, and finding a supportive network.

I still believe that even for those who are struggling the most, you need to help them to help themselves, rather than do it for them. Maybe at the start of the journey you stand very close to them and are more active in your support, but there comes a time when you must let them know they can fly solo. You need to sometimes let people make a decision that might not be in their best interests, because it's their decision; it's their life.

It is harder for the younger ones. By 41, I had kind of worked out who I was. There are some 18-year-olds in military hospital who are badly injured, and they hadn't worked out who they were before injury, so how can they know who they are now? That's a very tough place to come back from. It's no surprise that you have some angry young men and women in these places. You need to give them some space to be angry and support them. It's very easy to disappear into a dark place, and in some ways you need to help people into that place and then help them out again. With support, a lot of young people do recover and recover well. I have amazing admiration for them. We've had several young patients who became athletes for Paralympics GB.

I recognized with ever greater clarity the value of having a strong and supportive family. They are your first line of support. My relationships with my loved ones came out of the experience deeper. You see each other at your weakest, but also at your best, your most caring and most resilient. Don't hesitate to ask people if you think you need help – though sometimes the hardest part is understanding that you do need help, rather than a fear of asking.

I neither wish it had never happened nor am pleased that it did. You make sense of it over time, by talking about it and by helping others who have had similar experiences. It brought one career to an end but it opened up other things. I just accept it. I could never picture myself as a victim. I was a combatant – these things happen.

I've met some brilliant people I never would have met and had some amazing experiences in the last few years, but I can also recognize that I might have done some great things if it had never happened. You are only an accident away from your life changing. It is easy to be glum about life – anyone can do that – but life has a lot to offer, so enjoy it.

MY THOUGHTS

It's easy to see why David must have been such an asset to the army and why his career continues to be a success. I met David thanks to Peter Smith (my brother's father-in-law), who got to know him through his amazing work for Help for Heroes.

David's story illustrates the importance of taking charge of your situation and active coping. His experience shows clearly that when you are able to make an active choice, it has a powerful impact – we can't choose what happens to us, but we can choose how we want to move forward.

Acceptance

Although what happened to David was clearly traumatic, his acceptance of the risks associated with being in the army meant he had a realistic view of his life and the fact that he might be injured. Unlike many of the stories in this book, David's meaning framework included the possibility of trauma.

When a gap was ripped open between the life he had known as an active husband, father and serving officer and his new reality, this clear-sighted meaning framework helped him through the initial phases of trauma more quickly than normal. There was the shock of outcry, but quickly he was on to working through it, without numbness and denial or intrusive re-experiencing. This immediate acceptance meant that he wasn't stuck in the victim role. It can take a long time to get to this point, but David was there from the start.

Don't get shot twice

When I spoke to David, I was struck by his ability not to overthink things. Getting pulled into rumination can be easily done, but avoiding it meant that he didn't get shot by the 'second arrow'. He didn't look back, only forward, and was naturally mindful and focused on the present. His approach shows the importance of taking ownership. This opened up his options, letting him move forward in a meaningful way.

A flexible approach

David's injury and recovery meant he had a constantly changing picture of what was happening. Initially he wasn't fully aware of how bad the injury was, imagining that he would be up and about in six months. Instead it was four years before he was fully discharged. This meant he had to adjust and readjust his expectations of how his life would be. His philosophy gave him a way to manage these changes, making progress much smoother. He let go of what he couldn't control and took firm charge of what he could.

The investment he put into his recovery and the effort he put into rehab gave him the best chance of recovery. Focusing on getting strong, fit and healthy meant he felt in control of his situation. He set himself clear goals, which acted as guiding lights, rather than a fixed plan or rigid timeline; even though he was driven and determined, he kept a flexible approach. David seems to bring this flexible approach to his life more broadly – he likes to see where things lead rather than having a master plan.

Things frequently didn't go to plan for David – the disappointment he must have felt following the bent femur is hard to imagine – yet his approach minimized disappointment and allowed him to weather any difficulties and obstacles without throwing him off course. This amazing mental resilience was rooted in not giving himself binary pass/fail targets for his recovery. This would have put him in a different space mentally each time things didn't go as expected.

I think his step-by-step approach and short-term focus also

really helped as he concentrated on what he could do next, rather than looking too far ahead at the mountain that was ahead of him. Mentally he took it as it came and believed in himself. He knew his capabilities and didn't waver in his self-belief, and this seems to be another key factor in his recovery. In many ways, the Ironman triathlon represented the completion phase of trauma and his recovery. An incredible achievement for anyone, let alone with quads only on one leg.

Too close to see clearly

I think the only cost of such a single-minded focus was that there was no chance for David to stop and catch-up with himself. He was so firmly in coping mode and trying to keep up with work, family and recovery that he didn't have a chance to look up at what was going on with his wider well-being. This is common in trauma. When you're pushed to overcapacity, you don't have the mental space to review how things are going, or whether you need to change your approach. You're just focused on trying to keep up with life. It sometimes takes time to see you need more help.

As David highlighted in his story, for himself and those he worked with, seeing it for yourself is important. Again it comes back to the importance of choice and feeling in control of your life. It needs to be your decision. It can seem obvious in retrospect, but not always at the time.

Letting support in

David took control, but not tight control, which would have been counterproductive. He allowed other people to hold responsibility where appropriate, trusting in the surgeons and the medical staff, allowing support from those who cared about him, especially his wife. He listened and asked for support and advice from those around him. Mentally this gave him more capacity and energy to focus on what he himself could do.

I love the combination lock analogy – finding the right approach for you alongside the common threads in all recoveries: taking ownership, accepting what has happened, looking forwards rather than backwards and finding a supportive network.

Telling your story

While David focused on his recovery, he did not avoid the trauma. Although he didn't have therapy, he talked about being shot and his recovery, speaking at events and meetings and in his work at Help for Heroes, as well as helping others who had had similar experiences. This provided a way to tell his story – a story of redemption, as you'll see in the next chapter. This meant he had different ways to express what had happened and allowed him space to make sense of his experience slowly over time.

Finding a meaningful way forward

David also found a meaningful way forward. He knew that being in the army wasn't enough; he had to be *in* it. He recognized his personality and approach and worked with that, rather than sticking with something he knew was not right for him. His meaning framework for army life meant being active and deployed, and this wasn't possible for him any more. He didn't overthink what leaving the army would mean. He listened to his instincts.

This opened the door to becoming director of recovery services at Help for Heroes, where he could use his skills and his understanding of what it meant to be injured. It was also a meaningful role for him, something I'll look at at the end of this book.

I admire David's ability to not have life pinned down. It has opened up more opportunities for him as a result. Seeing where things lead and enjoying the adventure, rather than having a master plan and being focused on the destination, not only helps in overcoming trauma but is a great approach to life too.

KEY TAKEAWAYS

- Disbelief and denial give you a chance to come to terms with traumatic events at a pace that is manageable for you, but avoidance becomes a problem when you keep yourself in this state.
- When you ignore your thoughts and feelings, they don't go away; they just reappear in a different place.
- The first step to looking after our emotions is simply to allow them.
- Active coping is the opposite of avoidance, letting you concentrate on doing something about what's happened and take charge of your situation.

9

TELLING YOUR STORY (STEP 5)

I n this chapter, we will look at the transformative power of storytelling to bring about positive change. In many ways, this is the most important part of the process; the 'working through' phase of trauma. Telling your story will help you overcome the challenges you have faced, find meaning in what has happened, and make changes so you can live a life that is right for you.

We will revisit the trauma, look at the story of what happened and then work towards creating a meaningful life aligned with your values. In essence, we will rewrite your story.

WHY IS STORYTELLING SO IMPORTANT?

Stories are the fabric of our lives. They are the way we understand and make sense of the world. Cave paintings, Gilgamesh carved on stone pillars, the Bible, Aesop's fables, fairy tales, Shakespeare. Stories brought to life in different forms – words, paintings, dance, song or drama. Stories that capture our attention and pull us into other lives and worlds, handing down learning and knowledge; building intimacy and connection; engaging our curiosity, imagination and emotions. Stories are kept alive through their telling and sharing, passed down through generations and across cultures. A way to entertain, but also to teach and bring insights.

Storytelling is part of our daily life. We are constantly telling and listening to stories in the conversations we have and the anecdotes we relate. They weave our lives together and bring connection. We long for meaning, we question our place in the universe: where we came from, what our purpose is, how we can make a difference and make our lives count. When we look at the sky at night, instead of balls of fire we see Orion the hunter, Draco the dragon and Lepus the hare.

The stories we enjoy the most are not perfect stories where everything goes well. We love stories of struggle, where things go wrong but somehow, against the odds, the hero overcomes their difficulties and rises stronger and wiser. And stories that show us the world in a different way.

Stories remind us how much we have in common. When we get to know someone, we share part of our story with them and ask them to share theirs in return. When we hear a story that resonates, we feel connected, as hearing other people's stories allows us to make sense of our own experiences. Much like when we go through heartbreak and listen to songs that match our situation and mood, we seek out stories that reflect our own lives, as a way to feel less alone. I know that just hearing the stories in this book helped me shape and make sense of mine.

THE STORY OF OUR LIVES

We grow up being told stories; not just our favourite book at bedtime, but the stories of our lives. My kids love hearing the story of their birth, tales from our wider family and funny anecdotes of things that went wrong. (My middle daughter's favourite is the time I sent her to nursery and forgot to take her pyjama bottoms off, so she wore them all day under her skirt.)

It is also important to tell our personal stories. We give meaning to our lives and relationships by 'storying' our experiences. In its simplest form, it's telling someone about your day. It's a way to share thoughts, triumphs and struggles. Every day we weave more into the story of our lives.

The theory of narrative identity developed by Dan McAdams describes how we form our identity by integrating our life experiences into an internalized, evolving story of ourselves, which gives a sense of wholeness and purpose to our lives. It is a combination of our past, present and imagined future all happening together in our mind. Over our lives, we write and constantly rewrite our stories as we experience more and gain more perspective on our past and present.

Our life story isn't just a review of everything that has ever happened to us. Instead, we make narrative choices. We focus on the parts of our personal histories that we want others to know. What it was like growing up, the school we went to, how we met our partner, the job we do, how we spend our time. What led us to make major life choices; the extraordinary events, both good and bad. This creates a story of who we are and what we've done. Our stories do not follow a clearly defined path. There are many arcs, good times and those more difficult, suffering and success. Each story has its highs and lows, heroes and villains, challenges and obstacles to overcome. Each experience teaches us something about the world, our life, ourselves or our relationships.

We add this to our meaning framework, adapting and assimilating to fit with our core beliefs. Bringing things together so the different parts of our life join up and make sense. These are the stories that shape us. When we tell the story of who we are and what has happened to us, we create a coherent narrative that allows us to make sense of our life, giving it a sense of consistency and purpose. This is key to finding meaning – when we believe our lives are meaningful, our stories are defined by growth.

What we choose to focus on will differ. When I think about the stories from my childhood, one stands out. It's the story of when my parents were shoe shopping for my sister, when my mum was heavily pregnant with my brother. I was about three, and we walked past one of those mini carousels in the centre of town. I asked my parents if I could go on it, but they said we didn't have enough time. In the next shop, when they were busy finding shoes for my sister, I went back to the carousel. The police were called and they swept the town centre, eventually finding me having a great time enjoying free rides. The only upset in the story was for the man who ran the carousel, who was apparently put out when the rides didn't get paid for.

The story of what happened lives on far longer than the true experience. When you recall a story, the parts you focus on get bigger and the other parts shrink. In our family, this was told as a funny story that summed up the sort of person I was. Someone strong-minded who gets caught up in new ideas without always thinking things through.

It's a story that gives me a sense of who I am now, but in some families it might have been told in a different way. A story about the trouble I got into, what a naughty child I was, or how much I scared my pregnant mother. It could have been the story of a near miss of something much worse happening, or the horror of a lost child and the police being called. In some families, it might have been a story that didn't get told.

The stories we tell ourselves don't just shape our personalities, they become intrinsic to our self-identity, letting us understand how previous experiences have shaped us. By making sense of our past, we can take more control of our future. Importantly, we all have the power to shape our story to live with more meaning and purpose.

TRAUMA

When we experience trauma, it shatters our fundamental assumptions and disrupts our story. This challenges our existing belief system, tearing up our mental map and bringing us face to face with a different reality that pushes us into that unsettling in-between place. Working through it and growing from trauma means rebuilding the framework and creating a new set of beliefs about life.

Stories can become a way of coping and creating shape out of the mess of trauma. It is through storytelling that we can ultimately make sense of our experience, piece together what has happened to us and gain greater clarity.

Stories empower us to master moments when we feel out of control, so that we can update our beliefs and close the gap between what we thought life was and what we now know it to be. Putting our experience into words lets us gain some distance from it. It lets us process the memories, feelings and thoughts connected to what happened, re-evaluate and gain new insights.

Thinking about the details of what has happened puts you in the best position for growth. It is this that allows you to begin to make sense of it and piece things back together in a new way. We need to look at our situation and acknowledge the gap it has created between the life we thought we knew (and all the expectations that ran alongside this) and the reality of how life is now. It is only when we look at all the shattered pieces on the ground that we can begin to work out where we stand.

This is the beginnings of 'rebuilding the house'. It's a challenging approach, but it leads to significant positive results. As much as we might want to, we can't jump straight to healing; we have to go through the pain. We have to reflect on what has happened and why we feel this way so we can address the feelings and release the pain and emotion from the situation. When we acknowledge and feel our distress, we also create space for growth. As we put things back together, it becomes possible to close the gap, moving us out of the unsettling in-between and letting us come to a new understanding about our life. This is post-traumatic growth.

Writing about the experience or talking with supportive friends helps us to update our old ideas about ourselves and build a new framework of meaning. This is something we see in all the stories in this book. We can mourn our losses, seek new perspective, step out of destructive emotions, think about blame more objectively, correct mistaken perceptions and find new insights.

Together we will do this in two parts. First we need to write the story of what happened to us. Then we can rebuild. The first story we tell about an experience is often different to the final one we settle on. It's only when we have space from it that we can update it. Once we have been through what happened to us, we can start to find a way to revise our old views of life to fit with our current reality.

WHY IS IT SO DIFFICULT TO TELL THE STORY OF WHAT HAPPENED?

Our brain has two sides, and although they look alike, there is a huge difference in how they process information. The left brain is rational and logical. It thinks in words and helps with sequencing, linear thinking, maths and facts. Our right brain is more visual and intuitive. It helps with imagination, intuition, holistic thinking and creativity, and communicates through facial expressions and body language.

When we experience something, the left brain, with its preference for facts and logic, explains it in words. The right brain carries the feelings of an experience. It stores memories of sound, touch, smell and taste, and the emotions they evoke. It reacts automatically to non-verbal cues, such as voices or music, to uncover deeper feelings within us.

Sadly, we remember insults and upsets most vividly. Our evolved threat focus and the adrenaline we feel at the time imprints these incidents in our mind. To show you what I mean, I want you to take a moment to think about something good that happened to you: maybe you completed a project, someone gave you a compliment, or you reached a goal. How long did you think about it for? How much did you go over it in your head? How long were you in the feeling? Now I want you to think about something difficult or bad that happened to you: something hurtful someone said, or something you felt you did wrong or could have done better. I'm guessing you spent longer on the negative stuff. This is a really simple way to see how we think about and attend to information.

Our memory of the event is also influenced by how personally meaningful it was and how emotional we felt at the time. We all have memories associated with particular people, songs, smells or places. If we think back to our mental maps, we are also more likely to remember things that fall outside of these maps. They capture our attention as they don't neatly fit what we expect.

Normally the left and right sides of the brain work together to filter and process information and store memories. When we experience something painful, scary or disappointing, however, we are faced with an overwhelming overload of information that doesn't fit into our meaning map. Thoughts, images, sounds, emotions and physical sensations flood the right brain.

When this happens, we are pushed into threat mode, and the left side of the brain can become deactivated, shutting down the structures concerned with higher-order thinking, memory storage and language. Often people question why they did things in a certain way. 'I wish I'd said…' 'Why didn't I do…' They didn't have a chance to respond as they normally would, as their brain was unable to function in its usual way.

With the left side of our brain shut down, we cannot put things in a logical sequence or translate what we are feeling into words. As a result, we often do not have a full memory of what happened, making it difficult to talk about coherently. The memories are not filed away as they normally would be. Instead, they remain in an active state, leaving us on high alert. The threat system doesn't shut off once the danger passes, so we can remain stuck in this state of high arousal.

When something scary happens, we retain an intense memory of the event for a long time, but because the memory of what has happened is not properly filed away, it is easily triggered by any reminders. Memory triggers can be outside conscious awareness and might not even be verbal; images, a certain song or smells can be particularly potent.

LAYING DOWN THE MEMORY

To process the trauma, we need to bring the left hemisphere back into action. One of the best ways to do this is to retell the story of the frightening or painful experience. By telling our story, we can use our left brain to understand what's going on – put things in order and name the overwhelming right-brain feelings so we can deal with them effectively. This links up the two halves of the brain and allows the memory to become integrated. We can then begin to re-author our story.

When a memory is not fully accessible, the mind is unable to change it, but as soon as we tell our story, particularly if it is told repeatedly, giving words to our frightening and painful experiences, we can integrate the left brain and right brain and come to terms with what has happened. Telling the story and feeling the emotions connected to the event makes it much less frightening and painful.

In my psychology training, this idea was explained to us using the stinging nettles metaphor. Imagine if someone throws you a duvet full of stinging nettles and shouts, 'Quickly, put it away!' The duvet hurts to touch with all the nettles in it. You might try to quickly shove it into the wardrobe and close the doors, but because it's been jammed in, the doors do not close completely and you have to push against them to keep the duvet inside. As soon as you try to get on with other things, the duvet pops out, stinging you all over again.

Traumatic memories are like the duvet, painful to handle, and so we try to avoid them. This means that they are not stored in the same way as other memories, and can pop up in our minds when we don't want them to. Avoidance may work for a while, but often the memories intrude into our consciousness again just as we begin to relax.

We need to take the duvet out and give it a good shake to get all the stinging nettles out. Doing this might hurt a bit, and we might need to get someone to help us. We can then fold the duvet up and make room in the wardrobe so we can place it carefully on the shelf. This will ensure it stays put.

When we tell our trauma story, we are shaking out the duvet and folding it back together neatly so we can put it away. Traumatic memories need to be processed. We need to talk through what happened, have a chance to feel the emotions connected to it and find a way to adjust our view of the world so we can fit the event into our meaning framework. Thinking the memory through enables it to be processed and stored with other memories so that it stays put. We can then choose when we want to look at it without being in fear of it popping up unexpectedly.

REVISITING THE TRAUMA

In therapy, when I explain that we need to revisit the trauma to move forward, a common reaction is shock. Many people fear opening up about how they are feeling; they worry the negative emotions will swallow them up and they will never get back to feeling good again. Every time, they find the reverse is true. They arrive feeling heavy with all they're carrying and leave feeling lighter. It might seem counter-intuitive, but looking at difficult feelings really is the best way to allow them to pass. Something I hope you have already begun to see in smaller ways with the exercises in Chapter 8.

Retelling the story of what has happened puts it outside of your head and brings it into focus so that you can do something about it. It's like the monster under the bed. Better to look at it, even in the most difficult situations. At least then you know what you're dealing with. When you avoid what's happened, there is no chance to rebuild, and you can be left stuck in how you feel and how you are looking at things. You're so close to it that you don't see it properly any more. It is only by starting to write things down that you can step back and gain a new view of what's happened, think about a different perspective and recognize how you've coped and what you might have learned.

Looking at what has happened, listening to how you're feeling and expressing the emotions connected to it lets you process your experience more quickly and puts you in a position from which you can take action. Symptoms reduce and growth occurs, something you will have seen in all the stories in this book.

When you feel distressed, opening up is a much better way to manage feelings than closing down. It is a way to actively deal with the problem, remind yourself of your ability to manage, and build a new understanding of what life looks like. It's also important to remember that feeling emotions after a difficult experience is a sign that you are human; a strength rather than a weakness.

Dr David Spiegel at Stanford University calls this 'supportive-expressive therapy'. He encouraged breast cancer patients to feel and express their thoughts and feelings, whatever they might be – death, loss of breasts or hair, harrowing experiences. He found that speaking openly and frankly about these difficult topics made them less scary, and that those who took part in the group showed improved mood, decreased anxiety, reduced physical pain and fewer symptoms of traumatic stress.

Use the idea of supportive-expressive therapy when you write your story in the next section. It is only by facing up to what has happened that you will find a way to make sense of it and a new reality can take shape. Doing this does not mean that you will always have your emotions under control – no one does. Your emotions want to communicate a message to you; they are there to help you rather than harm you. But it will stop the thoughts catching up with you when you don't want them to, in the middle of the night, or when you stop to sit down for the evening.

As you write your story, be careful not to be pulled into rumination, replaying what happened over and over in your mind. Rumination can make you believe that events could have been different or that things never change. That nothing ever works out or bad things will always happen to you. It moves you from a specific issue that you can look at and do something about to a problem with your life that feels impossible to overcome, and this type of thinking can become a self-fulfilling prophecy. The focus of attention shifts to all that's wrong in your life, and you are more likely to engage in problematic coping strategies. No rumination is good, but it's worse when you negatively evaluate your emotions and are self-critical and judgemental of how you're feeling.

This type of thinking will not help you to process what happened. It might feel like you're trying to work things out, but while these are all understandable thoughts, you have to be careful of getting stuck in them, as they are questions that do not have an answer. This type of analysis has a negative effect on mood, increases negative thinking and is a predisposing factor to depression. Rather than helping you work things out, it impairs problem-solving, saps motivation and makes it very difficult for you to enjoy your life. Research finds that rumination is one of the critical differences between how happy and unhappy people construe themselves and their lives.

You can't change what has happened, but you can help yourself navigate it by giving yourself space to process it and decide how you wish to move forwards. This will leave you with so much more capacity for the present, with more energy and clarity to function in your day-to-day life.

STEP 5: TELLING YOUR STORY

It's now time to take the next step and tell your story. Finding a way to put your experience into words is transformative. It allows you to take back control of it and to confront the reality of what has happened. It is a chance to see the past differently, so that in time, you will be less negatively impacted by your trauma and more comfortable in your life.

To do this, I want you to write your story down. Before you start, set up your space so you feel you are in a safe and supportive environment. Make sure you are comfortable, with a cushion or blanket, a drink, anything that makes you feel relaxed. Try and find somewhere quiet where you won't be interrupted. It is important that you are feeling calm and grounded in the present. It can also be helpful to let someone know what you are doing so that you can check in with them when you are finished.

Often when I do this in therapy, people tell me that they feel worse before they feel better. It can be painful writing about these things. In studies, despite participants crying or being deeply upset by the experience, the overwhelming majority reported that the writing experience was valuable and meaningful. It is shown to produce long-term improvements in mood and well-being, and is also associated with significant reductions in distress. If you don't want to write things down, find another way that works for you. It could be talking it through with a friend or therapist. Even recording your thoughts on an audio device is shown to make a difference. This is also a point in your journey to think about therapy as an additional support. I know personally that going through these steps with a therapist made a huge difference to me.

How to Write Your Story

When you feel ready, I want you to write down what happened. Starting before the trauma and ending when things felt safe again. You are in charge of telling your story. Move at your own speed and stop if you need to. You are in control of this process; do it in the way that feels best to you. As you tell the story, it's important to find compassion for yourself. This was not your fault. You were doing your best in an awful situation.

We know this exercise works best if you write it in the first person, as if it's happening to you now, a bit like the stories in this book. If you find it too difficult to tell the story first person, try writing about your experiences as if you are telling someone else's story. This can be a way to give you some distance from what's happened and let you see it though different eyes.

Unpack what happened and recount the key scenes. Give the story a beginning, a middle and an end. Think about the important moments. What were the highs and lows? What was your understanding of what happened? Include the worst parts and what they meant to you. Add as much detail as you can and try and make it clear and easy to follow. The more coherent your story is, the better the outcome will be.

Try to use words that express causality and insight in order to make sense of what has happened. Think about your personal beliefs and values and the impact on these. What is the story's central theme and what was the turning point?

As you go back through the events, bring in all your senses. It can be helpful to think it through as if you are watching a film of what happened. If someone else went through those things, what might they feel? As you think about what happened, try to understand the significance of your experience. Allow yourself to feel the emotions connected to what happened – pain, anger, doubt, disappointment, grief. It is only as you do this that you can move forward to the life you want.

As you write, don't ignore disappointments or let them take over the narrative. It's important to acknowledge and accept what's happened. This allows you to process the event, letting your mood pass naturally and freeing you to move forward. It teaches you that emotions aren't the enemy and that bad feelings aren't permanent. If there are certain things that bring up strong emotions, think about doing these sections with someone else or getting some additional help. Try to work out what it is about these parts that makes them so difficult to look at. It often links to feelings of blame, shame, guilt, anger or resentment.

When you have finished writing, check in with the person you talked to about doing this, and then go and do something to look after yourself or that makes you feel cared for. Have a break from thinking about your story before you come back to it and tackle the next chapter.

KEY TAKEAWAYS

- Telling your story will help you overcome the challenges you have faced, find meaning in what has happened, and make changes so you can live a life that is right for you.
- The stories we tell ourselves become intrinsic to our self-identity, letting us understand how previous experiences have shaped us.
- Stories can help us create shape out of the mess of trauma, piecing together what has happened to us so that we gain greater clarity.
- Retelling the story of what has happened puts it outside of your head and brings it into focus so that you can do something about it.
- Giving words to our frightening and painful experiences allows us to come to terms with what has happened. When we tell our story we link up the left brain and right brain and this allows the memory to become integrated.

10

GRIEVING, LETTING GO AND ACCEPTING (STEP 6)

Grieving, letting go and accepting is the next step to overcoming your trauma. It is important to grieve for your losses before it is possible to make space for what you have gained. Growth occurs as a result of the struggle with trauma. If you think about it, that makes sense, as trauma forces you to confront how you live your life, what you thought you knew and the beliefs you want to hold on to. It's important to acknowledge this struggle and the emotions that can arise during this process, and to validate your feelings as you navigate the stages of grief. It is then possible to move forward in the way that is best for you.

When trauma first happens, it can leave you locked into negative emotional states. Writing your story of what's happened might bring up these feelings again. It can be easy to hold on to resentment, hold grudges or even seek retribution, especially if someone else is involved, but while this is a very normal and human reaction, research shows that holding on to resentment and hurt has a negative effect on mental health and can contribute to poor physical health too.

A study by Charlotte Witvliet and colleagues involved interviewing 71 students, while monitoring their heart rate, blood pressure and sympathetic nervous system activity. The students were asked to call to mind someone in their life who had mistreated or offended them and to imagine both what it would be like to forgive this person and what it would be like to harbour a grudge. When imagining harbouring unforgivingness, the participants felt stronger negative emotions and experienced higher heart rate, blood pressure and sympathetic nervous system activity than when imagining offering forgiveness.

In follow-up studies, those who were unable to let go even reported higher rates of heart disease, cardiac arrest, high blood pressure, stomach ulcers, arthritis, back problems, headaches and chronic pain. The physiological response and agitation experienced seems to have a corrosive effect on health over time.

It is only when you free yourself from these destructive emotions that you can move on to updating your story. To do this, you need to bring these feelings out into the light so you can begin to examine them and see if they are helping or hindering recovery. It is of course important to allow these feelings and to express them, but if you become stuck in them, they can imprison you, robbing you of your life and keeping you forever in the past. It doesn't matter that you are now in a different place and time, no longer facing these threats; your mind is still replaying them, going over and over what has happened.

Flashes of these thoughts can come into your head unexpectedly, or you might purposely find yourself running over them. Your body responds to what is in your mind, so you feel a visceral response, hurt physically by the pain again. The stories you tell yourself can exacerbate the problem. You can become stuck wishing you could go back in time to life as it was before.

Not just the specifics of the situation or a wish to have done things differently, but your naive understanding of a life that was safer, where things wouldn't go wrong.

Wishing you could return to how things were is understandable, but it holds you back. Remember, don't believe everything you think. Shame and guilt can trick you. Be careful of 'should' or 'shouldn't'. In the moment, you are just reacting to what has happened – there's no choice in what you did or didn't do. Hindsight bias can be cruel, telling you that you could have predicted events, but no one can foresee every eventuality and outcome and we are programmed to trust. If you keep trying to get away from what's happened or change it, you're going to wear yourself out. Really question who these feelings are hurting the most.

Trauma leaves an indelible mark on you and changes your life. Things can never be the same again. When you try to go back, that's when you get stuck. You can't escape adversity; what you must do instead is confront your experiences and learn from them. As Akemi said in her story, once she'd gone through the process of grieving what she'd lost, she could then really focus on how much she had gained and how her life would be in future.

REDEMPTION AND CONTAMINATION STORIES

Writing down your story is the first step. You should now have a coherent narrative, and this will have already made a difference, allowing you to lay it down more firmly in your mind. In this next section, I want to look in more detail at your story. Reflection lets you unpack what has happened, refine your thoughts, evaluate your capabilities and increase your coping capacity.

Stories can be classified into two types – contamination stories and redemption stories. Redemption stories emphasize hope.

They have a sense that all you have been through has brought you to a better place. Even though you have experienced pain, you have learned more about yourself and emerged stronger, with a focus on what you have, rather than what you have lost. These stories are associated with long-term positive mental health and life satisfaction.

Contamination stories are when people interpret their lives as going from good to bad. They are tinged with regret. These stories emphasize a downturn and can leave you feeling stuck. They are often coloured by anger and resentment; you see yourself as a victim without hope of a different or better future. David noticed and talked about this in his story – the people who struggled most after serious injury were those who could not detach themselves from what had happened.

The stories in this book could have been contamination stories of how unrelenting life is or of things falling apart, but instead they are stories of strength, resilience, love and learning. Rather than becoming a single mother, Akemi and her boys became the three musketeers. Naomi (who you'll meet later) could have focused on the unfairness of a double cancer diagnosis, but instead saw it as a lesson to concentrate on what is important to her with a renewed determination to live life.

So how do we end up with a redemptive story rather than a story of contamination? It's our interpretation of what has happened that forms our sense of who we are, how we became this way, what we're capable of and what we want from life. What the experience means to us is key to our response. How we appraise an event can be different, as we saw for Jess and Finn. It's the subjective appraisal that is most important.

Essentially this is your choice. You are in control of your narrative and how you see yourself. You need to be aware of your story and think about how you wish to tell it. You can't change what has happened. The facts are the facts; you're not making up a story or conjuring up a positive spin. But by really looking at your experience and what it tells you about yourself, you can shape, strengthen or challenge your opinions and values. I hope you can already see that just getting through this and dealing with what is happening to you shows great strength. I'm sure that before all this, you never thought you would be capable of going through something so difficult.

LETTING GO

When we face challenges, trauma or obstacles in life, changing our story can feel difficult. When our losses are great, how do we find positive meaning from the experience? It can feel difficult or even wrong to acknowledge any beneficial changes.

Letting go helps you avoid getting lost in negative feelings. It doesn't mean forgetting or ignoring what has happened – it is important to acknowledge what you have been through – but it allows you to focus on the present and the future, rather than staying imprisoned in the past.

Negative emotions are difficult to get over, but you need to give yourself permission to move forward. This means recognizing that these emotions are having a detrimental effect on your life and your health. There is nothing you can do about the past. You cannot change what has happened. There's no going back to how things were. It is only when you acknowledge this that you can move forward. When you look at what has happened to you, you have a chance to process it, to acknowledge it, and this allows you to start to let go.

Edith Eger expresses this beautifully: 'When we don't allow ourselves to grieve our losses, wounds and disappointments, we are doomed to keep reliving them. Freedom lies in learning to embrace what happened.'

Edith Eger's book, *The Choice*, is her story of surviving the Holocaust, and despite the unbelievable horrors of that time and all she endured, it is a story filled with hope, showing that we can choose how we wish to move forward even after the darkest of times. It is incredibly humbling, thought-provoking, and a wonderful reminder of what we're capable of as humans. She poignantly describes how what happened to her can never be forgotten or changed, 'But over time I learned that I can choose how to respond to the past. I can be miserable, or I can be hopeful – I can be depressed, or I can be happy. We always have that choice, that opportunity for control.'

You will always be connected to the things in your life that have hurt you, but when you start to manage their effects, you leave space for growth. Seeing gains in what has happened is in no way minimizing what you have been through or how much you have struggled, but how you shape your story affects you. When you let go, it doesn't change the past, but it can change how you feel in the present and it can change your future – it's important to see this as something for you.

BEREAVEMENT

If you've experienced loss, it can be hard to think about yourself or the future. You might even feel survivor's guilt. But by living your life and looking after yourself, you are not forgetting the person you've lost. Imagine what they might want for you now. Or what you would want for them if it was the other way round. What did you learn from that person that you can bring into your life in honour of them? How can you keep that person with you while living your life. Letting go doesn't mean letting go of them. Instead, it's a way to keep them with you without always feeling sad. Like Finn knowing what his mum would say, or Jess making the most of life like her mum did.

Think about the feelings the trauma brought up and what they mean. Perhaps you feel you can't trust others, that nothing is certain, that life is unfair or that no one cares about you. Identifying these feelings is a way to understand your reaction, and it lets you look at how best to soothe and care for yourself. Find a way to let the feelings out and mourn what you have lost. Do what feels right to you. You might feel you need to cry or shout. You could write a letter that you don't send to get all the feelings down, or express yourself physically by punching a cushion or going for a run. Trauma moves us away from connection and comfort, and it's important we move ourselves back.

It is also important to remember that anger tends to be a secondary emotion and can be easier to express than grief. If you can, try to look behind the anger and see what the primary emotion is. Give yourself space to understand why you are feeling like this and to really acknowledge what you have gone through. Finally, let yourself see how far you have come since this happened and what you are trying to do to put it right – reading this book, for example, or working hard to put your life back together again.

Letting go is recognizing that you cannot change the past. You can't bring someone back. You can't go back to a time of naivety or innocence. Holding on to negative emotions will not bring those things back or reunite you with someone you have lost. You cannot change what has happened, but you can change your reaction and allow yourself to look forward in a different way. Rather than dwelling on the past, you can find a way back to hope and think about what you want now.

You have lost enough valuable time and energy to trauma.

Rather than fight what life throws at you, it is time to allow yourself to let go and move beyond the hurt. Try to use the emotional pain you are experiencing as motivation to think about letting it go. Sometimes we move to a place of letting go naturally, but other times it can take thought and effort. Ask yourself:

- Is this story serving me?
- Who are these feelings hurting the most?
- How would I see this if it was a friend?
- Do I want to hold on to this?
- Is there a way I can let go of it?

Giving up on the quest and responsibility to change what has happened breaks the ties that bind you to the past. Letting go allows you to stop looking back and to be present in your life. It is a chance to move from the gap of all that didn't happen, what was unfair or what you didn't get to the gain of what you do have. Being in the gap makes you a victim of your past. You have a choice: you can focus on the gap or on the gain.

It can also be helpful to update your story. When you went through the trauma, you might have felt scared, unable to cope; maybe you felt your life was at risk or you could have died. Updating means telling yourself that you are safe now. That you are alive and that the future is still there ahead of you with any number of paths you can follow.

Forgiveness can also be something to think about at this stage, but only when you feel ready. This could be forgiving others involved, or it might be forgiving yourself. Forgiving others isn't something that can be forced. There is no way to forgive until you feel ready, and you certainly don't owe anyone your forgiveness, but when the time is right, it can be helpful to start to think about things from their perspective. Remember, many perpetrators were once victims themselves. There's always context to what happens.

In Desmond Tutu's words: 'When I talk of forgiveness I mean the belief that you can come out of the other side...a better person than the one being consumed by anger and hatred. Remaining in that state locks you into victimhood, making you almost dependent on the perpetrator. If you can find it in yourself to forgive then you are no longer chained to the perpetrator. You can move on.'

He describes how the only path to recovery is to forgive: 'Until we can forgive, we remain locked in our pain and locked out of the possibility of experiencing healing and freedom, locked out of the possibility of being at peace.' This does not mean you condone what has happened, but it is another way to free yourself from the past, allowing you to move forward with your life.

ACCEPTANCE

The final part of the grieving process and letting go is to find a way to acceptance, something that shines through in Peter's story, which you will read next. To move forward, you need to accept what has happened and the reality of how life is now. Accepting what is rather than how you believe things should be allows you to complete step 6.

The serenity prayer that is used at Alcoholics Anonymous (AA) brilliantly sums this up: 'Grant me the serenity to accept the things I cannot change, the courage to change the things I can, and the wisdom to know the difference.'

Acceptance does not mean you feel glad about what happened to you. It just means accepting it, no longer fighting against it. Recognizing that this is how life works, not that it was something you did wrong or that could have been avoided. Life is fragile, but that's what makes it so special and important too. The one choice you do not have is rewinding back to a time when it didn't happen, but beyond that, your choices are infinite. How you approach life now is up to you.

Some people go beyond just accepting what happened to them. They feel it made them better human beings than they would have been without it. It made them wiser, and inspired them to take the risk of really living and being fully alive.

When we recognize what it means to be human, that it is human to suffer, it takes away shame and blame and connects us to others. When we tell our story, we hear from others about their experiences. We know we are not alone. That it is not our fault; sadly, this is how the world works.

It's important to take control of what we can but to let go of what we can't. It means riding the wave of life and recognizing that we can't be completely responsible for what happens. If we try to hold on to life too tightly, in a funny way it leaves us feeling less in control. It's only when we step back and let go of the wish to fix and control that we see everything is OK and will keep being OK even without us. Change is part of life.

Acceptance means allowing life to take its course. To recognize that although things will never be perfect, when you let go of your expectations, you will no longer be constantly disappointed. You will be free to experience life for what it is and appreciate it.

Letting go, forgiveness and acceptance is not an easy pathway; in fact, I think it is one of the hardest things I am asking you to do in this book. It's normal to move backwards and forwards on the path, but when you manage to get to this point, it's like finding freedom again.

The past will aways be with you, but you can learn to be less tuned into it. You can also channel what's happened into a different future, focusing on how you can change and allowing you to take responsibility for how you live in the aftermath, rather than blaming yourself for your fate. We'll be looking at this next.

For Peter, who you'll meet in the next section, finding a way to tell his story, looking back and coming to terms with his past was key to overcoming his addiction, alongside finding a purpose that fitted with his values. It was difficult to match up all he had been through with the unassuming man who sat before me telling his story. Yet it is incredible that he has managed to overcome so much. I was struck by Peter's ability to accept what had happened and use it to help others by being a sponsor in AA and setting up Peter Hutt Counselling.

PETER'S STORY: FINDING YOURSELF AFTER ADDICTION

I've been sober for ten years. I'm 57 now, so that represents the longest period of time without a drink I've ever had, as I'd already tried alcohol by the age of ten. It was a long time coming, but I have grown up and finally taken responsibility for myself. My life has been transformed as a result.

Like many alcoholics, my childhood was difficult. There was no great trauma but a string of problems that led to me having a feeling of not being quite good enough and of lacking a sense of belonging. I also spent a long time fearing responsibility and actively trying to avoid it. In essence, I didn't know how to *do* life.

I was the youngest of five, with three older brothers and an adopted sister. I was a mistake, and although my mother said I was the best mistake she ever made, the word I always remembered was 'mistake'. My parents were very academic and high achievers, in senior positions in universities and research companies. They worked long hours and valued the work they did. My dad was a volatile man who suffered from anxiety. He took Ativan, a benzodiazepine, for many years, which obviously wouldn't be allowed now. He was almost certainly thoroughly addicted. Within the house, what he said went. He wasn't physically violent, but I was very scared of him.

My mother did her best – they both did, I suppose – though I never felt very loved or really part of the family. I was never affirmed as being worthwhile or 'good'. I was very caring and sensitive. I remember crying quite a lot – my family nickname was 'Blubber'. It took me a long time to discover that part of myself again, but now caring is central to my whole life.

Like my older siblings, I was sent to boarding school. I was moved up a year as I had been excelling at my previous school. I think that was probably a mistake. I went from top of the class to being average and ended up not really trying or putting in the effort that was required. I was also one of the poorer kids, who didn't have the Levi jeans or the Kickers shoes. It seems silly now, but I resented that. It fed into this idea that I was not good enough.

By 15, I was drinking quite heavily, and by my final years of school, I was in the pub several nights a week. My study room had a load of drink inside and I had a pyramid of beer bottles in the window of my room. I liked strong English beers, anything with a higher alcohol level. Even then the standard beers didn't do it for me – I was already drinking to get drunk. Amazingly, my drinking was never mentioned by the school and I was never pulled up on it. I was once caught sneaking back into school on the way back from the pub, and the only consequence was that got I 'gated', a punishment that meant I wasn't allowed to leave the school for two weeks. To be honest, I think this is shocking as it must have been obvious that my drinking was getting out of control.

I escaped with decent grades. Nowhere near as good as they could have been, but as good as I could manage without doing any work. I was good at sport, so all my time was spent on the tennis court or the football pitch – whatever was available. I was always looking for that sense of belonging, and sport was the best way for me to get it at that age.

By the time I got to my late teens, my drinking was getting worse and I did very poorly in my exams. I was spending more than I could afford on booze and started stealing from other students and from my parents. It was my first addiction. I knew I would get caught but I didn't really care.

When I left school, I had no idea what I wanted to do. I was very lost. My parents tried hard to help me find a path, but I resisted. I managed to get accepted by a couple of universities to do sports science and maths, but I didn't take up the offers. I just didn't want to study any more and be in a school environment, I wanted to take my chances in the outside world. I could shine in the workplace because I had a good education and the right accent, which was important back then. I would take jobs I could manage easily, but every time responsibility came along, I would run away and find something else instead. When I was 18, I'd inherited some money, which meant I didn't have to find a secure job. I had 50 different jobs between the age of 18 and 47, more than one a year.

I'd always had an idea that I'd be successful by 30. By then I'd got married, had two kids, bought a semi-detached house and a Ford Escort. But I wasn't happy, and I was prone to depression. My drinking was getting increasingly worrying; I was already drinking on the drive to work. I was sent to psychologists and psychiatrists by my exasperated parents to deal with the alcoholism and depression, but soon afterwards I had my first suicide attempt, an overdose. I went through a period of sobriety then, after my first stay in rehab, maybe 18 months, but then I was back drinking as heavily as ever.

My first marriage lasted seven years and I left because of my unhappiness. I'd given in to a relationship I didn't really want – we were never compatible – but I thought it would make me happy. I gave her the house when I left and some of the last money from the inheritance. All I can say about that marriage is that my wife did a great job bringing up the kids, mostly alone, for which I will forever be thankful to her.

When I was 40, I tried to kill myself for the second time. Again it was an overdose, and I really wanted to die – I was very upset that it didn't work. I was severely depressed and drinking constantly. By then I was with my second wife – this time I had got married to someone who drank like me. Her kids from her previous relationship suffered badly due to our fights.

After the second suicide attempt, I went back into rehab and stayed sober for nine months. I started going to AA meetings but didn't get a sponsor and didn't do any of the work that was recommended. On holiday with the family in France, I fancied a bottle of Breton cider, and that was it, I started drinking again.

The following seven years were a blur of outpatient detoxes and psychiatric hospitals. My wife left and the bank stopped lending me money. I had another, this time half-hearted, attempt to kill myself. During those seven years I was drinking very heavily. I bought myself a motorbike and would drink half a bottle of vodka on the way to work. Unsurprisingly, I crashed, and was in a coma for seven days. I really didn't care about living.

The drinking was bad, really bad, and as soon as I left hospital after the bike accident I got a taxi to the off-licence. I felt awful, constantly terrible, and the only way to stop feeling like that was to wipe myself out. I did my third private rehab, but started drinking again straight after I walked out the doors. I had problems working at all and sold my house to pay my debts. I had £15,000 left over, so I paid the rent up front on a flat for a year and thought I would spend the time getting myself sorted. The reality was that by the end of the year I had drunk myself into oblivion. By then I had tried to kill myself for the fourth time.

I was still in touch with my children, and they were still putting up with me, just. It was a day with them that finally made me stop drinking. I was shopping with them – they would have been in their late teens by then – and I spent the day popping into off-licences to buy half-bottles of vodka to drink in secret around the corner. They knew what I was doing; they had done for a long time. They were constantly angry and upset with me. They had even been in a near-fatal car crash with me where I had fallen asleep at the wheel, drunk. At the end of the shopping trip, I remember putting the kids on the train back to Oxford and thinking, *I've had enough of this*. Really thinking it. I walked down to a recovery project and banged on the door and begged to come in. I finally knew that I couldn't carry on, that I had no other option. I couldn't even kill myself, as I had tried so many times and failed. I was desperate. The person at the centre told me to get detoxed and come back, so I did that (probably my ninth time), and then I rang them every day until they let me in.

I was in a place with 25 others, all from different backgrounds with different issues, some with quite difficult histories. A lot of them were heroin users and I thought I was better than them, which I now realize was absolute rubbish. I was being forced to take responsibility for my actions, and so something within me rebelled and I thought it was a good idea to have a couple of cans of Special Brew. I got chucked out and was told to not drink and to come back in a week. I drank every day that week.

That weekend, I was sitting on a park bench with my bag of alcohol, watching a football match (with my copy of *The Times*, as that made me a posh drinker and not an alcoholic), when someone came and sat next to me who was a bit rougher than me – a street drinker, probably homeless. He asked if he could join me. I saw something then that scared me. I realized what I was, what I looked like to others. I think that was the last drink I ever had. I like to think it was, anyway. I went back to the centre and begged to go back in, promising to do everything and anything. I finally got humble, as they say in AA, and I was willing to go to any lengths to get sober. I was willing to learn and to listen. I think that was the most important point of my life.

From then on, I went to AA meetings every day, sometimes twice a day. I had a great key worker, Cliff, who understood me and how traumatized people in general operate. He taught me a lot. Most importantly, he helped me to exist in the present and live one moment at a time. I discovered quite quickly that if I took responsibility for myself, I would start to feel better. That was the crucial thing – I didn't have to influence the world or change anyone else; all I had to focus on was myself and my own actions. I ended up in the centre for ten months. It was a real opportunity for me and I stuck with it.

I had finally found a way to consistently feel better about myself. I also quickly found a sense of purpose. I made my mind up while I was there that I would start studying. I took a counsellor taster course as soon as I left and started on the progression to my current role. I'd done a similar course after my first suicide attempt, when I had that initial brief period of sobriety. It had always been something that appealed to me, but I hadn't had the will to progress it previously.

They say in AA, and I totally believe it, that addicts stop developing emotionally from when they first become dependent. For me, that meant I was stuck as a 16-year-old with no tools to deal with my emotional state. I had to grow up, and Cliff and others taught me to understand my emotions, be comfortable with them and see why I was feeling the way I was. I was taught to relate my past to how I feel now, which was important.

The 12-step programme (the framework of recovery followed by Alcoholics Anonymous) is a huge part of my recovery, especially in looking back and coming to terms with my past. I had been in rehab countless times, seen counsellors, psychiatrists and psychologists, and knew that nothing external could cure me. I had to cure myself, and AA enabled me to do that.

While at the centre, I was known as 'Project Police', as I wouldn't let any rule-breaking go and would pull people up on what they were doing. I stuck to all the boundaries and rules, and I'd tell other addicts that if they weren't honest, I would be honest for them. Honesty is the foundation of recovery – it is an absolute must. These days everything in my life is based on honesty. I turn up where I say I am going to turn up, I do what I say I am going to do, and if I hurt someone or do something wrong, I try and rectify it immediately. Otherwise I will start down the wrong path again, and I can't afford that. I must take responsibility for myself and my recovery.

When I was nine months sober, my dad was terminally ill and I was able to care for him as he was dying. In a sense, my life became about caring. I've forgiven him for his part in my upbringing. While I was caring for him, I made my amends to him. He sort of made amends to me as well. We spoke honestly for the first time. I had the realization that I could make things better and find purpose even when it wasn't easy. This was a major step, as my previous life was all about taking the easier, softer path.

After I left the recovery project, I set myself a target of going back to work there at some point in the future. I'd never really had a goal before that, which I find quite upsetting. This really spurred me on. If I was to make anything of my life, that was what I had to do. I booked on to a course for the next two levels of counselling training, managed that and then continued to train. Recovery is progressive, much like alcoholism. Life became better quite quickly and my state of mind improved dramatically.

Coming out of the haze of alcoholism meant I had to confront multiple fears. When I started the counselling course, I really struggled with believing I could do it. I'd never risked putting my all into anything before, and that habit was hard to break. When I saw the syllabus, I found it incredibly scary, but I tackled it one day at a time, like my sobriety. I realized that if I faced things I was scared of, I could get through them.

There was hope in my life by then. AA gave that to me initially, and then I gave it to myself. Having self-belief came more slowly, but I could see that if I put the effort in, I could do it. I chose a very practical course that was more based on experience. A lot of AA is not about drinking, but about becoming a person who can live in sobriety. The counselling course was similar in that it was about becoming the type of person who could operate effectively as a counsellor. There was a lot of self-examination that built on the work I had done in AA.

I've always had that caring side and I've learned to be useful through my work on addiction. It's given me the opportunity to step up and help. I came to see how my experience meant I could help people out and be a better counsellor. I engaged with the course well. I knew I had to get through it, as I really wanted what it would give me.

I met my current wife, Kay, around eight months after getting sober, which is quite a 'higher power' moment. The more 'good stuff' I do, the more higher-power moments I get! I'm not religious, but I try and live a spiritual life. God isn't a thing to me; I just look for an immeasurable power of good.

Kay was a 'normal' person. On paper we were a total mismatch. I was a jobless alcoholic, fresh out of rehab. She was commuting to London and working in copywriting for a marketing company. She was divorced and her previous partners had been very, very different from me. She did try and dump me at one point, although her daughter told her to give me a chance, and fortunately she did. The relationship was, and is, very good for my self-esteem. That feeling of not being good enough for her does creep in, but it's been nine years now, so I must be doing something right. I work very hard at the relationship, always have.

She is a very sensible, well-balanced person and lives her life naturally in a '12-step way' – she works hard, she does things she enjoys doing, she doesn't mind what people think and she stays away from stuff she doesn't like. My previous relationships were based on a certain set of values and desires. But at the point I met Kay, I was starting to look at life in a completely different way, with different values. I moved in with her about nine months after we met and we got married three months later. It feels like a miracle.

While I was training to be a counsellor, I worked in a homeless hostel. My old key worker, Cliff, died of a brain tumour just as I qualified, and I was given his old job at the recovery centre. It was a very profound moment for me. Incredibly sad, but I know he would have been proud of me. He would have wanted that. I then worked in the recovery centre for two years, after which I set up my own counselling business.

My old life and my new life now feel like two completely different things. My old life feels like a dream, although it's still very real in my head. I accept all the things that happened to me and I don't wish to shut the door on the past. It has enabled me to be the person I am.

Acceptance is huge and it is a big word. I was very lost; I was very confused and I accept that. I can't change any of the past, but I can change the present and future if I want to. I have a way of living now that I know works for me. I have a feeling of safety and security that I never had while I was drinking. I know that when I put the effort in, good things happen. I don't crave huge amounts of money; I don't crave big holidays. I accept everything as it is and appreciate what I have. When I was younger, there was always a sense of something missing. That's gone now. Being in control of my life is very important, as well as accepting that I can't control others. I love being able to pick and choose what I want from life.

Around a third of my clients now have addiction problems. I often push them towards AA and stop formally treating them. Sometimes I even become their sponsor. It isn't great for my business, but it's the right thing to do. I see again and again that it isn't about the addiction, it's about the underlying trauma. The addiction is a way to cope in the short term. Something that we can control at first, that then starts controlling us and taking things from us.

I don't have to look back at my old life in detail. I can glance back. Every day I write a gratitude list, and part of that is the things that aren't in my life any more – the pain, the worry, the anxiety and the hurt I did to others. I don't live in fear. I get nervous, like everyone, but I don't run away from anxiety any more. I don't have a fear of fear. I respect it, but I know what is real and what is not. Little Peter still sits on my shoulder and tells me lies, but I can ignore him.

MY THOUGHTS

Peter's experience highlights the importance of acceptance and the power of telling your story. It also shows how problematic some coping strategies can become. How hard this makes it to change and the length of time it can take before things do work out, but the incredible difference it can make when they do. Peter is a friend of my husband, and I feel privileged to have met him and heard his story.

The impact of early experiences

Peter had a difficult childhood, something we know is a risk factor for alcoholism. Multiple experiences – feeling unloved, feeling like he was a mistake, changing schools – led to a sense of not feeling good enough and not belonging. This is likely to have been exacerbated by his relationship with his father. Living with a volatile parent who is inconsistent and unpredictable makes it very difficult for a child to work out how to be. You never know what to expect or what will cause a reaction, so you live life on eggshells, in fear of what will cause the next reaction, with little security or stability or sense of safety from your caregiver. This made it much harder for Peter to learn how to deal with his emotions, manage how he was feeling or develop adaptive ways to cope.

As we saw in Chapter 7, not feeling good about yourself often begins in childhood. You make sense of yourself through your experiences and your relationships with others. This can mean you begin to see yourself as the problem, as you have no other way to make sense of things. Once in place, these beliefs form your meaning framework, and your brain becomes invested in proving them right, making it very difficult to see or believe a different view.

I feel for Peter that no one picked up on how he was feeling. No one saw him struggling and he had no support. They missed that the behaviours were not him being bad, but were more likely an expression of not feeling good enough, feeling lost and finding it hard to cope. In therapy, I notice that sometimes people tell themselves they don't care as a method of self-protection. Caring is not worth the risk. It can feel too exposing or crushing when your sense of self is fragile. Perhaps Peter's fear of responsibility and potential failure meant it was easier not to care than to try and fail.

Alcohol as a coping strategy

Addiction is essentially a coping strategy gone wrong, as we saw in Chapter 8. Alcoholism is like depression, anxiety or an eating disorder – it's a sign that things are overwhelming and you're struggling with life. The trouble is, it's socially unacceptable and often the sufferer doesn't see it, which means they don't get the help they need.

Alcohol was a way for Peter to avoid or ignore how he was feeling. Although it worked in the short term, in the longer term it made everything worse. You might be able to ignore your difficulties when you're drinking, but they don't go away, and drinking feeds into the problem, making it bigger – more shame, increased loneliness and no chance to see that you are acceptable exactly as you are.

For Peter, the alcohol was covering up so much pain that taking it away would have meant having to find a way to look at his life and deal with everything that had happened. Alcohol can feel like the one good thing you have; it becomes prized over everything else, but it means you miss the fact that it's really the reason you're so miserable. The longer you drink for, the harder it becomes to stop.

Alcohol dependence also makes it more difficult to develop emotionally. Many people, like Peter, find alcohol at a young age, so they never have a chance to learn how to cope with those feelings naturally, halting their emotional development. It's their only coping strategy and when they're not drinking, they're left with very raw feelings that they are unskilled at dealing with.

Unfortunately, when you're in the midst of addiction, it obscures the truth. You really don't see it, and denial grows with the problem. Making a link between drinking and feeling awful would mean that you'd have to consider stopping. Instead, you find ways to make it OK and to differentiate yourself from others with problem drinking. Alcohol feeds into avoidance and tells lies about what it can do for you and the type of person you are. The brain is rewired, and eventually it sees only one solution to any problem. Drink.

Even when you do realize that alcohol is the problem, the solution is not simple. It can take repeated attempts. Making changes is really hard. The physical and emotional attachment to alcohol is very powerful, and the addiction causes significant changes to neural pathways and associated impulse control. You can know what you want and need to do but be unable to do it. In my professional experience, it is one of the most difficult things to overcome.

Often people wrongly have a very black-and-white view of alcoholism, but there's so much more nuance. It's about how and why you drink and the purpose it serves. A way to drown out or manage difficult feelings. Addiction is the symptom, trauma is the cause. It's only when you deal with what is underneath it that you have a chance to make changes.

Telling your story, grieving, letting go and accepting

Committing to recovery, taking responsibility and understanding his experience was a turning point and transformed Peter's life. Acceptance of the past without denying or avoiding it has enabled him to move forward and appreciate what he has. To live one moment at a time and live honestly, by his values.

The Alcoholics Anonymous programme allowed Peter to take charge of his life and find a new sense of purpose. Looking back gave him a chance to tell his story and come to terms with his past in a safe way, so he could process and make sense of what had happened and feel the emotions. This helped him to tackle the base issues that had contributed to his addiction – past experiences and pain – as well as the problems caused by his alcoholism. He also had to learn new coping strategies to take the place of alcohol.

Peter began to make choices about what he wanted from life, rather than being pulled along by it, and his goal to go back and work at the recovery centre gave him a clear focus to work towards. He stopped listening to what the addiction wanted and started listening to those who could support him and who he could learn from, slowly getting to know himself and his wants and needs.

Stopping drinking let Peter see that when he faced up to his fears, he could get through them. When you don't try something, it's easy to come to the false conclusion that you couldn't have done it or it wouldn't have worked out. It's only when you are in a position to test this out that you can see your ability to cope and your strengths. Sticking with his recovery and setting goals meant Peter had a chance to recognize all he was capable of and to consistently feel better about himself, slowly building self-belief and living a life where he dared to care – something he'd perhaps never had a chance to learn as a child.

Peter's story makes me think of the wounded healer, a term created by the psychologist Carl Jung – someone whose painful experiences enable them to help others. Finding a purpose in counselling, being a sponsor and sharing his story in AA has given his life direction and meaning and helped many others to overcome their struggles and change their lives for the better.

KEY TAKEAWAYS

- It is important to grieve for your losses in order to make space for what you have gained.
- Holding on to resentment and hurt has a negative effect on mental health and can contribute to poor physical health too.
- Letting go helps you avoid getting lost in negative feelings. It allows you to stop looking back and to be present in your life.
- The final part of the grieving process is to find a way to acceptance. You cannot change what has happened to you; it is only when you acknowledge this that you can move forward. Beyond that, your choices are infinite. How you approach life now is up to you.

11

BECOMING YOURSELF (STEP 7)

'And once the storm is over, you won't remember how you made it through, how you managed to survive. You won't even be sure whether the storm is really over. But one thing is certain. When you come out of the storm, you won't be the same person who walked in.'

– Haruki Murakami, *Kafka on the Shore*

The final step in this process is to take charge of your story – to look past the difficulty and value the positive changes. Finding meaning in what has happened is at the core of how we overcome trauma and whether we grow from the experience.

You have been through an incredibly difficult time, but you can use what's happened as a wake-up call. It can provide you with an opportunity to re-evaluate. As we've seen in this book, trauma leaves an indelible mark. It can tear your life apart but it can also make space for changes and give you freedom to review your life, reflect on what you have learned and confront anything that is no longer right for you. It can link you back to your natural motivations and desire to grow stronger – a chance to live again and live differently, bringing into sharper focus what really matters and letting you think about what you truly want from your life.

It is only by letting go of your old life that you can begin to consciously choose how you want your life to be. This means living 'intentionally', understanding yourself better and the things you need to do to be yourself. These experiences bring you new insights, opening your eyes again to life and all its potential. But you have to make the most of this moment in order to see it clearly and channel what has happened into a determination to change things for the better.

Sometimes these insights lead to immediate change and sometimes they need bringing more fully into the world. This is the focus of this chapter. I want you to go through the questions that follow, answering all of those that resonate with you. Write down your answers so you can capture what you've learned and what you now want from life (writing this down is *very* important).

LISTEN TO YOUR HEART

While doing this, I want you to listen to your heart and create a life that is aligned with your values and that gives you a sense of purpose and fulfilment – not what's sensible or rational, not what's practical or what others think is a good idea. Try and free yourself from the ideas and judgement of others. I want you to tune into your gut instincts and listen to your intuition, no longer allowing the noise of life to drown it out.

How we spend our time is the single most important decision any of us makes. This is a chance to bring your inner and outer lives back into sync, so that the life you are living day to day – the work you do, your role in your family, your interests and friendships – matches up with how you feel inside. Allow your inner voice to speak, become self-aware and listen to what you are feeling – your true wishes and wants, private thoughts, values, emotions and sense of meaning. Remember, there's no magic formula; you need to find out what works best for *you*.

When your inner and outer life are in sync, it brings a sense of wholeness, letting you feel grounded and anchored and giving a clear sense of what you are living life for. This is what makes life meaningful. Having meaning in life is one of the most consistent and strong predictors of psychological well-being and happiness. It helps you define your life, cope with adversity, find inner strength and have a clear picture of the future you wish to strive towards.

What do *you* want from life?

SEE YOUR STRENGTHS

First, I want you to go back through your story, but this time tell a redemption story of how far you have come. Write it down again and allow yourself to see it from different perspectives, so you can gain a new understanding and accommodate all you have learned. What is the story you want to tell about yourself? Is it one of difficult times overcome? Of beating the odds? Striving for something better and keeping going when things are tough?

Perhaps you have recognized that you cannot have ultimate control over everything in your life and that trying to do this is a waste of time and energy. Did you learn that you were stronger than you imagined? Did you have a chance to see your determination? Has it made you braver?

These lessons can then help you face whatever lies ahead, knowing you have the ability to cope even when things become hard. Look at the challenges and obstacles you have overcome and gain a greater sense of confidence and strength as you continue to live your life, all of which helps build resilience. You stood strong when you felt like collapsing, kept going even when it felt too hard. You did your best in a difficult situation. This is all part of growth.

Given that you have gone through such difficulty, what does it say about you as a person?

- What are your strengths?
- How have you grown because of this experience?
- How has this experience shaped your identity and how you view yourself?
- What lessons has it taught you?
- How do these lessons show up in your life now?
- What does this say about what you could do in the future?

GRATITUDE

Going through trauma shows you that you never know what each day is going to bring, but it also gives you a new perspective. When you see how difficult life can be, it can bring the things you do have into sharper focus. It can make you realize how much you value your life and help you recognize that you don't need a lot of the things you thought you did.

Trauma can remind you to enjoy each day to the fullest, celebrate life and be thankful for what you have. Not as a way to diminish or belittle how you might be feeling, but as an addition to your mental map of life. Personal growth occurs as a result of overcoming challenging times. Going through something difficult lets us see the things that really matter to us; it is like a mirror to 'normal' or 'ordinary' life and all the good things in it. Often we take 'simple' for granted, but trauma reminds us that it is something to be celebrated. Trauma can also be a reminder that it is not materialism or external success that is most important. When we become obsessed by that final goal – thinking, hoping and scheming about what's ahead – it can blind us to all that we already have and the importance of having a daily life that fulfils us, rather than waiting for a time that never comes. It's easy to miss out on the wonderful little things that are happening every day. All those good feelings. All those opportunities to see what you already have. Happiness and meaning comes from within us – from how we view our life and value it, and the actions we take.

Trauma can be a reminder to slow down and appreciate the things in life that are truly important. It's only by switching out of autopilot that we can really take things in.

- Has anything good come from your experience? List any benefits or opportunities that have emerged from what's happened, no matter how small.
- Think about how your experience has shaped you, your view of life and the world. Has it made you think about yourself or your life differently?
- Has it brought into sharper focus what you do have? Your family and friends? Your body? Your mind? Your work?
- What has it shown you about other people?
- How has it affected your relationships?
- Has it brought you closer to anyone or shown you who your true friends are?
- Has it given you a new appreciation for the world around you?
- What has changed that is harder now?
- Do you feel like there was a reason you went through this?
- How do you understand your life now?

LOOKING DEATH IN THE FACE

Death is something we are often discouraged from thinking about, but doing so can be empowering; it can clarify life and act as a reminder of how fragile it is. Your time is finite and valuable – you can't buy extra hours, so you need to make sure you use them wisely. Rather than putting off life, make the most of the opportunities that matter. Dare to try new things, move into that unsettling in-between place, change the routine. Make time for the things you care about. Wear your best clothes rather than saving them for a special occasion. Don't wait for a retirement that might never come.

I love the story of Candy Chang. In 2009, Candy lost someone she loved very much, who had been like a mother to her. The loss was unexpected and it left her thinking a lot about death. As she slowly came to terms with her loss, she found that thinking about death made her feel a deep gratitude for the time she'd had. It brought clarity to the things that were meaningful to her, but she foresaw a struggle between maintaining this perspective in her daily life and getting caught up in the day-to-day. With the help of some friends, she turned the side of an abandoned house into a giant chalkboard and stencilled it with: 'Before I die, I want to…' Anyone walking by could pick up a piece of chalk, reflect on their life and share their personal aspirations in a public space. She had no idea what to expect from the experiment, but by the next day, the wall was entirely filled out, and it kept growing.

Before I die, I want to be tried for piracy.
Before I die, I want to straddle the International Date Line.
Before I die, I want to sing for millions.
Before I die, I want to plant a tree.

Before I die, I want to live off the grid.

Before I die, I want to hold her one more time.

Before I die, I want to be someone's cavalry.

Before I die, I want to be completely myself.

The neglected space became a constructive one, and reading other people's hopes and dreams made Candy feel less alone with what she was going through.

Two of the most valuable things we have are time and our relationships, something that is easy to forget when we don't regularly cherish them. Try filling it out for yourself: 'Before I die, I want to...'

RE-EVALUATE: WHAT DO YOU PLAN TO DO WITH YOUR ONE WILD AND PRECIOUS LIFE?

What do you want to do with this gift of life? Don't just stop at this point and accept what life has given you; it is your time to go after the things you want and think about how you want to live.

I love Mary Oliver's poem, 'The Summer Day', in which she asks, 'Tell me, what is it you plan to do with your one wild and precious life?'

Use this experience as a chance to really think about who you are and what you want. What are the things that matter most? What are your dreams? What is your purpose? How can you contribute to the lives of others? How do you want to be remembered, and most importantly, how do you want to spend your time?

Moving out of autopilot is so important to gaining the most from life. What are the things that make you feel alive or give you a sense of freedom? Your favourite music turned up loud, running, the outdoors, doing well at work? Relationships? Kindness? Giving back or being part of something bigger?

Thinking about the previous question, what do you want before you die? Do you want to change jobs, get a promotion, set up your own business, take a sabbatical? Do you want to enter a triathlon, learn carpentry, teach yourself upholstery, have time for gardening or learn to paraglide? Remember that not everything you do has to be productive. Do some things for the sake of it, with no expected outcome or achievement. If you were at the end of your life looking back on it, what would you want to see? Do you want to live as you did before or go in a different direction? Are there things you had forgotten about or that were lost living life in line with someone else's expectations?

Think about Sophie, who moved to Bali, finding a sense of freedom, overcoming her insomnia and retraining as a yoga and self-worth coach. This is a chance to trust your gut instincts and find your voice again, like Akemi remembering herself and all she was capable of, forging a special relationship with her boys and training as a SENCO specialist. Has your experience shown you that you already have everything you want, like Naomi – you will meet her towards the end of this chapter – who realized that she had everything she needed and that she didn't need to prove herself? Has it reminded you of the importance of making the most of life, like Jess and Finn? Or do you want to give back and be part of something bigger, like Peter and David?

It's also important to think about what you need to say no to. What are the things you complain about or dread doing and no longer want in your life? It could be being too busy, or constantly feeling tired. It might be something bigger, like a person in your life or the job you do. When your values and behaviour align, it means you are living authentically. Which values belong to you and which belong to your family? What are the values you want to live by?

As part of this, it's also valuable to look outside of yourself and find something you believe in – charity, community, study, spirituality or a higher power. Find a sense of belonging, maybe by helping others or creating something you are proud of. Being part of something is central to a meaningful life. What do you believe in or care about? What are the things you stand for, and how can you bring this more firmly into your life?

Becoming myself

- What do you want from your life?
- What and who is important to you?
- How will your future be different as a result of what you've been through?
- What do you want to hold on to?
- What do you want to let go of?
- What do you want to make time for?
- Is there anything you are not doing that you want to do?
- What are the things that give you a sense of freedom?
- What makes you feel alive?
- What are your hopes?
- What are your dreams?
- What do you want from the future?
- What are you committed to doing and being because of what you've learned?
- How can you look outside of yourself, help other people or give back?

LIVE INTENTIONALLY

It's essential to not just think about these things, but to hold on to your ideas and put them into action so you live differently. Thinking about it and writing everything down isn't enough.

First, I want you to take some time to review everything you have done as you have worked through this book. This is something I do in therapy. It will consolidate your ideas while they are fresh in your mind. Writing them down gives you something to look at when you need it, so you have an easy reminder without having to go back through everything. It also provides a map to check in with and guide you on this new path.

- When you read this book, which ideas resonated most with you?
- What has been most helpful in terms of understanding trauma and how your body and mind work?
- Which chapters really struck a chord?
- Which skills and strategies did you find particularly helpful?
- Which are the key ideas you want to pursue?
- How can you do this?
- Who can support you?

Your work here has only just started. Together we have planted the seeds of change; it's now up to you to look after them, to water and nurture them, so they continue to flower year after year. Consider telling family and friends what you are doing, if you haven't already. Their encouragement will be invaluable. The more you build on these new ways of thinking and incorporate healthy coping strategies into your daily life, the easier it will be to put everything you want for your life into action.

Some days it will seem easy and other days it will feel hard. The difficult days are when you will need to remember the new ideas most; the more you use them, the easier it will become as you build those new pathways. It is worth persevering, I promise. When you need to, make sure you look back at your notes, remind yourself of this review and be kind to yourself so you can get back on track.

Next, I want you to note down all the different ways that growth and change is already showing up in your life. Recognize how far you have come. Don't underestimate what you have achieved. It's important to take time to regularly reflect, on both your internal thoughts and your external actions. Ask yourself: are you looking after yourself? Adopting a spiritual practice? Are you better at accepting yourself or doing something that matters to you? It might be taking a course or joining a new class, volunteering, social action or advocacy. It might be changing the way you speak to yourself or the standards you set, saying no, speaking up or expressing yourself differently. It might be an acceptance of how things are now, spending more time with your kids, giving back or opening up to others you care about. It might be working differently, looking forward to doing things or doing something you've been putting off.

Write down examples of where you are already doing this. The positive changes you have made in your thoughts and actions that demonstrate the ways you have become more self-accepting and purposeful in your life.

- How much are you already doing the things you have written down?
- How have you prioritized the things that matter to you?
- Who are the people you want to spend time with and when are you doing this?

- What are the things you want to make time for and how much are you already doing this?
- What have you said yes to and what have you said no to?
- Is there a gap between what you want and what you are doing? How can you change this – not next month or next year, but today?
- What more do you want to do?
- How can you live by these new values and lessons more fully?
- What is the next step?

When you look at all the different examples of how your life has changed, you can see how you've grown. Reflecting on these changes can also show you the type of person you are, your strengths and what this means about you.

BECOMING WHOLE AGAIN

At the beginning of the recovery process, it can be difficult to hold on to a clear sense of who you are. I hope that as you have gone through this chapter, you are beginning to find yourself again. Despite what has happened, you are still the same core person. What has happened is part of your life, but it is not all of who you are.

I hope you have reconnected to the person you were before all this happened; not necessarily right before (although that might be the case for some people), but the last time you felt yourself and in touch with your wants and needs. Bringing together the best parts of your life before trauma and the new things you have discovered as a result of going through adversity will mean you are ready to step back into life with an inner strength and a wish to live again.

In this final step, I want you to take some time to think about all of who you are. I imagine this as spokes on a wheel, and the exercise works best when you actually draw it out, like in the diagram below. Trauma (see pages 21–22) can feature as one spoke, but it's only a small part of the whole. Draw out everything you have written in this chapter, so you have a clear picture of where you are now. Your strength and courage; the things that you now wish to focus on in your life. Your family and home, your work, the hobbies or interests you have, the people and things that are important to you, the different roles you do.

I hope that when you look at this picture, your life feels meaningful and aligned with your values. Life is full of ups and downs; there will always be good days and bad, but meaning is deeper, creating an underlying sense of purpose and belonging that carries you through traumatic events and difficult times.

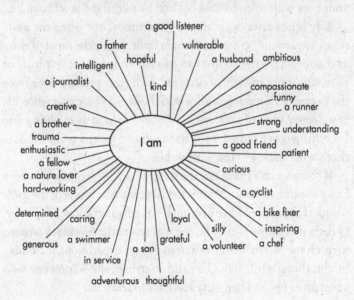

Obviously bad days won't disappear, but when life threatens to throw you off course, there is something stronger to keep you steady.

When you know why you are doing things and have a clear picture of what makes your life meaningful, it is like a guiding light. Meaning anchors you to your life and enables you to weather the storms. It will give you a new-found understanding of yourself and what you have been through, making you more resilient, with the courage to face problems and make changes, and more confident in your ability to manage in difficult times and grow.

The goal is to reach a place where you can accept how life is while still living to your fullest. This doesn't mean living your 'best life' or having to make every day count. It means living consciously and making active choices about what you want, with your eyes wide open to how big and beautiful the world can be.

Life is not always about the good times, but when the good times are around, grasp on to them tight. Make the most of them and appreciate them, instead of yearning for something out of reach or not in sight. Focus on the bigger picture, free from the pressure of having it all worked out, so you experience life at a deeper level of awareness. We are constantly evolving and becoming more ourselves. That's what it means to be human, that's what makes living worthwhile.

If there's a story that encapsulates this, it's Naomi's. I've been lucky enough to know Naomi for 10 years. She is one of the most wonderful people I have ever met – a truly incredible character. Quietly determined (in 2011, she was one of the few Black women to reach the North Pole after a four-day ski expedition), incredibly bright, thoughtful, articulate and so strong, she is someone who never gives up, and her story has a lot to teach us.

NAOMI'S STORY: A DOUBLE CANCER DIAGNOSIS

I was on a short holiday with my daughter when I found the lump. It was like a pea under my skin. I didn't think much of it and carried on with my holiday. I made an appointment with my doctor when I got back and was booked in with a specialist, but no one was particularly worried. The specialist thought it was most likely to be benign, a fibroadenoma, but they would do a biopsy just in case.

A few days later I had a message asking me to come in. I had always been concerned about seeing doctors for some reason; I had never liked being in hospital. The first thing the doctor said was, 'It's cancer.' At that point they didn't think they would need to take the breasts off as it was very early stages – stage 2. I was told there would be further tests, but they didn't think I would need chemotherapy as it was a type of cancer with a great recovery rate. They also said it hadn't spread, so I could have a lumpectomy rather than a mastectomy.

Everything about my lifestyle was good. I didn't smoke, I didn't drink, I didn't eat meat, I exercised all the time. It didn't make sense that I would be someone who'd get cancer.

I was in total shock. I received the diagnosis just a week after I had found the lump. I was also alone, as my husband was out of the UK with work, although he came right back. But I trusted what I was being told, so I convinced myself I was going to be OK. Everything was looking positive.

I had the lump taken out the next week and the tumour was analysed to see if I needed chemo. It came back as not needed, so I just had radiotherapy. I was diagnosed on 28 October 2020 and I finished the radiotherapy just two months later, on 28 December. All the tests had come back in my favour. I had even been able to finish my A-Level exams, which I did alongside completing a one-year undergraduate English Literature course. I hadn't had much time to process what had happened, but I did feel like I had lost some innocence. I allowed myself the time to grieve over the life I had before I knew I had breast cancer. I realized how incredibly vulnerable I was.

The hardest thing was telling my children, but they were amazing. My daughter wanted to give it a name, so she called it Jeffrey, which really helped as I could tell her all about all the procedures in an age-appropriate way. I went for a couple of months without worrying about my health, and then I got a couple of iffy symptoms around February. Every now and again I'd get this pain in my stomach. I went back to my doctor and he booked me in for another check-up. I had an ultrasound, and all was fine. In June 2021, I had my six-month check with the cancer doctor. She did a manual examination and all was clear, but I told her again about the stomach pain.

I went to see a stomach specialist and had more ultrasounds. During this period, weird things kept happening: my wrist would just give in, or my ankles would swell up to twice their normal size. I was still healthy, I looked fine and I was still exercising, but

I had a sense that something wasn't quite right. They did some more tests and nothing concerning came back, apart from some inflammation of the stomach wall, for which I got medication. They then sent me for one final test, to take samples from the stomach wall. The doctor who did the test came in afterwards and looked at me. He looked really sad. I know with hindsight that he realized it was cancer, but it wasn't in his power to tell me.

When my doctor told me I had stomach cancer, I was in shock. I thought there could be no way that it was cancer. I was feeling good in my body. I was starting university as a mature student, this time reading Classical Studies with English. I was devastated. It was a very dark time. I can't describe how awful it was.

My experience was very different the second time round. The waiting periods were much longer and the expected operation was much more complicated. I had loads of tests done to see the extent of the cancer. Usually, stomach cancer patients are very unwell and I wasn't, so there was some hope.

It was diagnosed as stage 2 as it hadn't spread, but I did have malignant fluid present, which officially made it stage 4. I said to my doctor that no one survives stomach cancer, but my gastroenterologist said some people can, which also gave me hope. I was prescribed six courses of chemotherapy. I started my chemo in November. I was OK then, as I was doing something about my situation and felt more in control.

The first cycle of chemo was awful. The next day I couldn't even walk up a small flight of stairs. I had to go back to hospital, where I was put on a drip. I was told that my white blood count was very low and I was susceptible to infection. I had to go into isolation for a week and wasn't allowed home. This was during the COVID-19 pandemic, so there was no way I could have visitors. My husband brought me stuff that made me feel comfortable – my favourite cushions, books. It made a real difference.

The very worst thing I could imagine, being in isolation in hospital, had happened, so I knew I could cope. While I was in isolation, I spoke to every nurse I could and asked them for advice. They were all amazing. They knew it was my second cancer diagnosis in less than a year. They all told me to keep well, push on and be positive, but understand that I would feel very low. I could either be utterly frightened and concentrate on the negatives, or embrace it as the pathway I had to take to get better.

After that, they decided to give me some additional medication, steroids, but to continue with the same dose of chemo, which I was really pleased about. I just had this feeling of real exhaustion, but the steroids made a big difference. After that, I knew I could do it. I had my COVID vaccine that December, which made me feel more comfortable too. I made the days I was in hospital for treatment as enjoyable as I could. I would download audiobooks, films, take in blankets and things from home that made me feel safe and relaxed.

After the six chemotherapy courses had finished, I had another endoscopy and some more scans. They both showed the cancer was in retreat and there was no metastasization or lymph node involvement. I was looking forward, feeling positive. But then I had a test that said I still had some free-floating cancer cells. The surgeon said, 'Sorry, I can't do the operation to remove the stomach.' The sense of failure was palpable. But I went back to the doctor and he said that the chemo was working well so they were going to carry on with it.

This time round, I told fewer people about the stomach cancer, largely because I was so exhausted and it was such a complicated situation. Instead, I chose a smaller group of people who had been with me all the way, and they gave me all the support I needed. I needed positivity at that time. Explaining it to some people was exhausting, but talking to the right people was cathartic.

I had another six courses of chemo. Towards the end, I was feeling bad. I was getting anxious and lethargic and increasingly worried about the new tests. I remember saying to my husband, 'I'm really tired of living in a house dominated by cancer.' I wanted to make sure I was living, so we started making plans again. It was my daughter's birthday the day after the second course of chemo finished, so we decided to give her a big party and invite ten of her friends, which was amazing. Then me and my husband started going on dates – we went to restaurants for lunch, as I was too tired in the evenings. And we started going on walks. I also kept up the exercise, doing weights and workouts. If you're feeling strong physically, it really helps your mood and your state of mind, and I wanted to be as strong as possible in case I could have the gastrectomy.

Finally the tests came back to say the cancer was inactive and that there were no free-floating cells. When the nurse read out the pathology report and said there were no malignant cells in any of the samples, it felt really, really great. I was then booked in for the operation. I was happy that everything was starting to go right medically, but I was still cautiously optimistic as I couldn't quite let myself believe it.

I remember waking up from what was meant to be the gastrectomy and being told that they'd had to call off the operation as they had found too much scar tissue near the cancer to be able to take it out safely. They couldn't be sure that they could remove it and it was too dangerous. If they had gone ahead and it had gone wrong, there would have been nothing they could do for me. I cried for two hours after that. I was distraught. I couldn't reconcile how I had done everything right with my lifestyle and had twice suffered from cancer. I had gone through all the treatment and they couldn't finish the operation. I allowed myself to break down then, but I also had to put myself back together. I had thought I would be cancer free, but now it seemed there was nothing they could do for me. I said to my husband afterwards, 'I am palliative now', the words you never want to say.

At my next appointment, they said they didn't know whether the treatment plan would be curative or palliative until the next set of scans. It was a real trauma. I had been hoping for better news. I was so exhausted with dealing with the uncertainty, I wanted to go to sleep and not wake up. We went away to the Cotswolds to try and relax, but I was so tired I couldn't enjoy it. I was fed up with being strong; sometimes you just can't be. I would stand in the shower screaming when the family were out. I just couldn't keep it in. They were the worst weeks of my life.

When I went back to the hospital, they said that the scans were good. The cancer was still inactive, but they didn't think there was anything they could do, so they were going to put me on a 'watch and wait' pathway. They told me that I could not have the gastrectomy, and there was no other surgery available. I felt that they had given up on me.

When we left, I was in floods of tears. The nurse took me to a room and said, 'It will take a while to get used to this.' I asked, 'Do people get used to the fact they are dying?' She answered, 'Eventually they do.' All they could offer me was a scan every three months.

I decided after that I needed to get my troops assembled. I called my support team together: my husband, my friends and my GP, and we decided to seek a second opinion. It was a death sentence; there's no way you can just accept that. The worst that could happen was that I was told the same thing; it couldn't be any worse. We found another doctor. I was terrified that he would come to the same conclusion, but he said that if the cancer was still contained and stable, they would do a radical surgery. Having that sense of hope has allowed me to move forward.

I started to put my affairs in order. That was one of the things I needed to do. It's like having a fire extinguisher in the house and never using it. It gives you some control. I was speaking to my friends and asking the closer ones to be there for the children after I was gone.

I have lots of useful coping mechanisms now, meditation most importantly. I've really enjoyed it: the concentration on my breathing and getting away from my head. I also started to use mindfulness to move away from the constant rumination, and that helped massively. If I don't get away from those thoughts, I become consumed by them.

I have learned a list of techniques to calm me and relax my body. I listen to a meditation tape most mornings. It allows me to 'see' myself post-treatment and in remission. I also started writing a journal, and that helped me process my thoughts. Getting things on paper is very beneficial. I'm doing a lot of exercise, but I stop when I'm tired. I'm doing stuff that is good for my body, but nothing that will cause stress. I need to enjoy it.

I have affirmations that I say to myself: 'I am healthy', 'I am strong'. I also have a vision board where I write down and pin up all the things I want to look forward to – travel, anniversaries – and a vision of what I will be like in the future. Oprah does this, and she hasn't done badly! It is all about forward thinking, putting it in writing and believing it.

I hate having this cloud over me. It stops me fully immersing myself in the day-to-day. I want to start enjoying life without cancer. There is only so much a person can go through, but I have the will and strength to recover. People ask me where it comes from, but when you are a parent, you just have to stick a smile on your face and move forward. A friend of mine said to me that the things that make it hard also make it easy, and that's right. It's the children, the family, experiencing the good things in life. Being told that you are not going to see your children grow up is really, really hard. I went to Paris with my daughter recently and had such a wonderful time, and I know that the experience I had with her will get me through. That's what I'm living for now, to have experiences like that. It's about finding whatever positive coping mechanism you can, even if that is screaming in the shower. There are different ways of coping, but I know I have the tools to help me. It is still hard; even now I can wake up and not remember that I have cancer. And when that realization hits, it can be devastating.

One of the reasons I didn't tell everyone is that I didn't want the cancer to define me. *I* am going to define who I am. And that's not going to be someone who is super-stressed and who doesn't spend enough time with their family. At the moment, I feel strong both physically and psychologically. I know what to expect now. When the operation goes ahead, it will last 14 hours at a minimum, with a long recovery period. I've set myself the task of getting my body ready. I know I have been through the worst possible time, but I am looking ahead.

If there is a lesson I have learned during all of this, it is that I need to concentrate on what is important to me. I have always put my family high up the priority list, but before, I was always trying to prove something, to whom I don't know. None of the things I have wanted to do since I have had the diagnosis have been about attainment. I don't need to prove myself to anyone.

I initially focused on getting through the treatment, and now I'm thinking about how I want to spend my time. I'm so excited about the future. I want to work hard, but on things that I find valuable, that give me pleasure and are worthwhile.

I can now see who I am as a person. I am kinder to myself. I can acknowledge my strengths and I can also find the pleasure in simple things. Everything from watching a documentary to appreciating walks outside – there is joy there.

The things I found most distressing about potentially being palliative was that I wouldn't see the kids grow up or grow old with my husband. But it was also that I was now looking forward to life and didn't want to miss out. My husband's mantra is that we are only at half-time. The next half is going to be where I live the life I want.

My husband has been a big part of my recovery. My friends have been fantastic, but Richard has been there all the time for me. He's my best friend. We really enjoy spending time together. I want to spend the rest of my life with him. I know what I am doing all these treatments for. He's a scientist, but he believes the Universe does have energy, and he can see it lining up again for me.

MY THOUGHTS

In training as a therapist, you are taught to be a blank slate. There are many good reasons for this, but it's not the way I've come to practice. It's my work, but it doesn't feel like a job. I keep a small clinic, I see people each week and I know their lives. It's a relationship; not on the usual terms, but I am connected, I care about how they're doing and want to know what happens to them. It's a privilege to walk beside people in difficult times, and this is what makes my job so special.

This is certainly true when it comes to working with Naomi. I have known her for ten years, and from the moment I met her, she has always been extra special. She has this impact on everyone she meets without even realizing it. Her story shows the seven steps of working through trauma, and how it can allow you to truly become yourself.

Shattered assumptions

When Naomi first discovered she had breast cancer, it was a shock, but she quickly found a positive approach by trusting in what she was told and believing she would be OK. After two months, her breast cancer treatment was successfully completed. There was a loss of innocence about her life, but her meaning framework was still in place, if a little bent.

The second diagnosis shattered her meaning framework and burnt down the house. It came just as she'd started her second university course. She had worked so hard to reach this point and to get through the breast cancer, and she was in a brilliant place. To have to contend with a new diagnosis felt terrifying, as well as incredibly unfair.

At first Naomi approached the treatment as she had the breast cancer, so when the operation couldn't go ahead after the first course of six chemos, it was understandably a huge blow. She felt she had failed. Therapy provided a space to slowly work things out, to see how far from the truth this idea of failure was and to work out a new way forward.

I watched Naomi as she learned to bring a more flexible approach and reach an acceptance of her situation, letting go of what she couldn't control and no longer fighting against the uncertainty. This flexible approach has helped her move with all the changes and find mental resilience through what has been a constantly changing picture of treatment. Her mental strength allowed her to reflect on the gastrectomy not going ahead as planned and to seek out a second opinion, which has led her back to hope and a new route to becoming cancer free.

Step 1: Care

Naomi has an incredibly positive approach to treatment. The basics – sleep, rest, nutrition and hydration – were put in place early on. At times with stomach cancer it was difficult to eat, but somehow she managed to keep weight on and keep herself strong and fuelled for treatment. Hope has been key, a guiding light in the darkness, and she has been brilliant at seeking out support and surrounding herself with people who believe in her and lighten her load. By letting in those closest to her, she can also see how much she is loved.

Step 2: Looking after your body

Paying attention to her body and looking after it has helped Naomi cope. Calming her body has helped to calm her mind. The chemotherapy has been gruelling at times, but despite this, she has managed to thrive. She uses practices like meditation and qigong as a way to look after herself, and techniques like the butterfly hug at times of high anxiety. She has consistently used exercise to feel strong physically and to prepare for the operations, and this has also helped keep her mentally strong. She has also learned to listen to her body and what it needs each day, ensuring she does not overdo things.

Step 3: Looking back to look forwards

Therapy has been a place to think about the impact of Naomi's early experiences. This is something we did primarily in our early work together, and it has allowed her to see how these experiences have shaped her framework of beliefs – how her past has influenced her present – and the unconscious biases she carries. My role has been to help her to understand herself better and give her space to question whether her beliefs are helping or hindering her; to think about where these ideas of success and failure might have come from and why working so hard and proving herself was so important prior to the cancer.

Step 4: Coping with trauma

You can't choose what happens to you, but you can choose what you do next. In Naomi's words 'stay frightened or embrace it'. Like David, Naomi has taken a step-by-step approach, focusing on what she needs to do today without getting too far ahead. She took control of everything she could, and did this in a way that helped her, rather than making it a pass-or-fail situation. She has developed a toolkit of strategies, using the mind–body link, therapy, affirmations, visualizations, journalling and letting in those who support and care for her.

Step 5: Telling your story

Therapy is also a space for Naomi to share the story of what she is going through, talking about everything that is happening, allowing the emotions, but also focusing on the good things that have come from this time. It has been a redemption story from the start. Telling me the full story again for this book was another chance for her to see how well she has coped, the many lessons she has learned and how she has grown from the experience. She saw her worst fears happen – a double cancer diagnosis, being in isolation after her first chemo treatment, the operation not going ahead, being told she was palliative – and coped every time.

Step 6: Grieving, letting go and accepting

At each stage, there has been news that has been incredibly difficult to hear and make sense of. Naomi's approach has helped her to stay positive, but this hasn't been at the cost of ignoring the complex mix of emotions she has understandably felt in response to her situation. If she'd been blindly positive, it would have been at the expense of feeling her way through. She is incredibly strong, but she recognizes that you can't always be, and this makes her stronger. She has a realistic view of her situation; she doesn't try to hold everything in, and allowing her emotions is coupled with self-belief and determination.

Naomi has been open and honest about how she has felt throughout. Therapy has been a space to share both the highs and the lows. A place where she can say the unsayable. She has been able to talk about the days where it all feels too much, the unfairness, the fears; but also the successes, the triumphs and her constant progress. It would be easy to get stuck in the anger at being in this situation, but allowing all of these feelings gives space to acknowledge them, to validate them, and to see that they are understandable, without letting them take over. There is nothing she has avoided, but her focus has not been on how difficult life is. Instead she has kept hold of hope and recognized all the good things that have come from this experience.

Step 7: Becoming yourself

Death is hard to talk about when you care about someone. But opening up the topic and looking at the 'monster under the bed' has allowed Naomi to get her affairs in order and think about what she wants if she were to die. It has given her back a sense of control and made more space for living, showing her what is most important to her and letting her see that she has nothing to prove. It has allowed her to listen to her instincts and think about how she wants to spend her time, the people she wants to spend it with and the places she wants to visit. It's given her a freedom to focus on what is meaningful to her, to be kinder to herself, to take joy in the simple things and to feel excited about the future, enabling her to see what she truly wants from life and how she wants to live.

KEY TAKEAWAYS

- Finding meaning in what has happened to us is at the core of how we overcome trauma and whether we grow from the experience.
- Difficult times bring what we do have into sharper focus and lets us think about what we truly want from life.
- Listen to your heart – rather than putting off life, make the most of the opportunities that matter to you.
- See your strengths and all you are capable of.
- Look death in the face – what do you want to achieve before you die?
- Live intentionally – think about how you want to live and go after the things you want using all that you have learned.

AFTERWORD

Change is an ongoing process; like the seasons or the tides, it is not something we have control over. We are constantly learning, evolving and growing. When we move with change, stop fearing discomfort and stay curious about life, it flows more easily. Trying to fight against the unpredictability and toughness of life is a bit like trying to stand up against the waves – they just knock you down. It's better to swim with the current and accept that the waves will always keep coming. Making peace with this and working out what makes life meaningful to us is part of embracing life. As scary as that may seem, there's a relief in knowing it. It is only by doing this that we can really learn to *live*.

As we get older, we feel like we should be better at figuring it all out, but it doesn't get any easier. This realization can be hard to come to terms with, but it is also freeing. It means we don't have to keep pushing on through tiredness and difficult times in the hope that one day things will magically be different. They'll only be different if we change them.

As hard as we might try, we can't always have our life permanently in balance. There will be times when we are haunted by our past. There will be times when difficult circumstances will be thrown at us, sometimes more than we feel we can take. As we have learned in this book, no one can skip life's struggle or pain.

When something difficult happens, don't be blindsided. In these moments, you can hold on tightly to all you have learned in these pages and put yourself in the best situation to deal with adversity. You can listen to your feelings and fears, but you can also answer them back. You can remember that even when you are doing everything right, some days will be difficult; you are not getting it wrong, this is how life works. Remember that you can do this (even when you don't want to have to) and that you can find your way back to the people and things that will support you. Remember that you can trust in yourself and keep a clear focus and direction. Remember that you are strong, ready and resilient. Remember that you are more than you ever believed.

While writing this book, I have thought a lot about what life really means to me. For me, it is about the everyday moments. Conversations with my son as I drive him to school. Watching my middle daughter play football. A fierce hug from my youngest. Cycling with my husband. Being there for the people I care about through the good times and bad. It's having time for the things that matter to me. Quality time with the people I care about. A meaningful job, time outdoors, being on my bike, giving back. Making sure life doesn't feel like a chore, or always serious. Laughing at a familiar joke that has been going on for years. Seeing the moonlight on the sea. It is feeling like I am present in my life, rather than putting life off for another time. Not doing so much that I feel constantly exhausted. It's caring about what I think rather than what others might think. It's not always taking the hard route and constantly pushing. It's about letting life come to me, keeping my eyes open to the world and all its wonder. It is speaking to myself kindly and giving myself permission to look after myself. It is knowing I'll always be learning and looking for answers. That at times I'll be unsure what I'm doing and I'll be back in the struggle room questioning whether these techniques work. It's allowing these feelings, remembering why life is harder in the threat zone and trying not to judge myself for getting it wrong.

Life is not something we should try to control – it is an adventure packed full of experiences and lessons. A slow but sure process of becoming truly ourselves. Live a life filled with highs and lows and middling in-betweens. One filled with heartbreak, pain and loss as well as heart-bursting moments of happiness, delight and pride. This is what makes life so precious. Time passes quickly, so grab what you can and embrace it. Harness and cherish the good parts of life because you don't know what tomorrow will bring. The only thing you really have is right now. And right now you have a choice to *live*. Take chances, live passionately and love with all your heart. Make sure you belly laugh, try not to stay mad; forgive, be kind. And most importantly, don't worry about what others will think. Go for the things you want. Because what have you got to lose? Some day is now.

STRATEGY TOOLKIT

STRATEGY 1: BODY SCAN

think it works well to listen to someone running you through this exercise. You will find lots of recordings online; choose someone you like listening to. Or if you prefer, you can follow the instructions below.

1. Get comfortable. Lying down is preferable, particularly if you are doing a body scan meditation before going to sleep. If that's not possible, sitting comfortably is also an option.
2. Take a few deep breaths. Let your breathing slow down and start breathing from your belly instead of from your chest, letting your abdomen expand and contract as though a balloon is inflating and deflating in your abdomen with each breath.
3. Bring awareness to your feet. Now slowly bring your attention down to your feet. Begin observing sensations there. If you notice pain, acknowledge it and any thoughts or emotions that accompany it, and gently breathe through it.
4. Breathe into the tension. If you notice any uncomfortable sensations, focus your attention on them. Breathe into

them and see what happens. Visualize the tension leaving your body through your breath and evaporating into the air. Move on when you feel ready.

5. Continue this technique with each area of your body, gradually moving up until you reach the top of your head. Notice how you feel and where you're holding your stress. If there's any tightness, pain or pressure, continue to breathe into it. This can help you release tension in your body and become more aware of where you hold tension and how to let it go.

STRATEGY 2: BREATHING

4-7-8 breathing is a simple exercise to start with, but with a bit of research you'll find many different exercises you can try.

1. Exhale completely through your mouth.
2. Close your mouth and inhale quietly through your nose to a mental count of four.
3. Hold your breath for a count of seven.
4. Exhale completely through your mouth to a count of eight.

STRATEGY 3: BILATERAL STIMULATION

A great place to start with bilateral stimulation is the butterfly hug. Some people don't like to have their arms across their chest, so if you prefer, you can hold them either side. You can also adapt the strategy to work for you wherever you are – for instance, if you're out and about, you could have your arms at your sides and tap them alternately. Or if you're making a cup of tea, you could tap your feet instead. Once you're comfortable with the exercise, you can use it if you're feeling anxious or overwhelmed or if you need to recentre. There are lots of video explanations online if you prefer to watch a demonstration of this.

1. Cross your arms over your chest so that the tip of the middle finger of each hand is placed below the collarbone and the rest of your hands cover the area between the collarbone and the shoulder and the collarbone and the breastbone. Hands and fingers need to be as vertical as possible so that the fingers point toward the neck and not toward the arms.

2. If you wish, you can interlock your thumbs to form the butterfly's body and the extension of your other fingers outward will form the wings. Your eyes can be closed or partially closed, looking toward the tip of your nose.

3. Now move your hands in turn, tapping your collarbone with your left hand and then your right hand, like the flapping wings of a butterfly. Let them move freely. While you're doing it, breathe slowly and deeply. Feel your breath slowly moving in and out. Try and ensure you're using abdominal breathing, so you feel your stomach rise and fall with each breath.

4. Be aware of what is going through your mind and body – thoughts, images, sounds, smells, feelings and physical sensations – without pushing your thoughts away or judging. Just observe it all, a bit like watching clouds pass by. You might even find you can just think about the tapping and how it feels, grounding you in the present moment and bringing a sense of safety and security. Do it for as long as feels good; a couple of minutes is usually all you need.

STRATEGY 4: GROUNDING

You can use sight, sound, touch, smell and taste to get out of your head and into your surroundings.

Sight: Look around and say out loud to yourself what you can see. Take it up a level and name five things that are the same colour, and now five things that are the same shape. It's also good to have something to look at that can remind you of being loved, supported and safe. This could be an affirmation card with something written on it that personally resonates, a quote or your own words. Or something you have been given that made you feel cared for. Maybe a letter or a photograph that reminds you of these things.

Sound: Notice and name the sounds you hear. The birds singing, traffic, a clock ticking. Or tune into music, a podcast or an audiobook that fits your mood.

Touch: Find an object that feels nice to hold and has a texture if you stroke it – stones can be great as they can fit in your pocket, or perhaps a tension ball or fidget toy. Physical touch can also be really good; for example, just stroking your own arm or face feels soothing.

Smell: Notice the smells around you or carry a smell you like that makes you feel calm and relaxed: essential oils can have a calming effect.

Taste: Eat something with a strong taste, like extra-strong mints. This can provide a helpful distraction.

STRATEGY 5: THOUGHT LEAVES

Imagine yourself on a riverbank, watching the river run past as the sun sparkles on the water. You notice an oak tree overhanging the river, and as you watch, a leaf falls off and drifts downwards, landing on the water and then floating away downstream.

As the next leaf falls, place the thought in your head on to it, without thinking about it, and watch it float away. Do the same with the next leaf – put a thought on it and watch it being carried off.

Try this for a few minutes (or as long as you're enjoying it). The aim is to become aware of your thoughts in the moment, so that you're just being (it can take a bit of practise). It's a great way to get out of your head and a reminder that you don't need to analyse every thought. You can just let them come and go.

If this feels too much, you can simply breathe in and out, focusing your attention on your breath as it enters and leaves your body, noticing any sensations associated with it. If it helps, you can say to yourself: 'Breathing in, I know that I am breathing in. Breathing out, I know that I am breathing out.'

STRATEGY 6: A BREATH OF FRESH AIR

I'd recommend reading *Losing Eden: Why Our Minds Need the Wild* if you're interested in finding out more about the importance of nature. In it, Lucy Jones explores the science of nature and mental health, uncovering a wealth of research and proving categorically what we intuitively know – nature has a measurable effect on our mental health.

ACKNOWLEDGEMENTS

A huge thank you to Akemi, Jess, Finn, Sophie, David, Peter and Naomi. Your stories brought this book to life and made it so much more. It's been a privilege to speak to each of you and to hear your story. You have inspired me and I have no doubt that your generosity in sharing your stories will help others and remind them they are not alone. Special thanks to Naomi and Sophie, for allowing me to walk beside you and get to know you on your journey. Thanks also to Peter Smith for taking the time to share your insightful thoughts on overcoming trauma and for introducing me to David.

Jack, Max, Edie and Bibi, my dream team. I never knew a heart could be filled with this much love – you are more than I could ever have hoped for. I'm not sure how I got so lucky to share my life with four such amazing people, but I'm so grateful I get to wake up with you every day.

Jack – I couldn't have written this book without you. Thank you for being my number one supporter in everything I do, for inspiring me, for joining me on every (crazy) adventure and for never complaining along the way. Meeting you is the best thing that has ever happened to me.

My incredible parents, John and Deborah. It's difficult to put

HOW TO OVERCOME TRAUMA AND FIND YOURSELF AGAIN

into words my thanks for everything you have done. You provided me with the firmest foundations, support and stability and a steadfast love. I am also very fortunate to have the support of my brilliant mother-in-law Heather and her wonderful partner John.

I don't think you could find a better agent than Jane Graham Maw. Jane you really are the best. I still laugh when I think back to the early submissions I sent, when I was first trying to write on my own. Thank you for your faith in me and for your excellent advice.

With this book I've been lucky enough to have not just one editor but two. Thank you Nicky Crane and Natalie Bradley for your clever thoughts and suggestions. Your advice helped improve and bring together my ideas far better than I ever could have imagined. Huge thanks to the team at Octopus. Particularly to Sarah Allen for her hard work editing and managing the final steps to bring this book together; and Megan Brown for her fantastic promotion of this book and *The Imposter Cure*. Thanks also to Jane Selley, Clare Hoban, Claudia Connal, Constance Lam and Victoria Scales. I feel incredibly fortunate to have such an outstanding team to help bring my ideas to life.

I know this sounds more like an Oscars speech than a book's acknowledgements, but I wouldn't be where I am without the brilliant mentors I've worked with, who have shared their wisdom and given me a huge amount of support. Roger Ramsden who guided me to gaining a place on the clinical psychology course. Neal Gething, who understands people more deeply than anyone I know, Professor Neil Greenberg, who gave me a phenomenal introduction to trauma research. Dr Paddy Ruane, an exceptional GP and friend, and my supervisor, Dr Anna Lavender, who I continue to learn from. And finally thank you to the remarkable people I work with in my clinic – for letting me into your lives and continuing to teach me so much about life.

REFERENCES, RESOURCES
AND FURTHER READING

INTRODUCTION

'In his seminal book': Frankl, V.E., *Man's Search For Meaning: The Classic Tribute to Hope from the Holocaust*, London: Rider, 2004

'Self-actualization Theory': Rogers, C., *On Becoming a Person: A Therapist's View of Psychotherapy*, London: Robinson, 2011

'Existential Psychotherapy': Yalom, I.D., *Momma and the Meaning of Life: Tales of Psychotherapy*, London: Piatkus, 2006

'If you would like to read more on the topic, I recommend': van der Kolk, B., *The Body Keeps the Score: Mind, Brain and Body in the Transformation of Trauma*, London: Penguin, 2015

Perry, B.D., and Winfrey, O., *What Happened to You?: Conversations on Trauma, Resilience, and Healing*, London: Bluebird, 2021

LePera, Dr N., *How to Do the Work: Recognize Your Patterns, Heal From Your Past and Create Your Self*, London: Harper Wave, 2021

'I investigated the effects of working in a war zone': Hibberd, J. M., and Greenberg, N. (2011), 'Coping with the impact of working in a conflict zone: a comparative study of diplomatic staff', *Journal of Occupational and Environmental Medicine*, 53(4),352–7, https://pubmed.ncbi.nlm.nih.gov/21436732/ (accessed 27 January 2023)

CHAPTER 1: TRAUMA

'It is estimated that 75 per cent of people in the developed world will experience some form of trauma': Breslau, N., and Kessler, R. C. (2001), 'The stressor criterion in DSM-IV posttraumatic stress disorder: an empirical investigation', *Biological Psychiatry*, 50(9), 699–704, https://www.sciencedirect.com/science/article/pii/S0006322301011672 (accessed 27 January 2023)

'1 in 5 will experience a potentially traumatic event': Kessler, R. C., et al. (1995), 'Posttraumatic Stress Disorder in the National Comorbidity Survey', *Archives of General Psychiatry*, 52(12),1048–1060, https://jamanetwork.com/journals/jamapsychiatry/article-abstract/497313 (accessed 27 January 2023)

Kessler, R. C. (2000), 'Posttraumatic stress disorder: the burden to the individual and to society', *Journal of Clinical Psychiatry*, 61(5), 4–12, https://pubmed.ncbi.nlm.nih.gov/10761674/ (accessed 27 January 2023)

'The first UK-based study of its kind, published in *The Lancet Psychiatry*': Lewis, S. J., et al. (2019), 'The epidemiology of trauma and post-traumatic stress disorder in a representative cohort of young people in England and Wales', *The Lancet Psychiatry*, 6(3), 247–256, https://www.thelancet.com/journals/lanpsy/article/PIIS2215-0366(19)30031-8/fulltext (accessed 27 January 2023)

'Flooding in Pakistan from June to August 2022 killed more than 1,391 people': https://www.wsws.org/en/articles/2022/09/09/rkue-s09.html (accessed 23 January 2023)

'The highest ever number of rapes': https://rapecrisis.org.uk/get-informed/statistics-sexual-violence/ (accessed 3 July 2022)

'On average someone is diagnosed with cancer every 90 seconds in the UK': https://www.macmillan.org.uk/dfsmedia/1a6f23537f7f4519bb0cf14c45

b2a629/9468-10061/2022-cancer-statistics-factsheet (accessed 7 March 2023)

'Divorce rates are also currently at around 40 per cent': https://www.ons. gov.uk/peoplepopulationandcommunity/birthsdeathsandmarriages/divorce (accessed 3 July 2022)

'The DSM-5, the diagnostic statistical manual for mental disorders': Breslau, N., and Kessler R.C. (2001), 'The stressor criterion in DSM-IV posttraumatic stress disorder', *Biological Psychiatry*, 50(9), 699–704

'The DSM-5 is used as a route to diagnosing PTSD': American Psychiatric Association, *Diagnostic and Statistical Manual of Mental Disorders*, Washington DC: American Psychiatric Association Publishing, 2013 (5th edn), 271

'Stephen Joseph was a pioneer in recognizing this': Joseph, S., *What Doesn't Kill Us: A guide to overcoming adversity and moving forward*, London: Piatkus, 2013

'Bessel van der Kolk describes the imprint left by trauma': van der Kolk, *The Body Keeps the Score*, London: Penguin, 2015

CHAPTER 2: BURNING DOWN THE HOUSE

'we grow up with three fundamental assumptions': Janoff-Bulman, R. (1989), 'Assumptive Worlds and the Stress of Traumatic Events: Applications of the Schema Construct', *Social Cognition*, 7(2), 113–136, https://guilfordjournals. com/doi/10.1521/soco.1989.7.2.113 (accessed 27 January 2023)

https://people.umass.edu/janbul/ (accessed 27 January 2023)

Janoff-Bulman, R., *Shattered Assumptions: Towards a New Psychology of Trauma*, New York: Free Press, 1992

'Neil Weinstein's seminal study on this topic': Weinstein, N. D. (1980), 'Unrealistic optimism about future life events', *Journal of Personality and*

Social Psychology, 39(5), 806–820, https://psycnet.apa.org/record/1981-28087-001 (accessed 27 January 2023)

'People perceive their own future as more positive than the average person's': Lerner, M. J., *The Belief in a Just World: A Fundamental Delusion*, New York: Springer, 1980

CHAPTER 3: CARE (STEP 1)

'Psychiatrist Mardi Horowitz': Horowitz, M. J. (1993), 'Stress-response syndromes: A review of posttraumatic stress and adjustment disorders', in J. P. Wilson and B. Raphael (eds.), *International Handbook of Traumatic Stress Syndromes*, New York: Plenum Press, 1993, 49–60 https://doi.org/10.1007/978-1-4615-2820-3_4 (accessed 27 January 2023)

'I love the poem "The Guest House"': Rumi, J., *Selected Poems*. Translated by C. Banks and J. Moyne. London: Penguin Classics, 2004

'This process is similar to the grief model': Kübler-Ross, E., *On Death and Dying*, New York: Macmillan, 1969

'The good room plays an essential role in our survival': Fredrickson, B. L. (2001), 'The Role of Positive Emotions in Positive Psychology: The Broaden and Build Theory of Positive Emotions', *American Psychologist*, 56(3), 218–226, https://ncbi.nlm.nih.gov/pmc/articles/PMC3122271/ (accessed 27 January 2023)

'Kerrie Glass, a researcher at the University of South Carolina': Glass, K., et al. (2009), 'Are coping strategies, social support, and hope associated with psychological distress among Hurricane Katrina survivors?', *Journal of Social and Clinical Psychology*, 28(6), 779–795, https://psycnet.apa.org/record/2009-10225-006 (accessed 27 January 2023)

'David Berendes and Francis Keefe at Duke University': Berendes, D., et al. (2010), 'Hope in the Context of Lung Cancer: Relationships of Hope to Symptoms and Psychological Distress', *Journal of Pain and Symptom Management*, 40(2), 174–182, https://www.sciencedirect.com/science/article/pii/S0885392410003271 (accessed 27 January 2023)

'A review of 77 studies examined the risk factors related to PTSD': Brewin, C. R., et al. (2000), 'Meta-analysis of risk factors for posttraumatic stress disorder in trauma-exposed adults', *Journal of Consulting and Clinical Psychology*, 68(5), 748–766, https://pubmed.ncbi.nlm.nih.gov/11068961/ (accessed 27 January 2023)

'it is the trauma survivor's *subjective* perception that support is available': Norris, F. H., and Kaniasty, K. (1996), 'Received and perceived social support in times of stress: a test of the social support deterioration deterrence model', *Journal of Personality and Social Psychology*, 71(3), 498–511, https://pubmed.ncbi.nlm.nih.gov/8831159/ (accessed 27 January 2023)

'In their excellent book *Supersurvivors*': Feldman, D.B., and Kravetz, L. D., *Supersurvivors: The Surprising Link Between Suffering and Success*, London: Harper Wave, 2015

'the research on social support': Guay, S., et al. (2006), 'Exploring the links between posttraumatic stress disorder and social support: processes and potential research avenues', *Journal of Traumatic Stress*, 19(3), 327–338, https://pubmed.ncbi.nlm.nih.gov/16788995/ (accessed 27 January 2023)

CHAPTER 4: POST-TRAUMATIC GROWTH

'One landmark piece of research': Tedeschi, R. G., and Calhoun, L.G. (1996), 'The Posttraumatic Growth Inventory: measuring the positive legacy of trauma', *Journal of Traumatic Stress*, 9 (3), 455–471, https://pubmed.ncbi.nlm.nih.gov/8827649/ (accessed 27 January 2023)

Tedeschi, R. G., and Calhoun, L.G. (1995), *Trauma and Transformation: Growing in the Aftermath of Suffering*, Thousand Oaks, CA: Sage, 1995

'Studies show a link between greater perceived growth and lower emotional distress': Linley, P.A., and Joseph, S. (2004), 'Positive Change Following Trauma and Adversity: A Review', *Journal of Traumatic Stress*, 17(1), 11–21, http://drjordankelly.com/Posttraumatic%20Growth.pdf (accessed 23 January 2023)

'This means that we are hardwired for growth': Deci, E. L., and Ryan, R. M. (2000), 'The "what" and "why" of goal pursuits: Human needs and the self-determination of behavior', *Psychological Inquiry*, 11(4), 227–268, https:/psycnet.apa.org/record/2001-03012-001 (accessed 27 January 2023)

Ryan, R. M., and Deci, E. L. (2000), 'Self-Determination Theory and the Facilitation of Intrinsic Motivation, Social Development, and Well-Being', *American Psychologist*, 55(1), 68–78, https://selfdeterminatiotheory.org/SDT/documents/2000_RyanDeci_SDT.pdf (accessed 27 January 2023)

CHAPTER 5: LOOKING AFTER YOUR BODY (STEP 2)

'numerous studies have shown that when we experience emotional pain': Meerwijk, E. L., et al. (2013), 'Brain regions associated with psychological pain: implications for a neural network and its relationship to physical pain', *Brain Imaging Behavior*, 7(1), 1–14, https://pubmed.ncbi.nlm.nih.gov/22660945/ (accessed 27 January 2023)

'Stephen Porges' polyvagal theory': Porges, S. W., *The Pocket Guide to the Polyvagal Theory: The Transformative Power of Feeling Safe*, New York: W. W. Norton, 2017

'The vagus nerve helps us with neuroception': Breit, S., et al. (2018), 'Vagus Nerve as Modulator of the Brain–Gut Axis in Psychiatric and Inflammatory Disorders', *Frontiers in Psychiatry*, 9(44), https://www.frontiersin.org/articles/10.3389/fpsyt.2018.00044/full?fbclid=IwAR3PA3EFjHZPgy0zsChJWyJMyVGkKyPM7SN7UDb2vCTuOCl97Ob2SQabkRo (accessed 27 January 2023)

'Tuning into our body is known as interoception': Price, C. J., and Hooven, C. (2018), 'Interoceptive Awareness Skills for Emotion Regulation: Theory and Approach of Mindful Awareness in Body-Oriented Therapy (MABT)', *Frontiers in Psychology*, 9, 798, https://www.ncbi.nlm.nih.gov/pmc/articles/PMC5985305/ (accessed 27 January 2023)

'Research suggests that bilateral stimulation': Engelhard, I. M., and van den Hout, M. A. (2012), 'How does EMDR work?', *Journal of Experimental Psychopathology*, 3(5), 724–738, https://doi.org/10.5127/jep.028212 (accessed 27 January 2023)

CHAPTER 6: WHY EXERCISE IS THE HOLY GRAIL

'There is an overwhelming amount of research': Firth, J., et al. (2020), 'A meta-review of "lifestyle psychiatry": the role of exercise, smoking, diet and sleep in the prevention and treatment of mental disorders', *World Psychiatry*, 19(3), 360–380, https://onlinelibrary.wiley.com/doi/pdf/10.1002/wps.20773 (accessed 27 January 2023)

Stubbs, B., et al. (2018), 'EPA guidance on physical activity as a treatment for severe mental illness: a meta-review of the evidence and Position Statement from the European Psychiatric Association (EPA), supported by the International Organization of Physical Therapists in Mental Health (IOPTMH)', *European Psychiatry*, 54, 124–144, https://www.europsy.net/app/uploads/2018/12/2018-EPA-Guidance-Paper-on-Physical-Activity.pdf (accessed 27 January 2023)

Mandolesi, L., et al. (2018), 'Effects of Physical Exercise on Cognitive Functioning and Wellbeing: Biological and Psychological Benefits', *Frontiers in Psychology* ('Movement Science and Sport Psychology' section), 19, https://www.frontiersin.org/articles/10.3389/fpsyg.2018.00509/full (accessed 27 January 2023)

'tracked 152,978 participants in the UK Biobank study':
Kandola, A.A., and Osborn, D.P.J., et al. (2020), 'Individual and combined associations between cardiorespiratory fitness and grip strength with common mental disorders: a prospective cohort study in the UK

Biobank', *BMC Medicine*, 18, 303, https://doi.org/10.1186/s12916-020-01782-9 (accessed 27 January 2023)

'self-worth coach and with her Move and Inspire online yoga platform': https://sophie-dear.mykajabi.com (accessed 27 January 2023)
https://www.moveandinspire.co.uk (accessed 27 January 2023)

CHAPTER 7: LOOKING BACK TO LOOK FORWARDS (STEP 3)

'The parent acts as a container for the baby's emotions and feelings': Bion, W. R., *Second Thoughts*, New York: Jason Aronson, 1977

'This awareness of ourselves as reflected back': Music, G., *Nurturing natures: Attachment and children's emotional, sociocultural and brain development*, London: Routledge, 2016

'When this happens, we feel responded to': Hobson, P., *The Cradle of Thought*, London: Macmillan, 2004

'These experiences also mean that we are more likely to be securely attached to our parent': Holmes, J., *John Bowlby and Attachment Theory*, London: Routledge, 2014

'It also puts you at greater risk of future problems': Keenan, K. (2000), 'Emotion Dysregulation as a Risk Factor for Child Psychopathology', *Clinical Psychology Science and Practice*, 7(4), 418–434, https://onlinelibrary.wiley.com/doi/abs/10.1093/clipsy.7.4.418 (accessed 27 January 2023)

Wills, T. A., et al. (2011), 'Behavioral and emotional regulation and adolescent substance use problems: A test of moderation effects in a dual-process model', *Psychology of Addictive Behaviors*, 25(2), 279–292, https://psycnet.apa.org/record/2011-06252-001 (accessed 27 January 2023)

Bahremand, M., et al. (2016), 'Emotion Risk-Factor in Patients With Cardiac Diseases: The Role of Cognitive Emotion Regulation Strategies,

Positive Affect and Negative Affect (A Case-Control Study)', *Global Journal of Health Science*, 8(1), 173–179, https://www.ncbi.nlm.nih.gov/pmc/articles/PMC4804021/ (accessed 27 January 2023)

'**Rewriting the Family Script**': Byng-Hall, J. (2008), 'The crucial roles of attachment in family therapy', *Journal of Family Therapy*, 30(2), 129–146, https://onlinelibrary.wiley.com/doi/10.1111/j.1467-6427.2008.00422.x (accessed 27 January 2023)

'**Corrective scripts are when we consciously choose to do things differently**': Byng-Hall, J., *Rewriting Family Scripts: Improvisation and Systems Change*, New York: The Guilford Press, 1995

CHAPTER 8: COPING WITH TRAUMA (STEP 4)

'**Excessive avoidance of feelings is associated with higher levels**': Littleton, H., et al. (2007), 'Trauma coping strategies and psychological distress: A meta-analysis', *Journal of Traumatic Stress*, https://pubmed.ncbi.nlm.nih.gov/18157893/ (accessed 27 January 2023)

'**Every time you manage a difficult situation or difficult feelings**': Sharma, N., et al. (2013), 'Chapter 1 – Neural plasticity and its contribution to functional recovery', *Handbook of Clinical Neurology*, 110, 3–12, https://www.sciencedirect.com/science/article/abs/pii/B9780444529015000010 (accessed 27 January 2023)

'**Writing offers a whole host of benefits**': Lepore, S. (1997), 'Expressive writing moderates the relation between intrusive thoughts and depressive symptoms', *Journal of Personality and Social Psychology*, 73(5), 1030–1037, https://www.researchgate.net/profile/Stephen-Lepore/publication/13864623_Expressive_writing_moderates_the_relation_between_intrusive_thoughts_and_depressive_symptoms/links/0fcfd50adafe9e991b000000/Expressive-writing-moderates-the-relation-between-intrusive-thoughts-and-depressive-symptoms.pdf (accessed 27 January 2023)

Lepore, S. J., and Smyth, J. M., *The Writing Cure: How Expressive Writing Promotes Health and Emotional Well-Being*, Washington DC: American Psychological Association Publishing, 2002

'Studies have shown that expressing a ratio of around 3 to 1': Fredrickson, B. L., and Losada, M. F. (2005), 'Positive affect and complex dynamics of human flourishing', *American Psychologist*, 60(7), 678–686, https://www.ncbi.nlm.nih.gov/pmc/articles/PMC3126111/?utm_medium=email&utm_source=other&utm_campaign=opencourse.QEXoJRBmEeWhsgqB1eduww.announcements~opencourse.QEXoJRBmEeWhsgqB1eduww.Iyy1h2nAEeiYGg5ylnfRYA (accessed 27 January 2023)

Fredrickson, B., *Positivity: Groundbreaking Research to Release Your Inner Optimist and Thrive*, London: Oneworld Publications, 2011

CHAPTER 9: TELLING YOUR STORY (STEP 5)

'We give meaning to our lives and relationships by "storying" our experiences': White, M., and Epston, D., *Narrative Means to Therapeutic Ends*, New York: W. W. Norton, 1990

'Supportive-expressive therapy': Spiegel, D., Bloom J.R., et al. (1981), 'Group Support for Patients With Metastatic Cancer: A Randomized Prospective Outcome Study', *Archives of General Psychiatry*, 38(5), 527–533, https://jamanetwork.com/journals/jamapsychiatry/article-abstract/492544 (accessed 27 January 2023)

Classen, C., Butler L.D., et al. (2001), 'Supportive-Expressive Group Therapy and Distress in Patients With Metastatic Breast Cancer: A Randomized Clinical Intervention Trial', *rchives of General Psychiatry*, 58(5), 494–501, https://jamanetwork.com/journals/jamapsychiatry/article-abstract/481764 (accessed 27 January 2023)

'The theory of narrative identity developed by Dan McAdams': McAdams, D. P. (2018), 'Narrative Identity: What Is It? What Does It Do? How Do You Measure It?', *Imagination, Cognition and Personality*:

Consciousness in Theory, Research and Clinical Practice, 37(3), 359–372, http://www.self-definingmemories.com/Narrative_Identity_shaped_by_SDM.pdf (accessed 27 January 2023)

https://psychology.northwestern.edu/people/faculty/core/profiles/dan-mcadams.html (accessed 27 January 2023)

https://sites.northwestern.edu/thestudyoflivesresearchgroup/ (accessed 27 January 2023)

'When you recall a story, the parts you focus on get bigger': Partridge, K. (2005), 'A systemic tale of assessment and formulation', *Clinical Psychology*, 46, 13–18, https://www.researchgate.net/profile/Karen-Partridge/publication/289657846_A_systemic_tale_of_assessment_and_formulation/links/5c7677aaa6fdcc47159eca3b/A-systemic-tale-of-assessment-and-formulation.pdf (accessed 27 January 2023)

'the stinging nettles metaphor': Ehlers, A., and Clark, D. M. (2000), 'A cognitive model of posttraumatic stress disorder', *Behaviour, Research and Therapy*, 38 (4), 319–345, adapted from: https://www.annafreud.org/media/4898/07c-david-trickey-handout-it-is-good-to-talk.pdf (accessed 27 January 2023)

'the writing experience was valuable and meaningful': Pennebaker, J. W. (1997), 'Writing About Emotional Experiences as a Therapeutic Process', *Association for Psychological Science*, 8(3), 162–166, https://journals.sagepub.com/doi/10.1111/j.1467-9280.1997.tb00403.x (accessed 27 January 2023)

'Research finds that rumination is one of the critical differences': Watkins, E., et al. (2008), 'Processing mode causally influences emotional reactivity: distinct effects of abstract versus concrete construal on emotional response', 8(3), 364–378, http://www.ncbi.nlm.nih.gov/pubmed/18540752 (accessed 27 January 2023)

CHAPTER 10: GRIEVING, LETTING GO AND ACCEPTING (STEP 6)

'A study by Witvliet and colleagues': Witvliet, C., et al. (2001), 'Granting forgiveness or harboring grudges: implications for emotion, physiology, and health', *Psychological Science*, 12(2), 117–123, https://pubmed.ncbi.nlm.nih.gov/11340919/ (accessed 27 January 2023)

Messias, E., et al. (2010), 'Bearing grudges and physical health: Relationship to smoking, cardiovascular health and ulcers', *Social Psychiatry and Psychiatric Epidemiology*, 45(2), 183–187, https://psycnet.apa.org/record/2010-02913-005 (accessed 27 January 2023)

'Edith Eger expresses this beautifully': Eger, E., *The Choice: A true story of hope*, London: Rider, 2018

https://dreditheger.com (accessed 27 January 2023)

'In Desmond Tutu's words': Tutu, D., *No Future Without Forgiveness*, London: Rider, 2000

https://www.theforgivenessproject.com/stories-library/desmond-tutu/ (accessed 27 January 2023)

'The serenity prayer that is used at Alcoholics Anonymous (AA)': https://www.alcoholics-anonymous.org.uk (accessed 27 January 2023)

'setting up Peter Hutt Counselling': https://www.peterhuttcounselling.com/ (accessed 27 January 2023)

CHAPTER 11: BECOMING YOURSELF (STEP 7)

'And once the storm is over, you won't remember how you made it through': Murakami, H., *Kafka on the Shore*, London: Vintage, 2005

'I love the story of Candy Chang': https://candychang.com (accessed 27 January 2023)

'I love Mary Oliver's poem': https://www.loc.gov/programs/poetry-and-literature/poet-laureate/poet-laureate-projects/poetry-180/all-poems/item/poetry-180-133/the-summer-day/ (accessed 27 January 2023)

Oliver, M., *Devotions: The Selected Poems of Mary Oliver*, New York: Penguin Press, 2017

'in 2011, she was one of the few Black women to reach the North Pole': https://www.icepeople.net/pdfs/icepeople042611.pdf (accessed 27 January 2023)

INDEX

Specific exercises and page numbers for tables and diagrams are in *italics*